Puerto Rican Chicago

LATINOS IN CHICAGO
AND THE MIDWEST

Series Editors
Omar Valerio-Jiménez,
University of Texas at San Antonio
Sujey Vega, Arizona State University

Series Founding Editor
Frances R. Aparicio,
Northwestern University

*A list of books in the series appears
at the end of this book.*

Puerto Rican Chicago

Schooling the City, 1940–1977

MIRELSIE VELÁZQUEZ

**UNIVERSITY OF
ILLINOIS PRESS**
Urbana, Chicago, and Springfield

Financial support was provided from the Office of the
Vice President for Research and Partnerships and the
Office of the Provost, University of Oklahoma.

Library of Congress Cataloging-in-Publication Data
Names: Velázquez, Mirelsie, 1975– author.
Title: Puerto Rican Chicago : schooling the city, 1940–1977 /
    Mirelsie Velázquez.
Description: Urbana : University of Illinois Press, [2022] |
    Series: Latinos in Chicago and the Midwest | Includes
    bibliographical references and index.
Identifiers: LCCN 2021038314 (print) | LCCN 2021038315
    (ebook) | ISBN 9780252044243 (cloth) | ISBN
    9780252086281 (paperback) | ISBN 9780252053207 (ebook)
Subjects: LCSH: Puerto Ricans—Education—Illinois—
    Chicago—History—20th century. | Puerto Ricans—
    Illinois—Chicago—Social conditions—20th century.
    | Puerto Ricans—Cultural assimilation—Illinois—
    Chicago—History—20th century.
Classification: LCC LC2698.C45 V45 2022 (print) | LCC LC2698
    .C45 (ebook) | DDC 371.82968/7295—dc23
LC record available at https://lccn.loc.gov/2021038314
LC ebook record available at https://lccn.loc.gov/2021038315

To Carina Inez and Xochitl Mirelsie

Contents

Acknowledgments

THERE ARE MANY PEOPLE TO THANK who have directly or indirectly played a part in the completion of this manuscript. Informally, the book began when I entered my kindergarten classroom shortly after my family migrated to Chicago from Puerto Rico. Little did I know that I inherited not only the mispronunciation of my name but a legacy of community activism that informed my schooling. This is my history.

Formally, the book began as a conversation early in my graduate school career at the University of Illinois at Urbana-Champaign, and I owe a great deal of gratitude to individuals with whom I crossed paths. Some remain at Illinois, while others have moved on to new institutions. I am thankful to those who entertained my ideas and fueled my excitement both in the department of Latina/o Studies and in the department of Educational Policy Studies: James D. Anderson, Julie Dowling, Mercedes Ramírez Fernández, Jonathan Inda, Cris Mayo, Laurence Parker, and Arlene Torres. I was lucky to share the space at Illinois with fellow students who made me laugh back then and inspire me today: Constancio Arnaldo, Richard Benson, Julie Griffin, Jon Hale, Chamara Kwakye, Brian Montes, Mario Rios Perez, Kamau Rashid, Ishwanzya Rivers, Gabriel Rodriguez, Steven Rosado, and Claudine "Candy" Taaffe.

At Illinois I was lucky to also make lifelong friendships, for which I am forever grateful. To Alicia P. Rodriguez and Laura Castañeda, you are two of the kindest people I have ever met, and I carry you with me wherever I am. I love you both. Yoon Pak, although I sat in only one of your classes as a student, I continue to learn from you. You have become one of my biggest supporters, and I consider myself lucky to now call you a friend. Adrian

Burgos Jr., thank you for tolerating our laughter as undergraduate students in your classes, challenging me as a graduate student, and now reminding me to remain kind as a professor. You flew all the way to Oklahoma to help me with this manuscript, but really, this began when you introduced me to the field. Mil gracias. My dear friend John McKinn, who never talked shop with me, and whose CDs I have never returned, I consider myself lucky to call you a friend and to share memories with you at Esquire and Mike and Molly's.

At the University of Oklahoma, I have been lucky to meet kind and generous colleagues and friends, some of whom have moved on from Oklahoma but remain important supporters of this work: Curt Adams, Karen Antell, Michele Eodice, Tim Ford, Siduri Haslerig, Kirsten Hextrum, Ben Keppel, Susan Laird, Rae Langes, Moira Ozias, Penny Pasque, Stacy Reeder, Gabriela Rios, Heather Shotton, Eric Sourie, Sabina Vaught, Janet Ward, and Alison Wilson. I am thankful for the patience and diligence of my research assistants, Jennifer Johnson and Rachael Tully. Jennifer, working with you has been such a joy. Our mutual attachment to home and our love for our communities have led to much laughter and many tears.

This project was also supported by generous funding from various departments at the University of Oklahoma: the Arts and Humanities Forum Manuscript Development Grant, the Jeannine Rainbolt College of Education Summer Research Grant, the Dean's Office, the Office of the Vice President for Research and Partnerships, the Office of the Provost, and the Department of Educational Leadership and Policy Studies. The amazing archivists at the Special Collections at the University of Chicago, the University of Illinois at Chicago, Northeastern Illinois University, DePaul University, the Chicago History Museum Research Center, and La Fundación Luis Muñoz Marín were all so helpful throughout the years.

I have been lucky to work with two kind (and patient) editors at the University of Illinois Press. Dawn Durante, although no longer at Illinois, was instrumental in seeing this project through and never allowed me to give up. Alison Syring, who inherited me, made me feel as if we had been working together all along. I am eternally grateful to you both. Thank you to both Jane Lyle and Jennifer Comeau for your assistance in preparing the final product, and to Miah Emano for the beautiful cover.

I am lucky to share a past with my Boricua sisters, but also glad to share a vision for a future for our community: Erica Davila, Delia Fernandez, Daynali Flores Rodriguez, María del Mar González, Lisa Ortiz Guzmán, and Kristina Medina Vilariño. I am indebted to those who have "shown up" and supported me in various ways throughout the years: Frances Aparicio, Dionne Danns, Dionne Espinoza, Merida Rúa, David Stovall, and Lourdes Torres.

Lilia Fernández, thank you for your generosity with time and resources, which have been instrumental to this project for the last decade. Laura K. Muñoz, whom I met as part of a manuscript development workshop to review an early draft of the book, has now become my academic hermana.

Some friends become family, and I would not have completed this project without you. Whether you supported my ideas, shared laughter, met me at Simone's for a drink, or offered a couch to sleep on, thank you: Ramona Arce, Ramzie Casiano, Miguel De Jesus, Maria Del Guadalupe Davidson, Ivette Del Villar, Mark Freeman, Lily Jimenez, Norma Marrun, Oscar Medina, Ebony Pope, Xavier Ramirez, Ariana Ruiz, Cindy San Miguel, and Berenice Vargas. To my dear friend Richard T. Rodríguez, I can't thank you enough. From the moment we met (well, almost), you have been my biggest supporter and have never let me give up on myself. It is rare to find a friend with whom I can laugh and cry, talk music, and wander the streets of London or Edinburgh, while also talking through ideas. You are my family. To my elementary school teacher Mrs. Rosa Navarro, thank you for instilling in me a joy for learning, but more so for creating a classroom space where my identity as a Puerto Rican child was celebrated every day.

Although we are separated by miles, I am grateful for my parents and the rest of my Velazquez, Gonzalez, and Salazar family, who have shown up to my school events, packed me meals, played board games, celebrated Chicago sports victories, or reminded me every day that I am just someone's little sister or daughter. Thank you. My late father did not live to see this book published, but I thought of him with every word I wrote.

And finally, to the two most important people in my life, my daughters Carina Inez Quiroz and Xochitl Mirelsie Quiroz. You remind me of what is really important in life: love. I am proud to be your mother. This is your history.

Puerto Rican Chicago

Introduction

The problem for the school is particularly acute with those children who have no knowledge of English. The unfamiliarity of their parents with continental, and specifically Chicago, ways of life complicates the problem of the children's adjustment in the new school situation. . . . The size of the population, its location and mobility and expected migration all affect administrative details in schools . . . the schools would find valuable such information as the sort of educational opportunity which the children have already had and the characteristics of the environment from which they have come.
—L. J. Schloerb, 1953

IN THE MIDDLE DECADES of the twentieth century, Chicago experienced a mass migration of Puerto Ricans. The Puerto Rican population in the city grew from a mere 240 in 1940 to 78,000 in 1970.[1] While their arrival helped alleviate the economic and labor needs of both the island and the city, the local schools were unprepared to contend with the influx of Puerto Rican children. Many Chicagoans, including L. J. Schloerb, the assistant to the superintendent of Chicago schools, assumed that Puerto Ricans lacked familiarity with U.S. customs and the English language, but in fact, American ideologies had influenced and framed education on the island since the territory's acquisition in 1898. Indeed, as Sonia Nieto reminds us, Puerto Ricans have been attending U.S. schools since 1898.[2] Framing the education of islanders under military rule and control after occupation, the dominant narrative surrounding schools and schooling highlighted the overall colonial project on the island, reminding Puerto Ricans how little agency they had over their own lives. Furthermore, the construction of Puerto Rico's schooling, both formally and informally, under colonial ideologies highlighted the frequency with which politicians, social organizations, and Puerto Ricans themselves negotiated the place of education and schooling in their lives. Chicago became part of that narrative. *Puerto Rican Chicago: Schooling the*

City, 1940–1977 is about more than just the schooling experiences of a population in constant flux; it is a story of how people met their daily needs within a colonial context, one that extends from the shores of San Juan to the streets of Chicago. Coloniality—including the experience of being subjugated to the will of an oppressive power—does not end when immigrants leave the colonized land and arrive in the colonizers' territory. Indeed, the everyday treatment of Puerto Ricans in Chicago during the mid-twentieth century served as a constant reminder that they were second-class citizens.[3]

Puerto Rican Chicago demonstrates that the work begun by schooling agents in Puerto Rico in 1898 was continued by Chicago officials after 1940. The book offers a historical reading of how the Puerto Rican community acknowledged and confronted the intricate ways in which their claim to space in Chicago was linked to schooling inequalities and challenges. Part of that history encompasses the role of the media and other print materials, which addressed the community's schooling concerns and also served as a vehicle for the creation and affirmation of Puerto Rican identities. Print culture created and maintained by the Puerto Rican community itself played a defining role in giving voice to an otherwise silenced community. Numerous women during this time, including Mirta Ramírez, María Cerda, and Carmen Valentín, were instrumental in creating newspapers and pamphlets, organizing activist groups, and serving in political positions. Their influential work was crucial in negotiating and forming a politicized Puerto Rican community in Chicago, especially within educational spaces. For some women, schools were the only venue in which they could gain a sense of power and control within the community. Indeed, these women's stories show that the fight to remedy educational inequality was very much a community effort. Although this book is not exclusively about women's contributions, it is important to point them out not only for their own significance but also as fertile ground for further scholarship.

After 1898, Puerto Rico's schools were swiftly transformed. This reflected the expectations of the American leaders, who sought to create an "acceptable citizenry" among the islanders by overseeing Puerto Rico's politics and social life. In 1901, Puerto Rico's commissioner of education, M. G. Brumbaugh, noted the enthusiasm of schoolchildren and teachers in celebrating American traditions. "The anniversary of the birth of our flag," wrote Brumbaugh, "was more generally observed than I have ever known it to be observed in the States, and more enthusiastically. . . . I am confident that it was the greatest day of patriotic devotion to our flag ever celebrated in the Tropics."[4] Puerto Rico's schools, and especially its schoolchildren, became imbued with the responsibility of aligning Puerto Ricans' loyalty and way of life with those of the United States, a responsibility that followed them across the diaspora. The complex relationship between schools and colonialism is noted in Solsiree del Moral's account of the cultural politics of Puerto Rico's schools from occupation until the shift to commonwealth status in 1952. Del Moral reminds us that "while U.S. school projects across the imperial archipelago and within the U.S. mainland were informed by the racist ideologies of Anglo-Saxon supremacy and Protestant missionary and civilizing visions, they were always specific to both imperial intentions and local conditions."[5] Further, there was overlap among the processes informing the schooling of marginalized populations (including American Indians, African Americans, and Puerto Ricans), their relationship (one not based on agency) with and within the United States, and "the larger intention of U.S. policy makers for the colony or people."[6] For Puerto Ricans, the position they inherited by virtue of the legalized second-class citizenship imposed on them similarly facilitated the schooling they received, and this phenomenon followed them across the diaspora.

For many parents and students, Chicago schools became an extension of the socializing agents and agenda of island schools, which sought to transform the population into "fellow Americans," albeit Americans who arrived in continental U.S. cities facing a reality different from that of white Americans. I argue that schools and schooling played both formal and informal roles in the everyday lives of Puerto Ricans. The nexus of competing agendas and interests of various stakeholders in Chicago, especially concerning the education system that Puerto Ricans encountered, affected the population's everyday life. More importantly, who was schooling whom shifted when power relationships were institutionalized and then challenged as the Puerto Rican population in Chicago encountered structures similar to those faced on the island. An unpacking of these relationships and agendas guides *Puerto Rican Chicago* in its historical and cultural analysis of Puerto Ricans' educational experiences following their mass migration to the city between 1940 and 1977.

The years 1940 and 1977 serve as bookends for this important story. The early 1940s saw the initial migration of Puerto Ricans to Chicago from the island as well as from other U.S. cities, although not necessarily in the large numbers we find in subsequent decades. The 1940s also reminds us that Puerto Rican migration was not limited to men's labor and economic interests or centered on a male reading of the migratory story. As we see through the lives of Puerto Rican women migrants, their bodies were tied to larger conversations about the future of the island and the diaspora. Women became part of both intellectual and labor migrations as the interests of University of Puerto Rico administrators and U.S. Department of Labor personnel intersected in the lives of these women in Chicago. But if the 1966 Division Street uprising ushered in a new era of community-based mobilization, awareness, and activism, 1977 reminded the now three-decades-old community just how little had changed. Like the events of June 1966, the 1977 celebration around the annual Puerto Rican Day Parade and festivities in Humboldt Park was marred by violence. Yet the 1977 event differed from the 1966 uprisings in that residents of the increasingly troubled and sometimes divided community were unsure of who or what, exactly, was the catalyst. During the 1977 festivities, Chicago police and community members faced two days of unrest that resulted in the deaths of two young Puerto Rican men, dozens of injuries and arrests, and property damage that lasted for years in the form of disinvestment by both property owners and the city.[7] If the 1940s marked the beginning, what would 1977 say about the community? Chronicling the community's evolution or genealogy is the focus of this narrative, and schools and education inform a much-needed reading of Puerto Rican Chicago. The book provides an account of critical moments in the lives of Puerto Ricans in the city during the mid-twentieth century as they confronted the structural inequalities they faced in education, employment, and housing. More importantly, it centers the critical nature of schools and schooling in their story. Although narratives on the history of island education exist, alongside pivotal works on Puerto Rican migration and settlement across the United States, this book serves as a critical account of the centrality of schools and schooling in the life of the diaspora. Whether seeking to adjust to life in the city in the 1940s and 1950s or challenging university administrators to acknowledge their needs in the 1970s, Puerto Ricans in Chicago positioned schools as a transformative tool in their quest to claim a sense of home and belonging in the city. In so illuminating these narratives, *Puerto Rican Chicago* contributes to a larger historical reading of the city as multiple sites experienced very differently by different groups of people.

The racialization of Puerto Ricans in Chicago resulted in schooling inequalities and community displacement, forcing the population to respond in various ways in the hope of alleviating concerns. For example, as Puerto Ricans found themselves relocated from (or pushed out of) their original communities in the city, including Lincoln Park, they created organizations and mobilized to confront the urban renewal practices that were forcing their geographic movement, reminding the community how schools were tied to this narrative. The Young Lords Organization, which originated as a street gang in 1960 but in the late 1960s transformed into a community activist organization, saw the loss of Waller High School in Lincoln Park for the African American and Puerto Rican residents as an expression of racially motivated oppression intended to disempower and marginalize the community. As the Lincoln Park community found itself in the midst of urban renewal projects, the school became a contentious site, as it symbolized to Black and Brown residents their impending displacement. A transformed community would need a new high school to welcome the white, more affluent residents, leaving African American and Puerto Rican students and their families without a space for themselves. Engaging in collaborative work with other marginalized populations in the community, the Young Lords confronted what they saw as the intentional and unjust work of the Board of Education and the city of Chicago to remove them from their community. In their view, the board and its supporters wanted "to consider school problems only and ignore the problems of our society and community, problems which directly cause bad schools."[8] The intersectionality of schools, oppression, and liberation for Puerto Ricans in the diaspora is the guiding narrative of *Puerto Rican Chicago*—a narrative that reminds us of the rich history of U.S. education and helps us unpack the life of a community and its people. Furthermore, this story complicates our understanding of citizenship as a privilege that does not always offer the benefits of agency, access to resources, or a better way of life.

Chicago is important in the story of the Puerto Rican diaspora, and schools and education played a central role during the middle decades of the twentieth century. But education and its values were not a monolithic ideal. The city's Puerto Rican community came to debate what education meant in their lives, and individuals' positions in this debate were sometimes marked by their gender or class identity. From the early participation of Puerto Rican women in Chicago organizing for labor rights to the struggle for community control of Tuley and Clemente High Schools, this conversation encompasses many threads reflecting how education and schooling were manifested in the life of Chicago's Puerto Rican community. These stories, however, are typically absent from the pages of textbooks and education histories. The history of Puerto Ricans in Chicago schools is a meaningful part of these educational narratives, and one I intend to tell. This is not merely a story about how Puerto Rican students were marginalized by a system of schooling inequality that led to marginalization. It is also a story of how their schooling served as a way for the community, including the students themselves, to mobilize and critically challenge the dominant forces within the city that limited Puerto Ricans' status. And further, it is an account of how the schooling of Puerto Ricans, whether as islanders or as part of the growing DiaspoRican community, was framed around colonial notions of schools' role in creating an "acceptable citizenry."[9]

Schooling Colonial Subjects

The commencement of U.S. rule in Puerto Rico brought new ideas about how to transform the United States' newly acquired people. The first appointed governor of the island, Guy V. Henry, was clear in his assessment of what was needed: "The work of Americanizing a new colony inhabited by an alien people, of a race diametrically opposed to the Anglo-Saxon in very many respects, incurs a responsibility that one cannot assume lightly. . . . In order to introduce American customs and forms of government on the island it was essential to educate those inhabitants of the island to our way of looking at things who were by nature and education best fitted for the work."[10] After 1898, education of Puerto Ricans on the island quickly became an "American" experience, with language and curriculum policies mirroring the schooling of mainland children. Perhaps more significantly, the schooling of island children became the starting point for forging ideological shifts both in Puerto Ricans' way of life and in their affiliation, transforming the former Spanish colonial subjects into quasi-Americans, something that followed the population as they migrated across U.S. cities. The head of the first Board of Education on the island, Vincent S. Clark, wrote, "If the schools are made American, and teachers and pupils are inspired with the American spirit, and people of both races can be made to cooperate harmoniously in building up the schools, the island will become in its sympathies, views, and attitude toward life and toward government essentially American."[11] The United States' hopes regarding islanders' education were clear, and they rested on the schools' influence on the students it sought to transform and educate. "The moral influence of physical environment of the pupil in the schoolroom cannot be computed in dollars and cents," detailed the *Teachers' Manual for the Public Schools of Puerto Rico in 1900*.[12] That influence "reaches far beyond the pupil himself; with his influence it goes into the home, placing new ideals before the parents, creating ambition for neater, more orderly home surroundings, and leading, indirectly, to the cultivation of industry, thrift and saving, and all those qualities that distinguish a highly civilized and enlightened community from the savages or from that lower strata of civilized society that approximates the savage state."[13] American island leaders assumed that Puerto Ricans were a people in need of intervention whose society lacked any attributes of "civilization." This stance was not uncommon. During the early decades of the twentieth century, the United States routinely wielded children's education as a tool for aligning oppressed groups, such as communities of color, with the national identity, even when the groups themselves did not stand to benefit from the alliance. However, as we will see with the Puerto Rican population in Chicago at midcentury, teachers, parents, and students were not passive participants in the colonial education project on the island. Educators there "carried forward the tradition of defending their practice and commitment to students before a colonial state."[14] Puerto Rican education, it seems, would frame the island's political and social discourse for decades to come, leaving its citizenry to contend with the residual effects of this complicated colonial relationship, both on the island and across the diaspora.

The United States wasted no time in reorganizing the island's education system by centering English language acquisition, American patriotism, and American customs as central themes in students' learning. Across the United States, school districts, religious institutions, and state and local governments similarly created Americanization programs targeting the growing (im)migrant population. As the headmaster of one Boston school wrote in 1910, "These schools not only educate the immigrant children, but from them knowledge of American customs and laws is carried by the children to the parents."[15] In 1915, the city of Detroit, "feeling that a vast but fertile field awaited only the scattering of the seed, . . . blazed the trail in Americanization work."[16] As reformers reiterated, "The American, even under the guise of benevolent paternalism, seldom offered anything more encouraging than words to the newcomers."[17] Adopting a curriculum to assist in the teaching of English and training teachers to carry out the work, Detroit invested various resources to promote citizenship and language acquisition. But Americanization programs in schools did more than just create an "acceptable citizenry." In the case of further racialized populations, such as Japanese communities in Hawai'i, these programs controlled and limited what officials viewed as subversive behavior.[18] Through its interventions across the world (and within its own occupied lands), the United States attempted to influence not only the economic and political futures of populations of people, "but also the opportunity to reinforce, reshape, and reorder the relations of power at home, including in the nation's growing public school systems."[19] Schools and schooling have been intricately tied to conversations on power and race that aided some while further disenfranchising others. Examples include boarding schools targeting American Indians; the industrial school movement, which limited opportunities for African Americans; and schooling policies that sought to create an acceptable citizenry of racialized and newly acquired populations. Schools also informed students, and by extension their families, about the disproportionate framing of power, as students swiftly learned their position within the racial and social hierarchies that schools reinforced. Puerto Rico's schools and Puerto Ricans in general were no exception. As articulated by Thomas Holt, "racial selves . . . were made in the social environments of theatrical and street performances . . . mediated between global economic and political forces and their local enactment."[20] The classrooms and neighborhoods inhabited by Puerto Ricans, first on the island and then in Chicago, similarly offered a platform for the population to negotiate their very existence amid these global economic and political forces. Unfortunately, these also became the spaces in which the population learned how little agency they had.

A decade before Detroit's own assessment in 1918 of its pioneering work on transforming the growing newcomer population, the mission of schooling practices on the island was already clearly aligned with political and military ideologies, with control of schools and pedagogical practices in the hands of American leaders. The implementation of American values, customs, and culture rendered the average Puerto Rican child well informed on such American figures as Abraham Lincoln and George Washington, and symbols such as the American flag.[21] Reports from the commissioner of education praised the early transformations.

> Almost every school on the island has an American flag. . . . In almost every city of the island, and at many rural schools, the children meet and salute the flag as it is flung to the breeze. . . . The pupils then sing America, Hail Columbia, Star Spangled Banner, and other patriotic songs. The marvel is that they sing these in English. The first English many of them know is the English of our national songs. The influence is far-reaching. In many schools the children also sing Borinquen, the canto provincial of the island. It was proscribed in former days, and is now all the more precious to the hearts of the people.[22]

Pedagogical practices in Puerto Rican schools enforced English language instruction, with teachers, most of whom were Puerto Ricans, required to practice everyday use of the language under the fear of suspension.[23] Legally, English and Spanish coexisted as the island's official languages, but a February 1902 law mandated the use of English for both governmental and instructional use.[24] The teachers' manual reminded island teachers of their responsibility in this colonial project: "If [they] keep the highest aspirations and ideals of their profession in view, they will be able to work a reform in public education in this Island in a few years as fundamental and far-reaching as that which has been accomplished in other countries only with the lapse of generations."[25] In addition to instructing teachers about their moral responsibility to the future of the island, the manual used illustrations depicting schools in far-off places such as Minnesota to demonstrate the proper placement of bookshelves, the importance of punctuality, and the need to enforce cleanliness in their students. Students, according to the manual, should have access to good books and manners within their classrooms, as these influences were assumed to be absent at home.

School-based approaches to Americanizing Puerto Ricans and other groups were not the only means through which local communities attempted to transform populations. As detailed in Vicki Ruiz's work on Mexican American women in the twentieth century, religious organizations' proselytization efforts utilized Bible studies, music lessons, scouting, hygiene, and citizenship classes as means to "assist" families.[26] In Texas, the push for an Americanization curriculum was met by the call for school districts to better serve the population, as detailed in the work of Carlos Blanton. But Blanton claims that "Americanizing through language meant that true academic achievement was made impossible."[27] He argues that because bilingual education failed to utilize the students' home language, it could not truly support academic success. In emerging barrios across the Midwest, the aims of Americanization programs were a bit more direct. Zaragosa Vargas argues that "Mexicans in the North were taught the principles of Americanization mainly to prepare them for the ordered and efficient world of factory work."[28] Puerto Rican students and their parents unknowingly and perhaps unwillingly became part of a similar history. However, the story of Puerto Ricans differs because even before they arrived in U.S. cities as an exploitable labor force in the early and mid-twentieth century, they had been subjected to Americanization efforts through their education on the island. Transformation of the island's schools in the early days of U.S. occupation ensured that Puerto Ricans carried the legacy of coloniality and its relationship to power as they moved from schooled bodies to labor hands.

In addition to infusing classrooms and students' lives with the virtues of good citizenship, the schools also asserted the importance of English language acquisition. In 1902, the Legislative Assembly of Porto Rico enacted the Official Language Act, reflecting the U.S. administrators' urgency to elevate English usage to the same level as Spanish usage in everyday life.[29] The recruitment of English-speaking American teachers and the training of island-born educators became a priority. "These American teachers," declared the commissioner of education, "know little Spanish. The children know no English. The people are anxious to have their children acquire the language of the United States."[30] According to the island's U.S. administrators, it was the responsibility of the American teachers to train "native" teachers how to provide effective instruction in both languages in their newly organized classrooms, especially in rural communities. Island officials were initially sympathetic to the need to retain Spanish proficiency alongside English acquisition and literacy improvements. In 1901, Commissioner Brumbaugh advocated for bilingualism, maintaining that "the Spanish language will not and should not disappear from these schools. . . . It will be a hindrance, not a help, to deprive these people of an opportunity to acquire both languages."[31]

In 1907, however, the commissioner of education on the island, Roland P. Falkner, writing about his appreciation of the Puerto Rican people's hunger for education, boasted "that the time seems not far distant when the graded schools throughout the island will be taught exclusively in the English language."[32] From the 1905–6 to the 1906–7 school year, the number of schools taught in English by American teachers increased from 37 to 74, with the number taught entirely in English by Puerto Rican teachers increasing from 37 to 128, out of the almost 700 school buildings in operation. Falkner gave credit for this to the Puerto Rican teachers who increasingly sought to qualify themselves in the learning and teaching of English. In addition to language enforcement, curricular interventions sought to introduce island children to textbook materials promoting Western ideals and history. The colonial project of schools, the legacy of U.S. intervention in the social lives of the population, had widespread effects, reaching far beyond the island itself. These curricular and pedagogical shifts meant that when Puerto Rican students enrolled in schools in U.S. cities, they and their families were already familiar with the aims and purposes of U.S. schools and with their own lack of agency in their education.

Despite intense Americanization policies persisting in the first half of the twentieth century, Puerto Ricans retained much of their culture and fostered what Felix Padilla refers to as "a Puerto Rican consciousness and solidarity," centered on maintaining linguistic distinctiveness despite U.S. colonial rule.[33] This resistance to full assimilation continued as Puerto Ricans migrated to various U.S. cities, including Chicago; at times, their conversations about their community's failures and successes were intricately linked to their linguistic identity and their perceived failure to assimilate and succeed in schools. Puerto Ricans across the diaspora faced unfamiliarity with the culture, language, and social landscape of these cities. This helped transform their relationship with schools: on the island, schools were a leading venue for Americanization, but in their new home cities across the United States, schools became sites of liberation. It is important to keep in mind that the story of Puerto Rican migration across the diaspora in the early twentieth century is shaped by Puerto Ricans' experiences in Puerto Rican schoolhouses. Their education in American practices, ideologies, and policies started in Puerto Rican schools but continued in their new host cities, where they faced inequalities in labor, housing, and schooling.

We can view Puerto Rican migration through a parallel reading of the history of American education in the twentieth century. Puerto Rican students across the diaspora entered schools and education systems immersed in their own discourses on the role of schooling within a national context, one with a complicated history. Even Americanization programs and initiatives came on the heels of a shift in the organization of schools that mirrored the rise in urban populations at the turn of the century. Simultaneously, Black and Indigenous populations were being pushed further toward the margins of educational spaces. Especially in the South and Southwest, they were forced to create their own schooling opportunities in spaces that offered better opportunities for their communities. Puerto Ricans thus inherited a system of education marked by social movements and historical shifts. From Americanization programs and progressive education to the growing civil rights movement, schools and schooling for the Puerto Rican community highlighted their lack of agency, irrespective of their location. *Puerto Rican Chicago* highlights the need to bring the Puerto Rican population into the conversation, and therefore out of the shadows of history.

Problematizing Citizenship for
Puerto Ricans in Chicago

The Jones Act of 1917 (also known as the Jones-Shafroth Act) granted U.S. citizenship to anyone born in Puerto Rico on or after April 11, 1899, and essentially established a U.S.-controlled government body on the island.[34] It also contributed to the freedom of movement between Puerto Rico and the United States. Puerto Rican migration has historically been quite diverse, with groups of students, merchants, and political exiles becoming fixtures in cities like New York from the mid-1800s to the early twentieth century.[35] Early works on Puerto Rican migration blamed the islanders themselves for the social ills, such as the island's perceived overpopulation, that contributed to their post-1898 movement. But those works ignored the various external economic factors contributing to their migration.[36] These conversations on "non-economic" factors ignored Puerto Ricans' lack of control over their own reality under U.S. rule, including their inability to vote for their own governor until decades later. In many ways, this "in-betweenness" and instability came to define the migrant population, who utilized their citizenship status to relocate to cities such as Chicago.

Both the Chardón Plan and Operation Bootstrap, which were closely tied to the struggle for political power between the U.S. and local Puerto Rican governments, contributed to the mass migration of Puerto Ricans.[37]

Scholars have claimed that the island's overpopulation was a factor driving Puerto Ricans to northern U.S. cities. Some have argued that this "excess" in population was caused in part by health improvements on the island following U.S. occupation.[38] Due to their concern about the island's perceived overpopulation, the U.S. and Puerto Rican governments recommended temporary migration "as a strategy for ameliorating the demographic pressures allegedly hampering Puerto Rico's economic development."[39] According to a report published by the Centro de Estudios Puertorriqueños, the island's population nearly doubled between 1898 and 1940.[40] This "excess population" needed new host cities, and Chicago was an attractive possibility due to its labor needs. Although the island's population did indeed increase in the years following U.S. occupation, that increase was tied to the better quality of available healthcare resources.

On the island itself, people's movement from rural areas to emerging urban communities was a clear response to U.S. expansion, triggered by the "critical social, political, and economic transformations in Puerto Rico."[41] This migratory pattern coincides with the island's shift away from a predominantly agricultural society as intense industrialization processes began to take shape. Industrialization was unable to sustain the resulting workforce, however, leading to chronically high unemployment rates.[42] The result was a mass exodus from Puerto Rico, "reflecting regional and gender dimensions of economic change and government policies."[43] Many people moved to cities in the United States in search of employment, a trend that accelerated in the years following the Depression. According to the Office of the Government of Puerto Rico, "Their 'Mayflower' is the modern airplane. . . . They come with the same hopes and aspirations of our forefathers. They bring the same resolve to make a better home for themselves than the one they left."[44] However, unlike "our forefathers," Puerto Ricans entered U.S. cities contending with racial politics that relegated them to the margins, racialized as foreigners despite their U.S. citizenship. Early migrants' lives point out the complicated racial hierarchies they left behind in Puerto Rico and highlight their introduction to U.S. politics and spaces.[45] The ramifications of U.S. imperialism and expansion created an in-betweenness for Puerto Ricans that followed them to the United States. Borrowing from Justice Edward Douglass White's assessment of Puerto Rico's status in *Downes v. Bidwell* (1901), Puerto Rico and Puerto Ricans continued to be seen as "foreign to the United States in a domestic sense."[46] This view framed the reality that the population faced as their numbers increased in U.S. cities. Puerto Ricans' movement to the mainland was informed not only by the granting of citizenship but also by the development of economic policies and plans, such as the Chardón Plan and

Operation Bootstrap, which served as driving factors in their migratory decisions. Consequently, the economic policies developed on the island by both U.S. and local interests, beginning with the Foraker Act in 1900, enforced the United States' control of island politics and policies and its subsequent corporate investment, leading to Puerto Rico's industrialization. These changes, which have been written about extensively by scholars, pushed Puerto Rican men and women to utilize their status as U.S. citizens to gain entry into U.S. labor markets. This rapid "spread of capitalism transformed the social class structure and the nature of political struggle in Puerto Rico," limiting the opportunities of many on the island.[47] The political relationship between the United States and Puerto Rico informed this movement, establishing Puerto Ricans as relevant and vibrant community members within major U.S. cities.

With the implementation of the Jones Act in 1917, U.S. cities became the destination of choice for many islanders seeking to escape unwelcome economic and political changes. The availability of educational opportunities outside the island informed the movement of some elite Puerto Ricans. Other islanders' migration was forced by economic disparities. Their migration to U.S. cities quickly filled a labor need created by U.S. military interventions around the world. In the years following World War I, the United States faced a shortage of semiskilled and unskilled workers because immigration reform acts, such as the Emergency Quota Act of 1921, seriously limited the number of workers entering the country.[48] The labor shortage and the expanding industrialization in northern U.S. cities prompted the movement not only of Puerto Ricans to the mainland, but also of African Americans from the South to northern cities. By 1920, forty-five U.S. states reported the presence of Puerto Ricans, with New York housing the majority. Understanding the experience of the population's migration to cities such as New York, including their residential, labor, and schooling struggles, is essential in we are to speak to the way this group became incorporated into Chicago communities.

The transnational ties between Puerto Ricans on the island and those in continental cities helped shape both places, as "people respond to, accommodate, and resist" the role of power in their lives.[49] The daily lives of Puerto Ricans in Chicago were influenced by their continuing ties to the physical island, including their work ethic and family structures, and affected the ways they interacted with and mobilized within the city. Despite their desire to maintain a sentimental (and sometimes physical) attachment to the island, Puerto Ricans quickly learned how to claim their rights and privileges as U.S. citizens and as Chicago residents, developing an understanding of the resources available to them. This process included politically and socially organizing the community to meet their needs, especially through schools.

Puerto Rican women, including mothers, similarly engaged in practices that ensured that the community's needs were met. Puerto Rican students faced numerous challenges: constant displacement across city schools, a curriculum that ignored their language and cultural identity, and educators who were either disinterested in assisting or unaware of how to assist the growing Puerto Rican population. In addition, these factors intersected with the day-to-day politics of life in Chicago for students of color. Schools became a site where Puerto Ricans claimed, reclaimed, and negotiated their place as rightful members of the Chicago community, but also as a community constantly facing displacement and having to reimagine or redefine home. Schools were also the place where the population again faced the idea that schooling should mold Puerto Ricans into "acceptable citizens." Their citizenship status allowed the population some form of mobility across the city, either because of dissatisfaction with employment or housing or because of displacement at the hands of developers. As their numbers and dissatisfaction with city life grew, citizenship also framed their overall engagement through community-based and religious organizations (as was the case for Los Caballeros de San Juan, discussed in subsequent chapters), as well as through their activism and political mobilization. However, citizenship did not always protect them from the misconceptions of city officials who viewed Puerto Ricans as deportable citizens. After community organizer José "Cha Cha" Jiménez had one too many encounters with the local police in Chicago, his family was given the option to send him back to Puerto Rico to avoid incarceration in a juvenile detention center. Jiménez's return to the island lasted less than a year but influenced his subsequent activism.[50] Similarly, some women migrants were offered "leniency" regarding their legal problems if they simply returned to Puerto Rico. The perceived deportability of Puerto Ricans, despite their status as U.S. citizens, complicated their early days in the city and perhaps played a role in their approach to life in Chicago. Furthermore, it influenced their view of the city's responsibility to them, and later sustained their political mobilization in the late 1970s and early 1980s.

The story of Puerto Rican Chicago is part of a larger history of Latina/o/x in urban cities.[51] This population is often missing from larger narratives, but Latina/o/x historians are writing it into an expanded reading of cities. Jerry González's work on Mexican Americans' movement into new communities captures the essence of what it means to reimagine oneself within new spaces, while also challenging contemporary readings of Mexican American identity and community formation.[52] Nancy Mirabal similarly challenges monolithic narratives of Cuban migration, settlement, and identity in her book *Suspect Freedoms*.[53] Mirabal meticulously historicizes sexuality and race and insists that they must be part of the narrative about how Cubans and Cuban Americans both reimagine and remake the story of the city. Often, however, these histories ignore the cultural and political importance of the Latina/o/x Midwest. Lilia Fernández's work on Mexicans and Puerto Ricans in postwar Chicago reminds us of the need to avoid limiting our conversations to the West and East Coasts in our quest to fill in the gaps in Latina/o/x history.[54] From the sugar beet fields to the growing auto manufacturing industry of the postwar years, Puerto Rican and Mexican migrants have been part of the economic, labor, and social history of the Midwest, but historiographers often ignore them or view them through a limited lens.[55] At times, historical writings depicted the population as laborers with little or no agency, often ignoring their contributions as community members navigating the social, political, and racial landscapes of their new home communities. The growing and critically important scholarship on Puerto Rican Chicago that began to emerge during the previous two decades helps unpack the role of migrants in the city. Felix Padilla's pivotal work on Puerto Ricans and other Latinos in Chicago presented a new understanding of the city through the history and community work of Puerto Rican migrants.[56] But the work of *Latina* historians, sociologists, anthropologists, and other scholars has truly transformed the field and mapped out this population's importance in conversations on migration, labor, and gender politics within a global city. Ana Ramos-Zayas's *National Performances* reminds us how the political and cultural consequences of the island's status were lived out on the streets of Chicago. The population, according to Ramos-Zayas, "perceived themselves to be empowered to claim these rights as U.S. citizens by constructing a popular nationalism that raised multivalent contradictions about the nation, national identity, and civil rights."[57] Thanks to new works on Latina/o/x Chicago, the diaspora is now center stage in any reading of the city.[58] This book adds to the narrative by focusing on the importance of schools and education in telling the story of Puerto Rican Chicago, highlighting the constant maneuvering, organizing, and rhetoric utilized by the population to facilitate change around schooling concerns. The life of a community often is centered on schools, as schools provide a reading of communities' day-to-day challenges in ways that mirror larger politics. The relationship between Chicago's Puerto Ricans and the city's schools offers us such a reading as we investigate the evolution of this community's status from the 1940s to the 1970s.

Chicago schools became contested spaces where communities began to reimagine themselves through decades of struggle, marginalization, and sometimes violence. The city of Chicago was the *space* that this population came to navigate, negotiate, and embody as a marker of who they are as ra-

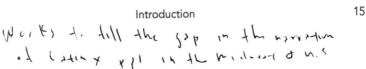

cialized beings. Schools then became the *place* where Puerto Ricans began to gain a sense of security and shared lived experiences, hoping to meet their practical needs through education. Further, schools served as a place where identities were created and maintained, especially for a community constantly facing displacement. James D. Anderson's seminal work on Black education in the South expresses the desire of a marginalized population to seek access to education in order to transform their status on their own terms.[59] For both Puerto Ricans and African Americans in Chicago, schools were a site where their growing populations in the postwar years could articulate their discontent with their status in the city and confront how their social and economic status was tied to their schooling inequality.

Community, Schools, and Home

With a population nearing eighty thousand in 1970, Chicago's Puerto Ricans held a substantial stake not only in *barrio* politics but as shareholders in the city's daily (and Daley) maintenance. Despite their citizenship, Puerto Ricans found themselves racialized as nonwhite, with their identities as Americans highly contested. In Chicago, New York, and Philadelphia, Puerto Ricans began forming critical alliances with other communities, building coalitions with other ethnic and racial groups to make gains following the civil rights movement. Organizations such as the Young Lords and the Black Panthers worked together to transform the institutional forces that plagued their communities in East Coast cities. In Chicago, Mexicans and Puerto Ricans actively developed and maintained ties with each other to gain momentum in addressing labor, housing, and political issues, all within a political context that had marginalized both groups for decades.[60] It is significant that these populations developed as a community during Mayor Richard J. Daley's administration; this affected their relationship with city and school officials.

These groups' schooling reality was truly a shared community concern. For example, in the fall of 1968, African American, Puerto Rican, and Mexican American students staged school walkouts to demand the development of relevant curricula and increased hiring of African American and Spanish-speaking counselors and teachers. School administrators quickly dismissed the students' grievances by claiming that outside agitators had encouraged their activism and the school disruptions. The appointment of both Alvin J. Boutte, an African American man, and María Cerda, a Puerto Rican woman, to the Chicago Board of Education in the late 1960s was a critical and shared win for these communities. This success demonstrated how communities of color could work to challenge the dominant forces limiting both their political growth in the city and their educational opportunities. *Puerto Rican Chicago* provides a narrative about these points of contention, showing that Puerto Ricans, at times with the help of other communities of color, mobilized across gender, class, age, and race to alleviate their growing discontent with the city and its schools. The population joined a generation of school-based, community-driven activism that challenged a system of education maintaining the social inequalities these communities faced daily.

During some moments of this history, Puerto Rican women in particular engaged in community activism and organizing, motivated by seeing their children underserved or ignored in Chicago schools. The familial ties that bind these (im)migrants, along with the gendered views within families and communities, similarly shaped and sometimes limited the educational trajectories of generations of Latina/o/x people and African Americans. Schools became the means for these women to critically engage in the development of their communities in ways previously denied to them. Their participation in school and community activism moved them beyond the traditional domestic sphere to which they had been relegated as wives or as domestic workers and into new roles as community leaders, schoolteachers, and administrators. This book places Puerto Rican women's experiences at the center of the story of Puerto Rican Chicago both because of women's involvement in community activism organized around schooling and because of their role as early labor (and intellectual) migrants to the city. For instance, while Mirta Ramírez was a young mother attending Northeastern Illinois University, she sought to facilitate educational change for Puerto Rican youth with the 1968 founding of Aspira Inc. of Illinois, closing a gap that local schools had not been able to fill. Aspira, initially a New York–based organization supporting Puerto Rican children's education, expanded to Chicago as part of an "effort to enable Chicago's Puerto Rican community to break out of its cycle of poverty thru self-help."[61] Media accounts chronicled women's role in the community, with young Puerto Rican women leading sit-ins at Chicago's largely Puerto Rican Tuley High School in 1973 to voice their discontent with the school's administration. These women fought for school equality as educators, through their participation in the development of local organizations such as Aspira and by serving on the Chicago Board of Education and in other leadership positions. For many women activists, the plight of Puerto Rican students across the city became a community affair. Yet their voices are largely absent from the archival records of community- and school-based groups. Even within these women's own Puerto Rican spaces, gender mattered.

During the late 1960s, Puerto Ricans in Chicago created space to come together, address local issues, and make demands of a city that had never imagined that they would become a permanent fixture. They did so through civic and political participation in community groups such as Aspira and the Young Lords Organization, as well as through publications such as the newspaper *El Puertorriqueño*. These activities forced the city to acknowledge the deplorable conditions in which Puerto Ricans lived, worked, and learned. Puerto Rican children's limited access to resources and quality education simultaneously marginalized and inspired this community as their numbers grew. Puerto Rican community members and parents engaged with city schools by participating in parent-teacher associations and organizing activist efforts, and the emerging cohort of college-age Puerto Ricans mirrored these efforts at state colleges and universities. Puerto Rican students chronicled their turbulent relationship within institutions of higher learning through newspapers such as Northeastern Illinois University's *Lucha Estudiantil* and *Que Ondee Sola*. Whether parents, community members, or students, Puerto Ricans entered a decade of community activism seeking to change educational outcomes for thousands of students while laying claim to a city they had called home for decades.

For many Puerto Ricans who migrated to Chicago or other U.S. cities, the political discourse surrounding the island's status framed how they participated in local politics and across the community. In the 1960s, nationalist organizations centered on Puerto Rican independence emerged in Chicago.[62] Nationalists' ideals for groups such as the Young Lords were filtered through the organizations' approaches to dealing with issues of equality and access for Chicago's Puerto Rican students. The school dropout rate for Puerto Rican students rose to over 70 percent by the early 1970s, leading to the creation of alternative schools through community-led efforts, including La Escuelita Puertorriqueña, later renamed Pedro Albizu Campos High School after the famed political leader.[63] This allowed the community to take charge of educating their youth, who were increasingly "pushed out" of city schools, as detailed in the work of Isidro Lucas.[64] The Puerto Rican community continued to be racialized as second-class citizens, albeit citizens nevertheless, with political power and the right to vote.

Puerto Ricans' organizing work in Chicago's schools is part of a long history of Latina/o school battles, especially in the southwestern United States, with some conflicts predating the *Brown v. Board of Education* ruling in 1954. Laura Muñoz's work on *Romo v. Laird* (1925) highlights the lives of central Arizona families "grappl[ing] with the concept of belonging in America and how they used the law to deliver the rights and privileges promised to white American citizens."[65] Although *Romo* is not always cited as a groundbreaking case, it highlighted the politics of belonging and was among the first cases to contextualize the role of Mexican and Mexican American families in filing lawsuits to challenge the relationship between schools and segregation. In *Independent School District v. Salvatierra* (1930), a group of Mexican parents in Texas claimed that their children were unjustly segregated due to their race.[66] In *Alvarez v. Lemon Grove* (1931), the court ruled in favor of a Mexican community, asserting that "separate facilities for Mexican American students were not conducive to Americanization and that they retarded the English language development of Spanish-speaking children."[67] *Méndez v. Westminster* (1946), a successful class-action suit brought on behalf of "Mexican-origin students" in Orange County, California, attempted to end racial segregation in schools on the grounds that separate was not equal. Lawyers in both *Gonzales v. Sheely* (1951) and *Brown* used *Méndez* to help frame their cases regarding the unconstitutional nature of school segregation.[68] I argue that this case marked the beginning of *Latina/o* challenges (not just Mexican or Puerto Rican challenges) to school segregation and inequality, as the main plaintiffs, the Méndez children, were indeed both Mexican and Puerto Rican. Although not historically cited as a landmark case in educational access, *Méndez* marks the beginning of a long history of community access to quality education for Puerto Rican students, who often found themselves in racial limbo and with their citizenship continuously questioned. "I married a Mexican, so I fought for the Mexicans," said Felícita Méndez, the children's mother. "Everybody that was minority was treated the same. I was a citizen, born a citizen in Puerto Rico. I could not even go to a theater and sit with the other people."[69] Chicago's Puerto Ricans were a part of this history of community-based activism, especially around schooling concerns—and this book will tell that story. At the same time, the constant reminder of Puerto Ricans' colonial status makes their story different from that of other Latina/o groups, a fact not lost on those actively participating in the movement to change schooling.

The Limits of the Archives

Just like the overall narrative of the history of U.S. education, the archives detailing Puerto Ricans' experiences in Chicago are limited in scope. The first two decades of Puerto Rican migration are documented mainly in the footnotes of the city's history and in the memories of others. When communities are denied a sense of belonging historically, even the archives work to exclude their contributions and realities. Oral history as a methodology in educational research has embraced the project of reconstructing a silenced past. To borrow from Eve Tuck and Angie Morrill, it is about "unforgetting," contending with "a ghost submerged in an archive."[70]

My visits to collections at the archives of the Chicago History Museum, the University of Chicago, and the University of Illinois at Chicago (UIC, formerly Circle Campus) documented the migration but also revealed Puerto Ricans' status as emergent community members. This frequently proved frustrating, because the information tended to be snippets that were not originally created to tell the story of Puerto Rican Chicago. These accounts were limiting and one-sided. But my visits to archives and special collections at the Chicago Catholic Diocese, Northeastern Illinois University, the Fundacion Luis Muñoz Marín, DePaul University, and the Rafael Cintrón Ortiz Latino Cultural Center at UIC helped move the community out of the footnotes. These collections included materials that documented the involvement of Puerto Ricans themselves in creating services aimed at their particular needs while also challenging misconceptions regarding their identities. Puerto Ricans in Chicago began developing their own newspapers in the mid-1960s. These publications bring the community's voice into the telling of their history. For information about the earlier years of the migration, I was forced to depend on mainstream newspapers. I found stories about Chicago's Puerto Ricans there, but the stories did not always include the community's own voices. Additional information comes from oral histories, some of which I conducted and some of which were provided by other researchers. Much like other historical works about and by communities of color, our community stories are collages, pieced together from a variety of sources.

A History of a Community

Puerto Rican Chicago is more than a history of schools and education; it is a history of a community. But to speak to that history, we have to begin with the island, as this introduction has done. Chapter 1 opens with a conversation about the historical consequences of U.S. colonial rule on the island as the population began to migrate to U.S. cities. Examining the role of community-based and citywide organizations in both New York and Chicago allows for a clearer understanding of the challenges faced by the population and the responses initiated to aid in their settlement in these cities—responses that often fell short. Groups such as the Mayor's Committee on New Residents, the Welfare Council of Metropolitan Chicago, the Chicago Commission on Human Relations, and the Chicago Board of Education are central to this story, as they demonstrate the common tendency to focus on schools and language policies without a clear understanding of the population itself. It is important to highlight a variety of readings of the migratory and settlement history of Puerto Ricans to the United States and Chicago, as these histories vary across different spaces. Chapter 1 fosters an understanding of Puerto Ricans' initial labor migration, the overlap between labor and education migration for Puerto Rican women in Chicago, and the responses of city agencies and organizations to the movement.

Chapter 2 details the evolution of the relationship between the city of Chicago and its Puerto Rican residents, with schools and education at the center of the conversation. The role of education in the community's life soon prompted debate about who would have a voice in deciding its future and the approaches to meeting the needs of the community. Aside from language policies and Americanization programs, the city had little else to offer the population. Exacerbating the issue, these policies ignored the city's rising racial tensions, which exploded in 1966 in the form of the Division Street riots. In this conversation, it is especially important to point out how the city's failure to provide adequate social and educational conditions inspired and encouraged the Puerto Rican population to shape their reactions in the form of community-based organizations. Groups such as Aspira were a much-needed response, and they highlight the role of women in forging their community's future.

The struggle for Tuley High School, discussed in chapter 3, shows how important it was for the community to take the lead in conversations about their children's future. These conversations both addressed the schools' physical structures and entailed intense battles over who would lead Puerto Rican children within the schools. The case of Tuley, subsequently renamed Roberto Clemente High School, is central to that story. To obtain justice for their children, communities of color spent the 1960s and 1970s battling with school administrators to combat oppressive school reform policies, sometimes with success. The late 1960s saw the appointment of a Puerto Rican woman and an African American man to Chicago's Board of Education, a sign of the permanency of these communities' voices in directing their children's schooling lives. But this was only the beginning of the Puerto Rican community's struggle to improve education, and this struggle followed them as they progressed into institutions of higher learning.

Although Puerto Rican students' school dropout rate was high in the 1970s, the number of students attending colleges and universities increased, both in Chicago and across the state. Two of those institutions, Northeastern Illinois University and the University of Illinois Circle Campus (later known as the University of Illinois at Chicago), quickly became sites of contention as the students sought institutional changes aimed at increasing the number of Puerto Rican and other Latina/o students and creating resources and opportunities to enhance their success. Perhaps having learned from their community's struggles during the previous decade, Puerto Rican students mobilized and utilized their community capital to challenge yet another system of education that they saw as impeding their progress. Chapter 4 serves to historicize the experiences of these students.

But whether at institutions of higher learning or in Humboldt Park, Puerto Ricans working for community change needed to find ways to communicate, document, and share their experiences. Chapter 5 focuses on the development of Puerto Rican print media and their importance in giving voice to the community's life. Newspapers such as *El Puertorriqueño* and *Que Ondee Sola* are central to the story; they enabled the community to retell their own history, particularly with regard to schooling. For example, *El Puertorriqueño* regularly informed parents and community members about critical news from local schools, including PTA meetings, open houses, and the hiring and firing of teachers and administrators. By contrast, mainstream newspapers did not have local Puerto Rican writers providing community accounts; nor did they celebrate the successes of the community and their children. Instead, they created a monolithic portrayal of Puerto Ricans in the city, perpetuating misconceptions about the community.

The conclusion shows that the Puerto Rican community in Chicago, a community in constant flux, created and continues to create real change in the lives of schoolchildren. And central to this story is an understanding of the space and the place the community occupies in the city's history.

How people create meaning in their lives, both within and outside school spaces, informs us in ways that can enrich and expand educational research. For Latina/o populations, this can help challenge preconceived notions regarding the problematic relationship between schooling, education, and home. As Yi-Fu Tuan reminds us, "The home provides an image of the past. Moreover in an ideal sense home lies at the center of one's life."[71] Schools became such a place for communities of color in the United States, a place where a sense of belonging and economic and social mobility could be demanded and fought for. Unfortunately, struggle and inequality still exist. That is why we need to situate the Latina/o/x experience in U.S. schools within an understanding of the overall history of American education. As James D. Anderson points out, "It is crucial for an understanding of American educational history . . . to recognize that within American democracy there have been classes of oppressed people and that there have been essential relationships between popular education and the politics of oppression."[72] In many ways, the schooling experiences of Latina/o/x groups mirror those of other communities of color, as Latina/o/x students' struggles for equality have been fought not only in courtrooms but within the community as well.[73] Education historian Guadalupe San Miguel's work on Chicano education reminds us that although many studies have been written since the 1960s on minoritized groups such as Mexicans, there is much work that still needs to be done.[74] The growing scholarship on Latina/o/x history is bringing these stories out of the footnotes of history. David García's work on the segregation of Mexican Americans in Oxnard, California, and its aftereffects shows the intentionality of policies that limited access to equitable school opportunities for communities of color.[75] Mario Rios Perez brings Mexicans in Chicago into the conversation by examining how transnational networks, postrevolutionary thought, and popular education were critical to community formation.[76] It is no coincidence that, decades after their initial migration to the city, the Mexican community faced similar battles for the creation of their own community school, campaigning to name it after a former Mexican president, Benito Juárez. But Puerto Ricans' history in U.S. education also differs from that of other, or othered, populations. Puerto Ricans' relationship with schools and schooling cannot be separated from their history as a people subjugated by a colonial empire. Centering schooling as an essential element in the history of Puerto Rican migration to the Windy City, this book is the first full-length study to bring Puerto Ricans into the history of education beyond the island. *Puerto Rican Chicago* writes this community into Chicago's history and into the history of American education, demonstrating how groups of students, teachers, and community members worked together to confront the contentious educational sphere to gain a sense of belonging and equality.

Exploring the education of Puerto Ricans in Chicago lends nuance to the complicated trajectory of the community's struggle for access to resources and their quest for equality, while also providing a narrative for the creation and maintenance of a Puerto Rican identity grounded in community activism and collaboration despite group differences. Indeed, scholars have studied and written about the deleterious effects of schooling on the lives of Puerto Rican students and the nature of schooling on the island, as well as the language and cultural challenges faced by educators. But this book fills a gap by demonstrating how in one diasporic community, Puerto Ricans fought for and at times reclaimed and reframed their schooling, not just as colonial subjects, but as a people reimagining their lives amid the racial, political, and cultural reality of life in the city.

CHAPTER 1

Al Brincar el Charco

Urban Response to
the Puerto Rican "Problem"

Puerto Rican migration to the continental United States
has fluctuated ever since the first decade of the twentieth
century as a function of the demand for labor in the
United States and the living conditions on the island . . .
and partly as a reflection of the greater self-confidence
of Puerto Ricans as American War-veterans whose
aspirations and ambitions could not be satisfied any
longer by the limited opportunities on the island.
—Mayor's Committee on New Residents, 1960

WHEN A GROUP OF FOURTEEN Puerto Rican laborers arrived in Chicago
in 1946, the first of a larger group of fifty-three recruited by the Chicago
Foundry Company, the *Chicago Tribune* lauded their English language skills
and adaptability.[1] The workers were hired in the hope of "filling a labor need"
resulting from a housing shortage and what the company perceived as the
"preference of some workers to live on unemployment compensation."[2] The
fifty-three men, many of whom were veterans, made the long trip from San
Juan to Chicago as part of the *guagua aérea* (flying bus) and settled into their
new shared homes: seventy-foot-long railroad cars fitted with beds, show-
ers, and clubrooms. A Puerto Rican chef cooked for them, and coffee was
flown in from Puerto Rico to suit their preference. According to the article,
this group faced two problems: obtaining materials for their work shoes and
procuring "a good supply of rice for their table."[3]

These Puerto Rican migrants were part of a larger social and cultural
shift on the island that had begun in 1898, informed by the imposition of
citizenship via the Jones Act of 1917. The journalist's comment about the
laborers' familiarity with English might seem benign to the average reader,
but it highlights significant cultural and political changes that migrants had

experienced on the island, especially regarding education and the imposition of U.S. norms experienced by the migrants prior to their move. These workers would have been the very students whom the early commissioners of education in Puerto Rico had discussed and, at times, celebrated in their reports. Whether laborers or students, the islanders were subject to colonial practices in their daily lives that gave them familiarity with the continental way of life they would encounter after migration, but familiarity would not necessarily make their experiences easier. For Puerto Ricans, life in U.S. cities in the 1940s mirrored the social, political, and economic milieu they had left behind. These migrants arrived at a time when those cities were facing their own cultural, political, and economic shifts. In Chicago, the postwar years were marked by racial conflict that permeated every aspect of city life, from housing opportunities to schooling. In the words of Arnold Hirsch, "More than a simple legacy of the past, the contemporary ghetto"—the city, as I argue—"appeared a dynamic institution that was continually being renewed, reinforced, and reshaped."[4] The city of Chicago here is read as an institution in which conflicting voices struggled to renew, reinforce, and reshape the lives and futures of Puerto Ricans and other racialized populations. Violence within and resistance to this institution became part of daily life in the city. Although these conflicts primarily targeted African American residents, their effects would trickle down to Chicago's Puerto Rican community and its classrooms, and the early Puerto Rican migration to New York offered a similar experience.

Life in the Diaspora

Many early migrants' knowledge about Chicago was limited to news from family members and friends who had already moved there, as well as media accounts that positioned the city as a place eager to welcome Puerto Ricans. The Chicago encountered by early migrants was very much defined by racial, class, and gender lines that, although sometimes blurred, were supported by city politics. Black and Mexican residents had already experienced decades-long struggles to gain access to housing, labor, and school opportunities for their emerging communities. Indeed, in a city increasingly led by its growing white ethnic population, race was embedded in every aspect of life, and Black and Mexican residents faced a tumultuous and sometimes violent struggle for survival. The influx of European immigrants, especially Irish, in the late nineteenth and early twentieth centuries set the stage for ingrained markers across city spaces that limited the movement of subsequent migrant populations. These invisible lines distinguished one community from another, enforced by community members, and reminded city residents of color where they belonged or did not belong. In one incident of racial violence reinforced by social and physical markers of space, tensions erupted in July 1919 as white residents on Chicago's South Side sought to maintain a racial order that further pushed Black residents to the margins. The perceived trespassing of a Black youth's body across the invisible line in the water at the 29th Street Beach was the catalyst for white men and teens to violently target the city's Black residents. The death of seventeen-year-old Eugene Williams on July 27, 1919, ignited already smoldering racial tensions throughout city neighborhoods that positioned Irish youth gangs as protectors of white political and economic control of Chicago, aided by other white ethnic gangs.[5] Mexican residents similarly were tied to the 1919 Race Riot, although this fact is often ignored in the larger writing of the history. Like the southern Blacks who were migrating to the city, Mexicans escaping the political and economic upheaval in their home country during the Mexican Revolution viewed Chicago as a place of opportunity. During the 1919 riot, however, Mexican bodies became yet another opportunity for white mobs to exhibit their perceived racial dominance. The murder of Elizondo González at the hands of white rioters and the subsequent trial of José Blanco were "critical to the formation of Mexican ethno-racial understandings of themselves and their place in the ethno-racial orders of Chicago."[6] Less than a decade later, Mexicans again had to defend themselves physically and legally. While protecting her ten-year-old son from what she perceived as an assault at the hands of a Polish teenager, Juana Guevara shot and killed a former police officer who intervened.[7]

The increased number of non-Irish European immigrants in Chicago, especially Eastern and Southern Europeans, contributed to the racial tensions (and violence) across the city. These populations struggled to distinguish themselves from nonwhite residents and worked and fought (as in the case of youth gangs) to align themselves with whiteness, and thus power. The fact that white European immigrants sought to set themselves apart from other populations reflected "how thinking about race became an important part of the consciousness of immigrants."[8] In the first decades of the twentieth century, white residents viewed the growing population of Mexicans and southern Blacks as a challenge to this social order. As a result, nonwhite residents found themselves navigating a social, political, and economic landscape that impelled them to accept the racial hierarchy, whether in housing or the labor market. The various "ethnic" white groups, such as the Irish and Eastern and Southern Europeans, were fully invested in challenging the status of Black and Mexican residents in the city, and city neighborhoods (and beaches) provided the space to do so. Straying out of place, or stepping out of bounds, as Eugene Williams did, could prove dangerous, and sometimes deadly, to nonwhite residents. Yet at the same time that neighborhood boundaries limited their freedom to move about the city unhindered, Black and Mexican residents became invested in their new neighborhoods. The lives of teens and young adults, especially males, were framed by the constant need to protect, claim, and control the physical and imagined boundaries that these neighborhoods embodied. This became the early catalyst for Chicago youth gang culture in ethnic and racial communities. The city encountered by Puerto Ricans in the decades to follow would look very similar.

City officials' early measures to encourage migration to Chicago were marked by efforts to create a situation different from Puerto Ricans' experiences in New York City. Frustrated with life in New York, including language barriers, "many Puerto Ricans come to Chicago feeling resentment," according to a *Chicago Tribune* article.[9] According to a detailed and informative report published in 1960 by the Mayor's Committee on New Residents, the migration of Puerto Ricans to the mainland was prompted not only by social and economic conditions on the island but also by migrants' understanding of the opportunities available to them as citizens and war veterans.[10] But as city officials came to recognize, the "paradox of citizenship and 'alienness' aggravated by the factor of color, may tend to lead to disorganization rather than to adjustment and assimilation."[11] The report asserted that Puerto Ricans were to be welcomed as "fellow Americans"; however, this statement came too late to influence the city's treatment of earlier migrants. And despite being publicly welcomed as new residents with citizenship rights, Puerto Ricans soon realized that citizenship would not give them full access to equitable housing, labor, and educational opportunities. Even when islanders and subsequent mainland-born generations occupied neighborhoods and communities across the diaspora, their movement within cities was rapid and frequent. Economic necessity and de facto racial policies challenged their rootedness as they faced constant displacement. These migrants were initially welcomed, often discussed, and racialized by the media and social service agencies. The city's increasing population in the mid-twentieth century led to scarcity in housing and jobs, and these shortages had a disproportionate effect on the growing Puerto Rican community. This led Puerto Rican Chicagoans to question their position within the city's racial, political, and economic landscape, even though earlier accounts had depicted a city eager to include them.

From the 1930s to the 1960s, new capitalist ventures on the island displaced thousands of Puerto Rican workers, creating a willing and available workforce eager to emigrate for employment. According to Padilla, they were "attracted to the idea of migration primarily by its promise of an immediate improvement in [their] material life."[12] Places such as Chicago and New York benefited from the influx of labor, as economic shifts on the island left few employment opportunities for workers.[13] However, the outmigration, which was encouraged by both island and U.S. officials to alleviate the supposed strain on population growth, did little to reduce the numbers; Puerto Rico's population grew from just under a million in 1899 to more than two million in 1960.[14]

Gender played a significant role in this migration. Island and mainland governments encouraged women as well as men to migrate in order to ease the perceived overpopulation. This economic narrative depended on a sexist reading of Puerto Rican women and their bodies. The sexual habits of working-class Puerto Rican women, and more importantly their reproductive practices, became intertwined with discourses about economic policies, poverty, and even Puerto Rican nationalism.[15] The perception of U.S. and some island officials was that reproductive intervention was needed in order to transform these seemingly "backward" Puerto Rican women, and thus facilitate economic and social change.[16] The use of female sterilization on the island became one such program and was highly encouraged as a means of tying economic and social programs in Puerto Rico to women's bodies. When island officials moved to encouraging migration to U.S. cities, women were "exported" through labor contracts, becoming unknowing participants in both governments' quest to transform the island. As one scholar noted, the use of domestic training programs was seen as an "effort [to] solve the island's overpopulation issue by relocating women of prime reproductive age."[17] The bodies of Puerto Rican women became sites of negotiation where political and economic battles were waged, an agenda that followed them to their new home cities, as seen in both the organizing work of women in Chicago and the targeting of Puerto Rican women by school and city officials in New York.

On the island, many Puerto Ricans had been agricultural workers, but in New York they found employment in garment manufacturing, light factory work, cigar making, and domestic service, as well as other sectors of the local labor market.[18] Like earlier waves of European immigrants, the Puerto Rican migration to New York encouraged the formation of ethnic enclaves. But although Puerto Ricans had been exposed to the "American way of life" on the island, their transition to life in the city was not necessarily smooth because of misconceptions regarding the population. City leaders engaged in conversations about the status of Puerto Ricans in the city and their ability to become successful (read "acceptable") community members. One of the authors of a 1935 study titled *Reactions of Puerto Rican Children in New York City to Psychological Tests* recommended "1. That steps should be taken to prevent the immigration into this country of individuals of subnormal mentality from all nations, since these individuals become an educational, social and financial burden to the community, as well as the victims of their own inadequacy in our complex environment. 2. That the projected grant of statehood to Puerto Rico should be held in abeyance, pending a thorough and impartial investigation of economic and social conditions on the island, and of the mental qualifications of its inhabitants."[19] Puerto Ricans settling in New York and other U.S. cities found that the era's racial politics framed and dictated their lives, including where they lived, what employment was available, and what kind of schooling their children received. Such politics racialized Puerto Ricans as "others," a population in constant need of intervention, deemed to be perpetual foreigners despite their status as U.S. citizens. These views not only affected their relationship to their new home but at times also led to contentious relationships with other populations.

While adjusting to life in New York, Puerto Ricans faced problems similar to those of previous immigrants and migrants. Migrants from the island tended to physically situate themselves in established ethnic enclaves, alongside not only European immigrants but African Americans as well. In writing about the first or "old" wave of Puerto Rican migration to Chicago in the first two decades of the twentieth century, Elena Padilla speaks of Puerto Ricans' need to maneuver along these existing racial hierarchies. During this early wave, Puerto Ricans who were part of professional or business circles and had some fluency in English gained access to living accommodations in "predominantly American" (read "white") neighborhoods.[20] But Puerto Ricans positioned in other places along the racial and class spectrum found themselves living alongside African Americans or within the young Mexican community. Padilla notes that Puerto Ricans who had access to whiteness via their class status shared white residents' contempt for "Puerto Rican Negroes." She argues that "there is, however, a stronger similarity between the Puerto Rican in New York and the Mexican in Chicago insofar as there is a great similarity in their background and both share to much extent 'color visibility,' which is a sociological phenomenon demanding a type of adjustment not required by American society from most European immigrants."[21] This exact "color visibility" often placed Puerto Ricans in New York in conflict with African Americans, even for Afro–Puerto Ricans migrating to the United States, as they found themselves almost in direct competition for the already scarce resources afforded to communities of color. In New York, "the day-to-day tensions between African-Americans and Puerto Ricans were undoubtedly exacerbated by the struggles of nonwhite *boricuas* to come to terms with the monolithic 'Negro' identity imposed upon them from the outside by a racist North American society."[22] Puerto Ricans in U.S. cities were viewed as nonwhite and were expected to socially and physically (residentially) align themselves with "other" racial and ethnic groups.[23] Although Puerto Ricans on the island were not devoid of color consciousness or prejudice, scholars have argued that racial categories there were quite different from those in the United States; they often ranged along a "white to black" continuum that depended very much on one's phenotype.[24] According to Padilla, race in Puerto Rico was not easily understood, and not always "necessarily linked to the biological implication of race or even to color visibility."[25] Racial implications were often said to be tied to a person's economic status on the island, whereas racial lines could be blurred, and an individual who brought capital to the table could gain a superficial sense of social mobility.[26] In other words, islanders at times negotiated their status in Puerto Rico, whereas their new position across the diaspora would offer very little room for negotiation. In many ways, these articulations in previous scholarship on Puerto Rico deny the legacy of Puerto Rican anti-Blackness, which existed on the island both during and after Spanish rule and continued as the population migrated to U.S. cities. This is evident in Elena Padilla's work. However, more recent scholarship, such as Isar Godreau's work, provides space to interrogate how intersections among race, class, and gender were "reinforced by the politics of colonial nation building historically fostered by Puerto Rico's relationship with the [United States]."[27] The reality for many islanders was one not of "blurred" racial lines, but of experiencing the very same racial conflict and marginalization experienced by African Americans.

New York's Puerto Rican population increased from about forty-six thousand in 1930 to over sixty-two thousand by 1940, with the overwhelming majority of those residing in New York City.[28] Immigrants and migrants in New York historically have filled the need for low-wage laborers, making them susceptible to exploitation because of their "new" status, their linguistic limitations, and their economic conditions. Puerto Ricans assumed the role of the underemployed and even served as an industrial reserve army in times of labor strikes and shortages during and after wartimes. Puerto Ricans' skills and capabilities influenced the jobs available to them, but language limitations, prejudices, and institutional barriers also affected their employment opportunities. Inadequate schooling was one of those institutional barriers. The Migration Division office in New York City played a critical role in educating new migrants about the city and in assessing how Puerto Ricans could best contribute in the labor market.[29] Similarly, New York's Welfare Council maintained that the migration of Puerto Ricans to the United States must be an "organized" process between the two governments, with the new host cities allowed sufficient planning time to avoid or alleviate overcrowding issues, an issue that would arise again in Chicago.[30] "Migration under favorable circumstances is beneficial both for the migrants and for the people among whom they settle," it maintained.[31] The council also sought ways to protect Puerto Ricans against discriminatory practices that it saw as unfortunately still prevalent in U.S. culture. It acknowledged that while Puerto Ricans were targeted by these prevailing views, they adopted the racial attitudes of their new environment.[32] Once in New York, many Puerto Ricans sought to distinguish themselves from other communities of color, in particular African Americans, to liberate themselves from the racial discrimination faced by other groups. Patricia Sexton claimed that "though conflict is still open, Puerto Ricans are closer in life style, religion, and attitudes to their Italian rather than their Negro neighbors."[33] This need to disassociate themselves from African Americans stemmed from Puerto Ricans' early awareness of how deeply race and racist ideologies were embedded in every aspect of U.S. life: housing, health care, labor, and of course education, as was the case for European immigrants in Chicago. Yet Puerto Ricans quickly found themselves affected by the very "color lines" constraining African Americans and other groups, as is evident by the physical space they occupied, their labor opportunities, their schooling experiences, and the rhetoric used to describe them.

The population would also see themselves targeted because of linguistic differences. Cases of violence against Puerto Ricans began to surface in New York City in the mid-1930s. For instance, two Puerto Rican men were stabbed and beaten by strangers in separate incidents in Harlem on the same day in December 1936.[34] Misconceptions and suspicions were exacerbated by the media and other groups that challenged Puerto Ricans' belonging by referring to them as deportable noncitizens. In 1937, the State Department of Social Welfare announced its intent to "send forty-one destitute Puerto Ricans back to Puerto Rico."[35] Across the country, widespread repatriation programs fueled by both the post-Depression economic downturn and the rising xenophobia targeted Mexicans and Mexican Americans, regardless of their legal status. By some estimates, the early 1930s saw the repatriation or deportation of more than three hundred thousand Mexicans, many of whom had initially come to the United States to meet labor needs in the Southwest and in northern cities.[36] But as employment opportunities decreased in the 1930s, an estimated 20 percent of Puerto Ricans on the mainland returned to the island.[37] According to a *New York Times* article, some had found that the city was not the "port of opportunity" they had expected, even as "many Puerto Ricans regard New York as a haven from poverty, poor nutritional diet and tropical disease."[38]

The Puerto Rican population in New York faced high unemployment rates, even though the Department of Labor worked to place newly arrived migrants in the few jobs available from 1930 to 1936. During this period, nearly two thousand individuals found employment in construction, laundry work, hotels, restaurants, carpentry, and other fields.[39] Limited job availability affected all kinds of workers, from unskilled laborers to professionals and college graduates. At a 1940 congressional hearing, migrant Florentino Irizarry spoke of his struggle to obtain employment despite being well educated, noting that he was "living on $6 a week . . . earned by teaching English."[40] Nonetheless, migrants found the alternative (returning to Puerto Rico) unappealing.[41]

Puerto Rican women in New York typically found jobs as domestic workers, in the garment industry, as office helpers, and in the service sector as restaurant servers, retail staff, and so forth.[42] New York offered many women their first employment opportunity outside their home and a chance at independence from their families. However, Puerto Rican women had often worked outside the home prior to migration, as seen in Carmen Teresa Whalen's work on Puerto Rican women in Philadelphia. On the island, women contributed to the economy, and to their families' situations, through their participation in a gendered labor market.[43] Moreover, for some of the women who migrated to Philadelphia, and perhaps to other cities, the availability of indoor plumbing and modern appliances eased their household work, thus freeing them to participate more in employment outside the home.

Although the development of Puerto Rican enclaves in New York City was limited by the community's employment opportunities, their settlement patterns allowed them to engage in and maintain their own cultural practices. According to one report, "the inability of the majority to understand the English language makes them cling to the heavily-populated, overcrowded Puerto Rican settlements in Manhattan, the Bronx and Brooklyn."[44] While island officials endeavored to infuse English language use into every aspect of Puerto Ricans' lives, the population themselves sought to maintain their Spanish language in order to maintain a cultural distinctiveness amid colonial rule. This followed them as they migrated. However, their customs and culture had to coexist with those of other immigrant and ethnic groups (such as Italians, Jews, and African Americans) as their presence in communities such as Harlem, the Bronx, and Brooklyn grew and began to overlap with the long-standing presence of other groups in the area. This move into already established communities was fueled by the need for cheap housing, access to shopping sites (aiding in the retention of their ethnic ties), and reliable transportation to their respective labor markets. These settlement patterns were seemingly independent of direct local government intervention. However, as we see with the emerging Chicago population in the 1940s, evidence suggests that city officials sometimes dictated where Puerto Ricans were expected to reside and, by extension, with whom they would interact. By the late 1940s, an estimated sixty thousand to eighty thousand Puerto Ricans were living in the East Harlem area, centered at 110th Street and Madison Avenue, in dilapidated units where property owners neglected to make costly repairs.[45] To address these living conditions, the Welfare Council of New York held a conference to deal with "unmet needs in neighborhoods where the concentration of Puerto Ricans, already great, was daily increasing."[46] But their move into historically ethnic and poor communities that were already overcrowded led to housing and health problems. The city's welfare commissioner in the 1940s publicly discussed this reality, mentioning that a reported "twenty-three Puerto Ricans live in four small rooms" in one Harlem residence, while "fifteen occupy a two-and-one-half-room apartment" in the same community, with "a day school for ten children on the premises."[47] However, a council report assumed that overcrowding was not a new experience for the migrants, implying that Puerto Ricans would continue their migration to the mainland for better work, wages, and food.[48] The presumption, of course, was that these substandard housing conditions were a vast improvement over Puerto Ricans' life on the island.

Perhaps learning from the efforts in New York, Chicago officials soon began to organize themselves to contend with the growing population in their own city. In the early years of Puerto Rican migration to Chicago, Mayor Richard J. Daley created local organizations and agencies to tackle the problem, in hopes of understanding not only who these new people were, but also how to facilitate their move to the city. "The Puerto Ricans are citizens who do not speak English, and are usually unfamiliar with the city and the weather. They have colonized in several areas of Chicago—Near North Side, Near West Side, Woodlawn, etc.—frequently occupying all the apartments in a building and thus providing the basis for self-help (one mother baby-sitting several working mothers' children)."[49] Daley, himself a member of the 1919 Race Riot generation, came to power in the 1950s, during the middle of an increasing Puerto Rican migration. In the early days of his administration, the city began to develop programs and resources to aid Puerto Rican migrants in their transition to life in Chicago. But their participation in the city was marred by long-standing misconceptions about Puerto Ricans as well as emerging racial politics that limited their full participation and settlement.

Life for Puerto Rican migrants in Chicago in the 1940s was complicated, and their status as American citizens was frequently unhelpful. However, during these early years they began to mobilize, utilizing their citizenship to bring about change to boost their community's development.

In her 1947 master's thesis on the migratory experiences of Puerto Ricans in Chicago and New York, Elena Padilla identified two distinct migrations to Chicago. The pre-1940 "old migration," discussed earlier, settled in established ethnic (Polish and other European) communities, with the 1920 census reporting the number of Puerto Ricans in Illinois at 110.[50] By contrast, the Puerto Rican population in New York City in 1920 was almost 8,000.[51] Members of the "old migration" were scattered throughout Chicago and consisted of native-born Puerto Ricans, and in Padilla's study, their non–Puerto Rican spouses were counted, along with their children. Padilla wrote about 86 individuals she identified as part of the "old migration," discussing their demographics and families, including information on interracial marriages.[52] Although the "old migration" was a relatively small group, these early migrants and their descendants mirror the heterogeneity that defines today's Puerto Rican population in Chicago, both in their racial and ethnic identities and in their economic and social status. Padilla's 1947 study also points out the complicated and sometimes damaging racial ideologies that Puerto Ricans brought with them to Chicago and that became embedded in their socialization in the city. Padilla was careful to note that none of the Puerto Ricans who were married to non–Puerto Ricans were married to "American negroes."[53] By 1940, the population of Puerto Ricans in the city had climbed to 240, and this increased rapidly as employment agencies implemented contract labor programs in collaboration with Puerto Rico's Department of Labor.[54] The recruitment of Puerto Ricans to Chicago was in part a result of growing tensions in New York's already established community. Puerto Rican and local city governments and the Migration Division offices in New York and Chicago launched an intense public relations campaign to encourage migration to the Midwest. Unlike their New York counterparts, Chicago's Puerto Ricans initially received praise for their ability to integrate into their new environment. Local newspapers such as the *Chicago Tribune* and the *Chicago Daily News* regularly published stories in the 1940s and early 1950s speaking to Puerto Ricans' "gentleness" and "docility." In a *New York Times* article titled "Chicago Good City to Puerto Ricans," journalist Donald Janson wrote that "Puerto Ricans have adjusted to the new environment without strife."[55] Many Puerto Ricans were steered toward Chicago by news from relatives in New York, who spoke of the decline in manufacturing jobs there. In addition, an increase in direct air travel to Chicago and the development of the Migration Division office in the city created opportunities that had initially been available only in New York and other East Coast cities.

By extension, the educational experiences of Puerto Ricans in cities such as Chicago and New York mirrored their labor and housing experiences, with limited resources in a system ill-prepared and ill-informed to assist the population. According to accounts compiled by the Welfare Council's Subcommittee on Education, New York City public schoolteachers found Puerto Rican students slow to learn English and, compared to their European-born counterparts, less prepared to enter their age-appropriate grade level even when their English was sufficient.[56] Further, this committee questioned the pedagogical techniques and qualifications of teachers on the island, viewing them as a possible cause for Puerto Rican students' educational inadequacies, even though teachers in Puerto Rico were required to pass a U.S. certification exam.[57] The history of teachers in Puerto Rico is complicated and very much informed by the island's racial and class distinctions, especially during the early years of colonial rule. As detailed in Solsiree del Moral's work, Puerto Rican teachers on the island were instrumental in critiquing the aims and mission of colonial education, and "the new generation of teachers that took over the classroom in the 1910s and 1920s directed public schools in the 1930s and 1940s when they replaced US administrators."[58] In the 1930s and 1940s, students who initially had been taught by this generation of island teachers were enrolled in New York schools. The population of Puerto Rican students in Manhattan's public schools grew to over twelve thousand by 1947, and the Subcommittee on Education sought ways to improve their learning of English.[59] Schools experimented with English language instruction, one-on-one instruction, and a "big brothers and sisters" program that linked English-speaking students with English learners.[60] The subcommittee also recommended the establishment of "mothers' clubs" to help parents understand "child care in an urban community, consumer problems, nutrition, home making and other subjects designed to strengthen the home."[61]

Although these measures were not explicitly referred to as an Americanization project, the aims and services outlined by the Subcommittee on Education were similar to the contemporaneous Americanization projects in Puerto Rico's schools in the first decades of U.S. control. Such practices were likewise underway in southwestern communities, aimed at transforming Mexican families by focusing on their home lives, particularly the transmission of "culture" through women. Because these parent organizations were called "mothers' clubs," women (or mothers) were explicitly tied to the success or failure of the Puerto Rican community, as was the case for Mexican and Mexican Americans in the Southwest. By targeting Mexican women in

Americanization projects in states such as California and Texas, these groups hoped to use women's roles to transform the second generation's family life and values to mirror those of the dominant group. Reflecting Americanization efforts on the island, organizations working with Mexicans and Mexican Americans found "the most potent weapon used to imbue the foreigner with American values was the English language."[62] But some of these women were strategic in their relationship with such projects. Understanding how their economic, housing, and educational opportunities were limited by their status as second-class citizens, Mexican women at times participated in such programs "as women who made choices for themselves and for their families."[63] Women utilized the opportunities offered by church organizations, schools, and community associations as a form of survival or as a space to gain opportunities for themselves and their children. Puerto Rican women also worked across and within their positions to create such opportunities for themselves and their community, as we see in Chicago.

Although overlapping themes emerged from the population's presence in New York City and Chicago, the New York experiences influenced early migrants' lives in Chicago. The two cities are very different spaces, informed by their own histories, which is evident in how New York's history framed Chicago's approach to the growing population. Whether in Puerto Rico, New York, or Chicago, women shouldered the responsibility for bringing the community to its full potential as active participants in their assimilation process through the acquisition of the English language and success in school, and through their participation not just as mothers but as workers. Women became agents in their community's economic, labor, and migratory history, even though they are often missing from historical narratives. Conversations about the various factors affecting Puerto Ricans' inclusion in labor, housing, and educational spaces followed the population to Chicago. Likewise, narratives emerged regarding the movement of Puerto Rican women across the diaspora and their role in the island's economic and political future. Initiated by both government agencies and private businesses, programs seeking to capitalize on Puerto Rican women's labor, especially as domestic workers in Chicago and in the manufacturing industry in places such as New York, promoted the population as a convenient and valuable labor force. However, as an unintended consequence of these promotional measures, women took on community activist work in addition to paid labor. Their organizing efforts focused on education, labor, and reproductive justice. In Chicago, migrants' labor and schooling lives began to overlap, with women as active participants. Puerto Rican women's movement from the island to Chicago both aids and complicates our reading of migration history, while showing that we must situate the population's labor migration history in the context of a larger reading of the history of education. Puerto Rican women historically have been central to the story of Puerto Ricans in Chicago as they worked across the city, whether as students, teachers, community organizers, or mothers, to confront the myriad issues afflicting their community with regard to schooling, housing, the labor market, and the intersections among them.

From *Domésticas* to Activists

As was the case for other migrant and immigrant populations, Chicago became a site for both labor and educational opportunities for Puerto Rican women, offering them an opportunity to mobilize to confront the realities of city life. In segregated Chicago, Black women, including students and university graduates, similarly negotiated their role and responsibility to the larger community. Black collegiate and professional organizations such as Alpha Kappa Alpha led the call for creating programs to provide school and career opportunities for the growing young population.[64] In the 1930s and 1940s, during a period of Blacks' mass migration to Chicago, Puerto Ricans became part of labor migration programs aimed at alleviating both labor shortages in the city and the perceived problem of overpopulation on the island. A labor recruitment program brought Puerto Rican women to work as domestic employees for affluent Chicago families. Simultaneously, the daughters of affluent Puerto Rican families on the island were recruited to attend the University of Chicago, and they eventually encountered the workers. As the university students and local workers crossed paths, their initial interactions and subsequent activism set the stage for the activism and mobilization that would mark life in the city for Puerto Ricans in the decades to come. Similarly, this diverse population of Puerto Ricans in Chicago in the 1940s challenged views that portrayed them as monolithic (working class and uneducated). From university students to domestic workers, the Puerto Rican community occupied many spaces in the city, and these relationships created a narrative about women's role in the life of the community. The narrative of Puerto Rican women in 1940s Chicago sheds additional light on migration, especially as the springboard for a conversation about community settlement and education.

Meeting with government and education leaders in Washington, DC, in 1946, the chancellor of the University of Puerto Rico, Jaime Benitez, was asked which American institution had most influenced his educational outlook. Benitez "unhesitatingly and emphatically" responded that as a student in the late 1930s, he had found "intelligence, purpose, and efficiency" at the University of Chicago and hoped to bring those ideals to his own campus.[65] Benitez and others at the University of Puerto Rico initiated partnerships with U.S. institutions of higher learning to provide opportunities for students on the island. These partnerships encouraged students to seek degrees at prestigious U.S. institutions to help create an intellectual elite on the island. But the students did more than maneuver their way through institutions such as Columbia University, the University of Michigan, and the University of Chicago. Some found themselves living alongside labor migrants from Puerto Rico and utilized their social capital as students to aid the local community.[66]

When Muna Muñoz Lee and Elena Padilla relocated to Chicago in the mid-1940s to attend the University of Chicago, they had little knowledge of or relationship with the community of Puerto Ricans who were settling in the city. However, as they encountered Chicago's Puerto Rican community, in particular the women, they became aware of the substandard pay and living conditions of workers recruited through formal labor contracts. As the daughter of then–Puerto Rican Senate president Luis Muñoz Marín (who later was the first democratically elected governor of Puerto Rico), Muñoz Lee had access to island officials, and she informed them of the workers' complaints regarding local labor violations. Padilla made contact with New York–based Puerto Rican labor activists, seeking to utilize their work with labor migrants to assist the Chicago community.[67] In 1946, Muñoz Lee wrote to her father depicting life in Chicago for both the University of Chicago students and the workers now in the city. She told him that the employment agency Castle, Barton and Associates strategically utilized racial politics and ideologies in placing Puerto Rican workers in cities across the country. The agency encouraged the placement of "white" Puerto Ricans in northern cities, such as Chicago, and sought to "import" Puerto Ricans of color to work in the South.[68]

> Tu sabes hasta que punto llega el prejuicio racial en el Sur de los Estados Unidos; es una situación injusta y peligrosa que un grupo de trabajadores de color que no estan acostumadrodos ser tratados como un grupo inferior y a quienes jamas se ha debido poner en una situacion en que tengan que acostumbrarse a esto—se envien a un area donde existen fortísimas sanciences sociales y donde se recurre hasta a la violencia fisica y la destrucción de la vida misma para mantener a la gente de color en un estado de subordinacion.[69]

(You know how far racial prejudice reaches in the South in the United States: it's an unjust and dangerous situation for a group of workers of color, not accustomed to being treated as inferior, to be placed in a situation where they should become accustomed to it—they've been sent to an area where strong sanctions exist and where even physical violence occurs, even death, in order to keep people of color subordinated.)[70]

Muñoz Lee recognized the need for discussion about the reality of life in Chicago for these migrants, particularly how the era's racial politics informed Puerto Rican migration.

Puerto Rican women in Chicago, such as Muñoz Lee, were at the forefront of discussions on the needs of Puerto Rican migrants in the city, even though their voices are often absent from historical writings about the community. As Muñoz Lee shared with her father, "Me parece que la situación de este grupo es aún más grave . . . y que urge remediarla inmediatamente" (It appears to me that the situation for this group is grave and must be remedied immediately).[71] Collaborating with social worker Carmen Isales, University of Chicago graduate students compiled a report on Puerto Rican migrants' working and living conditions. It stated that Castle, Barton and Associates deducted large sums of money from workers' wages, forced the *domesticas* to work long hours with little relief, and consigned the men to live in substandard conditions.[72] In 1946 alone, nearly four hundred Puerto Rican "girls" were brought to work as *domesticas* for Chicago families. They earned sixty dollars per month, with deductions taken not only for housing but also for transportation from and to Puerto Rico. The Mayor's Committee on New Residents claimed that importing young Puerto Rican women accomplished two things: "it brought one of the most attractive 'products' of Puerto Rican culture to Chicago and after some of these girls became established in the city they caused many of their relatives and friends on the island to follow them and settle here."[73] Speaking of Puerto Rican women as "attractive 'products'" further highlights the role of gender in city officials' poor understanding of the labor migration, particularly with regard to women's experiences.

In a letter to Luis Muñoz Marín, Isales detailed the everyday complications of life in Chicago for the workers. She informed Muñoz Marin about the tribulations of some Puerto Ricans who had broken their employment contracts, as Castle, Barton and Associates pursued the workers to their new homes and employment sites. Isales described one underage Puerto Rican worker's plight:

> Tengo un caso de una niña de 14 años. La madere que tenia 10 hijos mas, aparentemente falsifico el certificado de nacimiento para salir de la hija. Aqui se econtro con una señora que no la dejaba salir. . . . Un día la muchachita se escapo y se fué con otras a un bar donde se emboracho con

'wiskey.' Al llegar a la casa a la 1:00 A.M. la señora no la dejo entrar y le cerró la puerta en la cara. Un mexicano (de los que en ingles le dicen 'pimp') la obligo vivir con el una semana y luego la quiso meter a la prostitucion.[74]

(I have a case of a 14-year-old girl. The mother had 10 other children and apparently falsified her birth certificate in order to rid herself of her daughter. Here she found herself [working for] a woman who did not let her go out. One day the young girl escaped and went to a bar, where someone got her drunk on whiskey. When she arrived at the house at 1:00 a.m., the woman did not let her enter and locked the door of the house. A Mexican man [who in English people refer to as a pimp] forced her to live with him for a week and wanted to force her into prostitution.)

After the worker escaped the "pimp," Isales placed her in a group home for young women. Yet the employment agency's only concern was to locate her in order to help her employer sue her to recoup perceived losses.[75] In another case that Isales recounts, YWCA health officials diagnosed a young Puerto Rican woman with appendicitis. They sent her back to her employer with detailed information regarding her health status, expecting the employer to ensure that she received treatment. However, they did not have the employer's contact information, so they were unable to follow up. Isales added in her letter to her father, "En enero 23/47 al empezar mi trabajo el primer caso que tenia a mi oficina es el de esa muchacha. Aún con apendicitis. La lleve rápido a una clínica y fué operada, como caso de emergencia." (Upon beginning my work January 23, 1947, the first case I had was of that young girl. The one with appendicitis. I quickly took her to the clinic, where they performed emergency surgery.)[76] Following the surgery, the employment agency and the employer both disclaimed responsibility for paying the young woman's medical bills, with the employer insisting, "Yo no tengo que ver con eso" (I have nothing to do with that).[77] Isales believed the young woman would have died without the YWCA's intervention and claimed that Castle, Barton and Associates had been well aware of her condition upon her arrival in Chicago.

Lawyers believed to be representing the employers tracked down men and women who left their initial job placements. After locating some of the workers at their new places of employment, they attempted to coerce them into signing notices of their intent to pay lost wages back to their previous employers, despite the unscrupulous contracts they had entered into. Isales wrote to Muñoz Marin:

No se como se el F.B.I se entero, y estan investigando la cuestion dede el punto de "peonage." No hay organizacion aqui que no esté almada de lo que llaman "ruthlessness" de parte de Castle Barton y siempre surge la pregunta, "But why did the Department of Labor of Puerto Rico approved [*sic*] such a contract. Are they crooks!" Si yo no fuera Popular tendria la gran oportunidad de desacreditar el gobierno de PR. Lo que le digo siempre es mi opinion personalisma—que hubo buenas intensiones pero faltá de visión.[78]

(I don't know how the FBI became aware, and now they are investigating it as possible cases of peonage. There are no organizations not alarmed by what they call the ruthlessness on the part of Castle, Barton, and the question always arises, "But why did the Department of Labor of Puerto Rico approved [*sic*] such a contract. Are they crooks!" If I weren't a member of the Popular Party, I would have a great opportunity to discredit the government of Puerto Rico. What I always tell them is that my opinion is a personal one—that there were good intentions but a lack of vision.)

Isales was employed by the Puerto Rican government, which meant she was not allowed to fully engage in conversations about the island's responsibility regarding these labor contracts. As she clearly states, however, while the government's intentions may have been good, there was very poor planning with respect to both implementing the contracts and following up with migrants.

Newspaper accounts in 1947 spoke of both the status of the labor contracts and the alleged participation of these women in organized prostitution. As one journalist maintained, "Comparative peace and quiet reigns in relations between the Puerto Rican girls who came to Chicago as domestic workers and their employers, but the employment agency that brought them here does not plan to bring any more. . . . Altho[ugh] Castle Barton tried to comb out the undesirables when the girls first came over, some were found to have venereal diseases when they arrived in the United States, and some were underage." One civic organization had "indicated that some of the girls, because they cannot speak English, were lonely and were frequenting Spanish-speaking night spots, were they fell into or were enticed into prostitution."[79] The article did not mention that some women who left their jobs were forced into city shelters, where employers attempted to take away their winter clothing despite the freezing temperatures.[80] Puerto Rican men working in Chicago faced some of the same issues, as some of the foundry workers contested deductions from their wages for shelter, transportation, meals, and even medical expenses due to work-related accidents.[81] Newspapers and city officials devoted little attention to the employment agency's failure to ensure these women's well-being and placed much of the blame on the women themselves. According to one journalist's account, when officials at Castle,

Barton and Associates were asked what would happen if an employee left a position and sought employment elsewhere, an official replied, "We could make it pretty miserable for them."[82] The *New Republic* reported that when the agency realized it was "manufacturing a 'displaced-persons' problem, [it] halted its imports temporarily," but hoped to continue with improved contracts and better screening of workers.[83] Again we see that the employment agency attributed the problem to the quality of the workers, not their working conditions and the inadequate resources afforded to them.

Following the intervention of the women students, Isales, and others, Castle, Barton and Associates ceased the "importing" of "girls," but did not acknowledge its alleged unethical labor practices and responsibility to the employees, many of whom remained in the city.[84] The work of the University of Chicago students implicated the deeply gendered migration in causing substandard housing and working conditions. It also highlighted the involvement of the governments and employment agencies in controlling the lives and opportunities of *domesticas* in the United States.[85] This exchange of sorts between working-class women and those in higher education created gains for both groups, as the *domesticas'* deplorable working conditions became the subject of labor disputes and changes within the city thanks to the help of the University of Chicago students. Utilizing the information gathered by the students, Isales, and city officials, the Department of Labor in Puerto Rico restructured policies related to women's labor migration.[86] Working with the Puerto Rican community in Chicago inspired Elena Padilla to write her master's thesis about the community.[87] Her intellectual contribution, which has become foundational for researchers writing on Puerto Rican or Mexican Chicago, in conjunction with the work of early community activists, forged a clear understanding of the role of education and community in the development of a distinct Chicago Puerto Rican identity. These initial events in Puerto Rican women's lives set the stage for the subsequent social activism and civic engagement that came to define the lives of Chicago's Puerto Ricans in the 1960s and 1970s, with schools and education at the center of life for decades to come. Women such as Padilla and Muñoz Lee were students, there as part of a social program aimed at elevating the status of island institutions and organizations. The city moved them from the classroom into roles as community leaders, reminding them of the overlap between schools and community life. As the Puerto Rican population continued to grow, city officials and agencies discussed migrants' roles in Chicago. For decades to follow, where Puerto Ricans should live, work, and attend school would be topics of sometimes heated but always crucial debate.

Puerto Rican Settlement and
Organizational Response

Because of the limited employment opportunities available to Puerto Ricans and encouragement by city officials, migrants from the 1940s through the 1970s tended to settle in or near the center of the city in neighborhoods such as Lincoln Park, Lake View, and the Near North Side. However, they had a presence in dozens of neighborhoods, which is evident in their participation in South Side Catholic parishes. Their settlement in Chicago was closely linked to prevailing housing segregation patterns that similarly affected Mexican and Black residents. And just like Mexican and Black residents, Puerto Ricans faced displacement from the neighborhoods in which they initially settled.

Puerto Ricans entered the city at the height of public debates about housing and land redevelopment, which especially targeted Black residents. The 1940s and 1950s found Black Chicagoans pushed further and further into segregated housing as white residents retreated from shared neighborhoods, and as communities were targeted for citywide urban renewal plans. Two such plans were spearheaded by institutions of higher learning and fully backed by city officials. "Chicago's black community was [not only] unable to locate new housing, it had to fight tenaciously simply to hold on to its current dilapidated stock."[88] The 1949 American Housing Act aimed to offer opportunities to working-class residents living in substandard conditions and to transform urban areas that cities considered slums. But even though the new law enhanced lives for some, it further exacerbated the housing divide along racial lines. As Black residents soon realized, "by providing funds to destroy areas . . . the housing act effectively destroyed the support system that Black communities across the nation relied upon."[89] High-rise housing projects took the place of neighborhoods with strong community bonds, resulting in isolated and segregated populations. This was the Chicago that awaited Puerto Ricans: a city invested in maintaining a spatial racial order, but one very much limited to a white-Black binary. Mexicans and Puerto Ricans worked "to make sense of their own identities in relation to others at the same time that they were being assigned sometimes competing and contradictory labels by their neighbors and by the state."[90] They sometimes found themselves serving inadvertently as a physical border between communities, not quite fitting within the racial divide that had been prevalent in the cities for decades.[91]

Perhaps learning from the experience of other cities in "dealing with" the influx of Puerto Rican residents, Chicago officials and local organizations engaged in conversations about strategies for serving the community, discussions that at times influenced their settlement across the city. Representing the Department of Labor of Puerto Rico in Chicago, Anthony Vega spoke of the need to discourage Puerto Ricans from settling "with any Spanish-speaking people"; instead, he said, they should "distribute themselves all over the city in Polish, Italian, Czechoslovak and other areas, so that they will soon learn English."[92] But Puerto Ricans and others found this difficult because long-established ethnic communities did not necessarily welcome new migrants. Puerto Ricans' own agency was very much absent from these discussions. One side (Chicago officials) sought to ensure that the population would live in proximity to their worksites and labor opportunities, while the other side (Puerto Rican officials) encouraged integration within already existing immigrant communities. Only a decade or two earlier, Mexican immigrants in Chicago had navigated the complicated housing market, sometimes by attempting to pass as European Americans and sometimes by living alongside African American residents, although their relationship with the latter was frequently contentious.[93] As was the case for other migrant and immigrant populations in the city, the work of social agencies and organizations became central to life for Mexican and Puerto Rican residents. With its settlement houses and local universities, Chicago offered a perfect opportunity to engage in the development of Americanization programs, promote assimilationist strategies, and center schools as an essential (or essentialist) tool in supporting these aims. The city managed multiple interests and communities framed by nationalist views and ideologies. Settlement houses, such as Chicago's Hull House, and religious organizations were important in aiding the Americanization process. Hull House targeted Mexican immigrants with the same Americanization programs it had used with European immigrants, who had been in the city for decades. As the Mexican population increased, reformers sought to "win over" the community, hoping to "ensur[e] civic order" across the city "by curtailing what were believed to be sources of potential unrest and turmoil" attributed to their cultural ties and nationalist ideologies.[94] However, no matter the intent, these Americanization programs would not supersede the role of whiteness, which allocated space and power to some groups (including Irish and Italians) and not others (Mexicans and African Americans). Puerto Rican migrants were similarly at the center of organizational responses to the growing "problem" of life in Chicago for these "fellow Americans."

The work of two local associations was instrumental in leading conversations about Puerto Rican migrants' needs and the city's role in assisting their transition, even if the groups themselves at times demonstrated prejudicial views regarding the population. The Welfare Council of Metropolitan Chicago worked in the 1940s to bring together other organizations and interested parties to facilitate the acclimation of Puerto Ricans in the city. The Mayor's Committee on New Residents (formed in 1956) was also a direct response to adjustment problems faced by newly arrived migrants, including southern Blacks, white ethnic groups, and American Indians as well as Puerto Ricans, who faced unwelcoming and unsympathetic established residents throughout the city. Puerto Rican newcomers found both bodies to be helpful as they familiarized themselves with urban life. The council and the committee offered resources and information that encompassed health services, education, translation services, assistance in locating and reaching family, and voting rights.[95] Voting rights were especially important, because they enabled Puerto Ricans to become active agents in the city's political and social development and perhaps contributed to their involvement in community-based self-advocacy organizations. Interestingly, one report on the status of newcomers to Chicago spoke of the need to help them understand their responsibility and rights as voters: "Since the Puerto Ricans, particularly, are citizens and eligible to vote, the Committee has worked for the registration of qualified voters with the help of the Citizens Information Service (League of Women Voters) and community organizations. A 30-second film trailer in Spanish was tried out in one West Side movie house prior to registration in the precincts in the Spring of 1958."[96] It is clear that city officials recognized the need for collaborative work in assisting Puerto Rican migrants, even though they did not always fully understand the implications of Chicago's own prevailing racial politics and its effects on the population's settlement. These attempts by the city to facilitate the population's settlement demonstrated to Puerto Ricans how little city officials understood them. Just as significant, such efforts illuminate how quickly the city's initially welcoming views and rhetoric could change.

In 1954, the Welfare Council acknowledged that "the Puerto Rican problem is not new in Chicago." The council had worked with the Illinois State Department of Labor in the 1940s to help migrants deal with "unscrupulous employment agencies," as seen in the early work of Padilla and Muñoz Lee.[97] Now various agencies and businesses, including the Board of Education, the Chicago Council against Racial and Religious Discrimination, and the Community Fund of Chicago, were urging that a study be conducted on how to better serve the growing Puerto Rican community. The Welfare Council's Committee on Integration of Spanish Speaking Citizenry maintained that research into the problem of integrating Spanish-speaking migrants into the community, in particular Puerto Ricans, would benefit both the city and the Spanish-speaking population.[98] Aware of the deceptive practices of some employers, the council aided organizations in ensuring that local and state governments, as well as Puerto Rico's government, would have a vested interest in the treatment of these new migrants. The organization collaborated with federal agencies to create a committee "to meet the immediate problem as well as to plan for the Puerto Ricans that are here and should probably stay here," similar to their work with the "Japanese resettler problem."[99] For Puerto Ricans in Chicago, the council warned, "the problem of housing is severe. . . . In some ways it is more serious than found in other minority groups." The Committee on Integration of Spanish Speaking Citizenry informed the council that Puerto Ricans suffered from group tension, the development of ghetto communities, and educational difficulties because of linguistic differences. One Puerto Rican resident involved with local agencies, Jose Hernandez, spoke to the Community Fund of Chicago about his concerns regarding assimilation. His group, the House of Puerto Rico, served as a "family club" that created programs such as "instruction for housewives on how to buy and prepare American food and informing members of programs of nearby welfare agencies in order to make all community resources known to them."[100] Just as on the island, the discussion turned to Americanization practices to encourage the assimilation of Puerto Ricans. And as with other migrant and immigrant groups, Puerto Rican women and mothers faced the burden of aligning family life with others' expectations.

In 1956, the University of Chicago's Human Relations Center organized a series of workshops to help city leaders and social service personnel better understand and work with newcomers to the city. The center brought together leaders from the Puerto Rican, American Indian, Mexican American, and African American communities, as well as representatives from local associations including the Chicago Board of Education, the Chicago Urban League, and various religious groups.[101] One workshop, titled "Understanding Spanish Speaking Americans in Chicago," attempted to dispel prevailing views regarding Puerto Ricans, especially among city workers and school officials.[102] For example, one misconception centered on the belief that Puerto Ricans were not interested in speaking or learning English, when in fact the community's children were crowding into schools, and many adults attended evening classes to learn the language.[103] Similarly, institutions of higher learning offered training programs for Chicago Public Schools teachers working with the Americanization Division.[104] Americanization programs in Chicago were initially aimed at providing English language instruction, naturalization classes, and training in civics to help newcomers attain citizenship. But for Puerto Ricans, these programs were part of a larger colonization process that began on the island and sought to transform the population into "acceptable" neighbors and citizens—even though they were already citizens.

The council spoke of the "exceptional educational opportunities" offered in Chicago and promoted the vast resources available to Puerto Ricans to learn English.[105] It claimed that "anyone who has lived in this city more than a few weeks should have learned a substantial amount of English; otherwise he must recognize that he is failing in acquiring a fundamental skill and that he will not be able to find success in work nor meet the most ordinary obligations of life."[106] Helping newcomers adjust to life in the city meant encouraging them to assimilate and become "acceptable" citizens. The Mayor's Committee on New Residents initiated various programs in conjunction with the Chicago Board of Education and other groups to reach new residents in their workplaces. The city prided itself on the "growing recognition that Chicago is the only major city with a governmental agency concerned with the needs of the new residents."[107] Aside from increasing the budget for their Americanization programs, the Committee on New Residents advised the Board of Education that "in addition to teaching English and vocational skills, attention [should] be seriously given to teaching city living; budgeting, installment buying, child care, knowledge of city resources, etc."[108] Roosevelt University offered in-service training for teachers from the Chicago Board of Education Americanization Division.[109] These practicums were "designed to teach the newcomers language facility as well as understanding of American culture in the broadest sense."[110] The classes, which met for twenty-four sessions in total, focused on pedagogical practices for teaching adult learners. However, the Migration Services Department recognized that as U.S. citizens, both African Americans from the South and Puerto Ricans avoided Americanization classes, which initially focused on teaching the English that was necessary for the citizenship examination, something that neither group needed.[111]

Despite local groups' "attempts" to help Puerto Ricans, the Welfare Council claimed that the population had ongoing problems with "social personal adjustment, which manifest themselves in family breakdown, illegitimacy, and delinquency."[112] For some, the solution to this problem was to "issue widespread publicity both in this country and in Puerto Rico, warning the Puerto Ricans against coming to this country."[113] Some members of the council believed that "all that they [social agencies and city officials] can do with non-residents who become dependent is to ship them back in plane lots" and encouraged the creation of a committee to make it difficult for Puerto Ricans "to stay and bring others with them."[114] But the common notion that early migrants were dependent on public welfare was unfounded. As detailed in Lilia Fernández's work on postwar Chicago, Puerto Ricans made up less than 1 percent of the welfare rolls in Chicago in the mid-1950s, representing only 148 out of the over 18,000 cases of public assistance.[115] Moreover, island officials continued to speak favorably of the population's work ethic in conversations regarding their movement to U.S. cities. The comments by council members regarding the presumed deportability of Puerto Ricans clearly reflected not only officials' unease but also their lack of understanding and knowledge about Puerto Ricans' status. In short, officials continued to racialize Puerto Ricans as foreign, despite their U.S. citizenship. The council formed a committee to address the immediate and long-range problems and needs of Puerto Ricans, looking to the experiences of cities such as New York, Milwaukee, and Lorain, Ohio, which had dealt with their own perceived Puerto Rican problem.[116]

The resulting 1957 report from the Welfare Council provided the new residents with information related to housing, healthcare, education, and other resources, while also seeking to educate them on how to conduct themselves in their new environment. The council did "not want to give you the impression that life will be easy in Chicago, and that everything will be pleasant. . . . Neither do we wish to create a very pessimistic impression." Instead, officials wished to give migrants the "facts" so that they could "make decisions based on correct information."[117] Some of the advice was useful and much welcomed, especially for those experiencing the harsh Chicago weather for the first time. For those new to renting houses or apartments in Chicago, the Welfare Council provided information about the housing standards that property owners must legally maintain, although there was no discussion of the discriminatory practices migrants faced at the hands of property owners or real estate agents. However, the report also used language indicating that long-held misconceptions and biases about Puerto Ricans were still in place. For instance, it portrayed them as dirty and uneducated, reminding them that they could no longer simply dispose of their banana peels by throwing them out a window, as was assumed to be the norm in Puerto Rico. If every one of Chicago's millions of residents "threw his garbage out the window," the report said, the city would become impossible to live in within a few hours.[118] Aiding Puerto Ricans in becoming fellow, or perhaps merely "acceptable," Americans became the agenda for city and school agencies during the early years of the migration.

The Mayor's Committee on New Residents was aware of the increasing number of Puerto Rican families relocating to Chicago in the 1950s. According to one report, "Puerto Ricans were arriving at the rate of 400 families per month" in 1957, but that number dropped to 100 families per month as employment opportunities dwindled.[119] The growth in the number of families relocating to the city, of course, called added attention to the already limited and stratified housing market, which was increasingly affected by strategic political interventions that created and exacerbated segregation, afflicting the growing minoritized population.[120] The Welfare Council warned Puerto Ricans not to allow too many extra family members to reside with them, reminding them that overcrowding was generally illegal: "You cannot have more than one person per 400 cubic feet for each adult and 200 cubic feet for each child." Further, "When an apartment is rented for one family use, generally speaking it is against the law to have two or more families use it."[121] However, Puerto Ricans in Chicago found themselves in substandard living conditions, at times in large numbers, as opportunities for better housing and employment were scarce.

Chicago's Commission on Human Relations recognized the difficulty faced by groups such as Puerto Ricans and African Americans in obtaining housing as "the massive overcrowding . . . exploitation, segregation, and mortgage discrimination" limited their opportunities.[122] Officials at Hull House worked to assist the Spanish-speaking population with housing issues, although much of the blame for the problem was directed at the migrants themselves: "Many times the Spanish-speaking tenants do not fully understand the rules and the need for them."[123] In 1960, one in six Americans faced racial discrimination when seeking housing, affecting no fewer than twenty-seven million persons.[124] According to the study, providing housing for Puerto Ricans and others was difficult, and sometimes impossible, as established white communities sought to preserve the historical exclusion of "minority groups" from their neighborhoods.[125] From 1950 to 1960, segregation in Chicago was at its highest since the turn of the century.[126] The city's minority populations were paying rent at rates similar to those paid by their white counterparts, and yet they still found themselves living within their own communities or sometimes dispersed among other ethnic groups who did not welcome them, as was the case with Mexicans and Puerto Ricans in the early years of their migration. Before establishing their own recognizable ethnic enclaves in the late 1950s and early 1960s, Puerto Ricans were scattered across the city, a settlement pattern dictated primarily by their participation in and proximity to labor opportunities. After 1960, large numbers of Puerto Ricans began moving into communities such as Logan Square, Lincoln Park, and West Town on the Near West Side, as well as Garfield Park, Pilsen, Hyde Park, and Woodlawn on the South Side. This movement was both caused by and a response to white flight, the movement of white residents to suburban areas. Another factor prompting Puerto Ricans' move into these neighborhoods was the vacancies created there as the result of disinvestment by property and

Table 1. 1960 Puerto Rican Population in Six Chicago Communities[1]

Census Area	Population
Woodlawn	2,055
Lincoln Park	2,181
Near North Side	2,699
East Garfield Park	3,676
Near West Side	6,662
West Town	7,948

[1] Data from Local Community Fact Book: Chicago Metropolitan Area, 1960, ed. Evelyn M. Kitagawa and Karl E. Taeuber (Chicago: Chicago Community Inventory, 1963), 246–47.

business owners.[127] Many buildings in Chicago were converted into multi-unit dwellings to maximize owners' profits, forcing Puerto Ricans and others to crowd into illegal living spaces, some of which would normally have been deemed uninhabitable.

Despite the Welfare Council's advice regarding property owners' responsibility to maintain safe housing and tenants' responsibility to avoid overcrowding, very few housing options were available for Puerto Ricans, given the high cost of living and their meager wages. Absentee property owners subdivided apartments into single-room dwellings with small kitchenettes, making it possible to house twice as many families as the space was intended for. In 1963, *Chicago Tribune* journalists chronicled the harsh reality of one Puerto Rican family living in a tenement dubbed "Pork Chop Hill," named for the high number of Puerto Ricans residing there.[128] The Santiago family, consisting of Fernando and Joaquina Santiago and their three young children, paid ninety dollars a month for a furnished one-bedroom apartment in a "dirty, yellow brick tenement." At least 245 residents were living in 64 "furnished" apartments there, with 125 of those living in "Pork Chop Hill" identifying as Puerto Rican. Fernando Santiago had initially left the island in 1946 and spent two years in Utah's copper mines, but he had returned to Puerto Rico, married Joaquina, and relocated with her to Chicago. He labored in the local steel mills to provide as much as he could for his family in the hope of one day returning to Puerto Rico. As Fernando shared with the journalist, "There are 700 of us living in this area. I don't like the way I live. I don't think the others do, either. The Woodlawn neighborhood is sort of a port of call for the Puerto Rican. He comes here to get used to the city and to get a job. As soon as he does this, he moves away. He either goes back to Puerto Rico or on to a neighborhood where landlords charge an honest rent."[129] Fernando

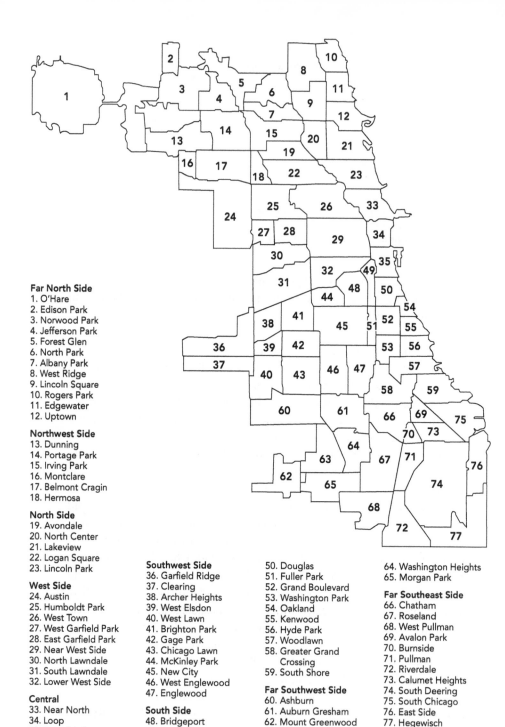

Far North Side
1. O'Hare
2. Edison Park
3. Norwood Park
4. Jefferson Park
5. Forest Glen
6. North Park
7. Albany Park
8. West Ridge
9. Lincoln Square
10. Rogers Park
11. Edgewater
12. Uptown

Northwest Side
13. Dunning
14. Portage Park
15. Irving Park
16. Montclare
17. Belmont Cragin
18. Hermosa

North Side
19. Avondale
20. North Center
21. Lakeview
22. Logan Square
23. Lincoln Park

West Side
24. Austin
25. Humboldt Park
26. West Town
27. West Garfield Park
28. East Garfield Park
29. Near West Side
30. North Lawndale
31. South Lawndale
32. Lower West Side

Central
33. Near North
34. Loop
35. Near South

Southwest Side
36. Garfield Ridge
37. Clearing
38. Archer Heights
39. West Elsdon
40. West Lawn
41. Brighton Park
42. Gage Park
43. Chicago Lawn
44. McKinley Park
45. New City
46. West Englewood
47. Englewood

South Side
48. Bridgeport
49. Armor Square

50. Douglas
51. Fuller Park
52. Grand Boulevard
53. Washington Park
54. Oakland
55. Kenwood
56. Hyde Park
57. Woodlawn
58. Greater Grand
    Crossing
59. South Shore

Far Southwest Side
60. Ashburn
61. Auburn Gresham
62. Mount Greenwood
63. Beverly

64. Washington Heights
65. Morgan Park

Far Southeast Side
66. Chatham
67. Roseland
68. West Pullman
69. Avalon Park
70. Burnside
71. Pullman
72. Riverdale
73. Calumet Heights
74. South Deering
75. South Chicago
76. East Side
77. Hegewisch

Figure 1. Chicago neighborhoods.

was well aware of the limited housing opportunities in the city and hoped for more for his family. City officials and local agencies were aware of the housing issues affecting Puerto Ricans, but migrants continued to encounter housing shortages and substandard living conditions. Unfortunately, once the migrants established themselves in their own Chicago communities, they faced impending displacement caused by urban renewal economic policies, which had a strong influence on educational opportunities. This scene played out all over the city as Puerto Ricans battled high rental rates and racial discrimination at the hands of white property owners. Similarly, the relationship between Puerto Ricans and their white ethnic neighbors indicated the limitations of their status as "fellow Americans," even when city agencies encouraged their integration and assimilation. This phenomenon was not limited to Puerto Ricans or to Chicago; it affected communities of color across the country. David García's work on Oxnard, California, reminds us that as whites continued to sit at the top of the racial hierarchy, "they sought to reproduce this hierarchy through the physical infrastructure of a city demarcated by racial spaces."[130]

Once Puerto Ricans settled in Chicago communities, their interactions with their new neighbors further hindered their adjustment. A 1960 survey by the Mayor's Committee on New Residents asked non–Puerto Rican community members about their views of their Puerto Rican neighbors. Forty-seven respondents were white and three were African American.[131] When asked whether they had seen any changes in their neighborhood since Puerto Ricans moved in, an overwhelming 62 percent said they believed it had changed for the worse, citing a drop in business volume and property values as the primary reasons for their discontent, especially due to the lack of maintenance on properties.[132] The survey similarly asked the non–Puerto Ricans about their social interactions with Puerto Ricans, with 22 percent acknowledging a close friendship with their Puerto Rican neighbors. As table 2 shows, the migrants' relationship with their new neighbors in Chicago clearly was complicated.

According to the survey, non–Puerto Rican Chicagoans did not necessarily oppose the migration of Puerto Ricans and their settlement in the United States, as they now understood the new arrivals' status as U.S. citizens and their contributions to the workforce. Yet these views did not translate into a desire to welcome the newcomers to their already established communities in Chicago. This ambivalence, with occasional hostility, forced migrants to create their own social networks to maintain a sense of cohesiveness and belonging in the city. The Mayor's Committee on New Residents study similarly pointed out the varying contradictions regarding views of Puerto Rican

Table 2. Non–Puerto Rican Old Chicago Residents and Puerto Rican Newcomers

Do you think that native Chicagoans you know would…	Non–Puerto Rican Chicago neighbors in sample area			
	Yes	No	Don't Know	No Answer
1. Intermarry with Puerto Ricans?	28%	30%	36%	6%
2. Willingly accept Puerto Ricans as neighbors?	12%	44%	28%	16%
3. Willingly admit them to their social clubs?	0%	56%	28%	16%
4. Like to exclude Puerto Ricans from employment in their occupations?	14%	62%	22%	2%
5. Like to exclude Puerto Ricans from working and settling in this country?	20%	66%	12%	2%

Source: Data from chart titled "Social Distance between Non–Puerto Rican Old Chicago Residents in Sample Area and Puerto Rican Newcomers," in Mayor's Committee on New Residents, Chicago Commission on Human Relations, *Puerto Rican Americans in Chicago: A Study of a Representative Group of 103 Households of Puerto Rican Migrants on Chicago's Northwest Side—and Their Adjustment to Big-City Living* (Chicago: Mayor's Committee, 1960), following 98.

newcomers held by Chicagoans. For example, although non–Puerto Ricans were unwilling to admit Puerto Ricans into their own social clubs, they were open to the idea of intermarrying with them (28%). The report pointed out that "discriminatory feelings of the continental 'neighbors' are more intense when directed against the group (as neighbors on the same street, or membership in their social clubs) than when projected against individuals (intermarriage)."[133]

The status of Puerto Ricans as U.S. citizens continued to complicate studies on the population: "Presence, degree and intensity of this pattern of prejudice does not seem to differ essentially from those found in previous immigrations, although this newcomer group has been exposed to the 'American way of life' for over half a century and, in fact, has fought under the American flag in three wars and has enjoyed United States citizenship for almost two generations."[134] That citizenship did very little to protect Puerto Ricans from prevailing racial attitudes in Chicago. The Mayor's Committee on New Residents articulated the troubling experiences of Puerto Ricans in dealing with dishonest business practices targeting the newcomers. One such incident led to the suicide of a twenty-four-year-old migrant who was left deep in debt and "hounded by creditors" after entering an "easy credit" business contract.[135] In 1960, William Rodriguez, a father of four small children, felt so burdened and desperate about his debt that he ate rat poison and died.

Noticing a trend in deceptive practices, the city took measures to educate consumers about exploitative local businesses, informing newcomers of the importance of thoroughly reading and comprehending the contracts they signed.[136] Educating the population, both formally and informally, would be crucial to their development and survival. But under whose terms would be debated in the decades to come.

Living to Learn

Chicago is a city of neighborhoods marked both officially and unofficially by various groups and spaces, and it is deeply rooted in the racial segregation and containment that has come to define, and map, the city and its people. The housing battles faced by Black communities in the postwar years, as areas of residency became too small, old, and decayed for both old residents and newcomers alike, reflect the city's vehement work to redefine racial borders.[137] The city "allowed" various ethnic and religious groups to situate themselves within their own enclaves in the already limited spaces, either by choice or by force, segregated from one another while working side by side in the limited labor opportunities available to them. Puerto Rican migration and settlement in Chicago at times complicate these historical patterns. For Puerto Ricans, who were simultaneously seen as domestic migrants and foreign outsiders, their movement into the city was influenced and troubled by their status as U.S. citizens, their "varying" racial identification, and the intervention of city and Puerto Rican agencies and officials regarding their settlement. For some Puerto Ricans, movement into the city was aided by familial ties that influenced their settlement and the availability of housing. Others were not so lucky; they found themselves isolated and alone in their new city, reliant on social organizations. The Chicago Land Clearance Commission was one of the groups responsible for assisting residents displaced by redevelopment projects. When the North La Salle redevelopment project left nearly four thousand residents in need of relocation, the Land Clearance Commission demonstrated that two of its biggest obstacles were the prevailing prejudice in the city and the Puerto Ricans' lack of sufficient income.[138] Similar scenes played out in neighboring communities, including Lincoln Park. New economic interests in the city rattled the young Puerto Rican community and further fueled racial friction among Puerto Ricans and whites, raising the question of who was responsible for assisting the population. As part of this conversation, schools become contested spaces. The redevelopment of Lincoln Park severely affected the schooling opportunities for Black and Puerto Rican residents and played out at Waller High School, a situation well documented in the pages of the Young Lords newspapers, as we will explore in chapter 5.

By shifting the focus of Puerto Ricans' Americanization courses to their home life, addressing cleanliness, food preparation, and so forth, city agencies presented an image of a community in need of intervention. The conversation about educating Chicago's Puerto Ricans was likewise infused with themes the migrants had faced on the island, centered on Americanization practices and ignoring the population's distinctiveness as displaced, underserved, and racialized "others." Local agencies viewed themselves as best positioned to facilitate the community's transition to urban life, yet also urged them not to fail at their "obligations of life," and perhaps their perceived obligations to the city. For Puerto Rican children in Chicago, these ideas made their way into the classroom as their education became intricately tied to this overarching public perception. Conversations about housing, labor, and assimilation centered their school experience as a site of struggle. The unstable housing market often uprooted Puerto Rican families, frequently forcing children to transfer to new schools. This placed them recurrently in classrooms that were ill-prepared to serve them. Because of this instability in housing and education, the second and subsequent generations of Puerto Rican migrants were not substantially better off than the first wave. High rent costs and discriminatory practices limited the mobility of Puerto Ricans in Chicago, perpetuating a de facto segregation afflicting already disadvantaged schoolchildren. The community's constant struggle with economic, labor, and housing displacement played out in Chicago schools, forcing local responses in the hope of alleviating schooling inequalities. This narrative would follow them for the next several decades.

CHAPTER 2

Community Visions of Puerto Rican Schooling, 1950–1966

THE CHICAGO BOARD OF EDUCATION in 1953 welcomed the help of outside agencies in dealing with issues pertaining to Puerto Rican students: "The Chicago Public Schools look forward with interest to the results of the proposed research study on the Puerto Rican population of Chicago. Any information which will assist the schools to improve the adjustment of any group of individuals is always welcome. . . . Knowledge of the background of the parents assists the school in relating the present environment to the parents' understanding on the basis of the great experience."[1] L. J. Schloerb, assistant to the general superintendent of the board, hoped that information gathered from the study would help principals and others "[gear] the work of the school to the individuals concerned," including in the development of adult education classes for those adjusting to life in their new city. The Welfare Council, which initially had seen no need for the study, later deemed it imperative due to the increase in the Puerto Rican population and their need for adult education.[2] According to these groups, the city was challenged by the growing migrant population and needed to work closely with officials on the island and in Chicago to determine the best course of action. But these conversations did not clarify whose interests took priority, the migrants' or the city's. Nonetheless, it is clear that city agencies in the 1950s and beyond struggled to comprehend the Puerto Rican population's status and needs and lacked an understanding of the migrants' lives prior to their move to the mainland. In telling the story of the Puerto Rican community in Chicago, it is important to center not only the city's struggle to define the community's needs but also the community's work to define itself. As the 1950s and 1960s unfolded, Chicago's Puerto Ricans saw a change in their relationship with the city. The narrative quickly shifted from schooling *in* the city to schooling the city itself, as Puerto Ricans continued to maneuver their way through Chicago and engage agency in their day-to-day lives.

"Fellow Americans"

Although Chicago's education officials did not acknowledge it (or were unaware of it), many parents of Puerto Rican schoolchildren had already experienced U.S. schooling practices and culture due to the United States' intervention in the island's schools after 1898. "Vestiges of colonialism extend beyond the Island itself," according to Jason G. Irizarry and René Antrop-González, "impacting Puerto Ricans in the Diaspora, the deleterious effects of which are evident in the experiences of Puerto Rican students in mainland schools."[3] As Irizarry and Antrop-Gonzalez remind us, Puerto Ricans' status as U.S. citizens and their familiarity with U.S. policies complicated their entry into Chicago schools. Migrants found themselves relegated to schools that were unprepared to contend with what was left of the "vestiges of colonialism," impairing the educational experiences of Puerto Rican schoolchildren, whose classrooms often were plagued by racist and prejudicial assumptions. Parents soon realized that school officials did not have an understanding of Puerto Ricans' history of schooling under colonial rule, something that might have helped officials better serve the emerging population.[4] Instead, Puerto Ricans faced prevailing views that labeled them as dangerous and ignorant, and these views followed them into the classroom.[5] Their Mexican American counterparts, who faced their own battles throughout the country, experienced similar sentiments. Mexican Americans "recognized that white middle-class educators viewed them as uncooperative consumers of public education," a belief that was "deeply embedded in the culture of schools as well as part of the defensive posture of educational practitioners."[6] As in the case of *Alvarez v. Lemon Grove* (1931), local politics and the racially motivated views of the dominant group and educators informed schools' social landscape for Latina/o/x children. In Chicago, city schools mirrored the evolving relationship between the city and its growing Puerto Rican population, who were initially welcomed as "fellow Americans" but soon became viewed as unassimilable.

For many Puerto Ricans, schools would serve as both sites of liberation and sites of oppression in their evolving lives and identities within the city. Although *Brown v. Board of Education* (1954) had promised to desegregate U.S. schools and encourage educational equality, Puerto Rican students still faced limited educational opportunities in a city that was not prepared to address their diverse needs.[7] Conversations about how to provide a better education for the population centered on English language acquisition by early migrants in the 1950s. School and city officials, as well as some Puerto Ricans themselves, viewed learning English as the key to inclusion, even though racial politics and increasing segregation presented greater barriers to Puerto Ricans' advancement.[8] Although touted as a city of immigrants, Chicago was also a city defined by the physical limitations that racial, linguistic, and ethnic identities imposed on the spaces occupied by migrants and immigrants. To promote their assimilation and English fluency, Puerto Ricans were discouraged from residing alongside other Spanish speakers and encouraged to live alongside European immigrants. However, as seen in the previous chapter, European immigrant neighborhoods were not necessarily welcoming to Puerto Ricans. This situation had a profound effect on Puerto Ricans' schooling experience and the opportunities available to them across the city.

In 1953, Chicago Public Schools hired an influential and controversial superintendent, Benjamin C. Willis. He was viewed as a progressive leader who could usher in a new "golden age" of reform, reminiscent of the first few decades of the twentieth century, when the city's school system was envied throughout the world for both its successful educational programs and its favorable workplace practices.[9] "Recognizing that the turmoil of dissatisfaction with the present necessarily precedes action," Willis wrote in 1954, "we should welcome the attention of those interested in the improvement of our American way of life through better education."[10] Willis saw a clear connection between schools and the improvement of society. For him, schools "[nurtured] an appreciation for the heterogeneity of our culture and the contributions made by the many racial, religious, and ethnic groups."[11] During his thirteen-year tenure as the head of Chicago schools, Willis faced much opposition to his colorblind approach to the persistent problems caused by school segregation. In combating segregation, Willis continually "invoked the image of the 'neighborhood school' which he argued was the best educational solution to the problems of inequality in education and to boosting achievement."[12] Across U.S. communities, the intentional planning of neighborhoods "stood at the intersection of descriptive efforts to map the city and prescriptive efforts to create a city ordered by distinct and homogenously grouped" communities.[13] Because housing segregation continued to plague Puerto Ricans and other communities of color in Chicago, there was little room to deny the increasing segregation experienced by these communities.[14] Housing and school segregation continued to feed one another, despite Willis's vision. Puerto Ricans' relationship to schools mirrored their troubled relationship with the segregated city. As this relationship evolved over the subsequent decades, the question remained whether and when they would have a voice in facilitating change in their children's schooling experience.

In 1954, Willis appointed a special committee to study the problem of educating Puerto Rican students and facilitate the relationship between the population and city schools.[15] Committee head Gretta Brown, who oversaw nineteen schools with growing Puerto Rican populations, argued that "many Puerto Rican youngsters chat in Spanish in school and the teaching of English is a problem."[16] As other organizations across the city had done, the Welfare Council of Metropolitan Chicago called for the formation of a citywide committee to conduct a study of Puerto Ricans to help school officials develop relevant curricula for language acquisition.[17] The high mobility of Puerto Ricans across Chicago schools was an important factor affecting their English language acquisition. Unsurprisingly, officials such as Brown faulted the youth and their families for their limited language skills, ignoring the role of larger circumstances such as housing and labor opportunities. While looking at ways to better serve the increasing Puerto Rican population in Chicago schools, city officials also traveled to the island to discourage migration to the city.[18] The city's welfare commissioner, Alvin E. Rose, visited with island-based labor and employment officials to discuss "what can be done to make sure that if Puerto Ricans are returned to the island they will have a means of support and not 'be dumped on the beach.'"[19] "The Puerto Ricans are very fine people," Rose pleaded, "but for their own sake immigration here at this time is inadvisable."[20] However, as U.S. citizens since 1917, Puerto Ricans could not be "dumped" or "returned" anywhere. Indeed, city officials and employers had initially approved of their migration because they viewed Puerto Rico as a source of U.S. citizens willing to labor for low wages. Yet in the 1950s, the common rhetoric about "deporting" or "dumping" Puerto Ricans ignored their status as citizens. Their perceived "illegal" status was a frequent topic of discussion as the city imagined ways to rid itself of the population, as it had regarding the women migrants in the 1940s discussed in chapter 1. But the legal removal of Puerto Ricans was not a viable option, so the city turned to schools to transform this population into acceptable "fellow Americans." One solution discussed by the committee was to study ways of "overcoming the language barrier" and "methods of adjusting the children to [the] social and school environment."[21] In the previous year (1953), the Chicago Board of Education had reached out to local groups, asking them to join forces in an effort to tackle the problems faced by Puerto Rican students. As L. J. Schloerb wrote to the Welfare Council, "In addition to statistical information outlined in the proposed study, the schools would find valuable such information as the sort of educational opportunity which the children have already had and the characteristics of the environment from which they have come."[22] We do not know whether Chicago officials made use of the yearly reports, dating back to 1899, generated by island officials on the status of schools, which would have clearly informed them about curricula that had been in place for decades in island schools, in many of which teachers trained in U.S. institutions used the same textbooks found in continental U.S. classrooms. These reports would have provided Chicago leaders with decades' worth of knowledge about Puerto Rican children's and parents' previous educational experiences under U.S. educational programs—a wealth of information not available about other migrant and immigrant groups.

In an interoffice memo in 1954, the Welfare Council recognized "the problem of education for children who know no English."[23] In response, some Chicago teachers volunteered to spend their weekends helping Puerto Rican children at local parochial schools, receiving praise for their efforts from the Chicago mainstream media.[24] Within the Catholic Church, similar efforts were underway by local priests to assist the population by "organizing social programs, establishing language classes, and other means."[25] Los Caballeros de San Juan and the Cardinal's Committee for the Spanish Speaking, both created in 1955 by Catholic organizations, became vehicles through which Puerto Ricans' needs could enter mainstream city politics.[26] Founded at Holy Cross parish, Los Caballeros soon became "the chief expression of social organization among Puerto Ricans" working to "structure a self-conscious community for ethnic advancement and betterment."[27] It and similar groups developed language programs to ease Puerto Ricans' transition to an English-speaking and English-serving community. One of the leaders of Los Caballeros, Wilfredo Velez, taught classes in English and American customs during his spare time.[28] As a 1959 *Chicago Daily Tribune* article highlighted, Velez had relocated to Chicago from Puerto Rico seeking better opportunities for himself and his family after viewing the film *Chicago, Capital of the Industrial World* at his San Juan school: "Leaving his family temporarily, he arrived in Chicago with $125. His hopes were high. He could even speak English. But alas, his teacher had been a Bostonian. When Wilfredo was confronted with our Chicago English, communication temporarily broke down for him. . . . Wilfredo is one of tens of thousands of Puerto Ricans who are adjusting well to life in our city. They never make headlines. They are so busy holding down jobs that they cannot even stop on a street corner to talk."[29]

Velez and his peers in Los Caballeros de San Juan sought to ease their fellow community members' transition to life in Chicago as part of the Chicago Catholic Diocese Cardinal's Committee for the Spanish Speaking. "'Our people need much advice,' Wilfredo said. He explained that in Puerto Rico, in the relaxed atmosphere of an island street, it is considered a gallant gesture for a young man to murmur his appreciation of a pretty girl as she passes."[30] Understanding the cultural norms of their new host city, especially around gender and social expectations, would aid in the population's adjustment to life in the city, perhaps as much as English language acquisition. Language instruction and job placement were the organization's initial aims. But as some Chicagoans came to question Puerto Ricans' presence, Los Caballeros sought to change islanders' behaviors to ensure that they were seen as a welcome and positive addition to the city, and schools played a role in these behavioral shifts. Los Caballeros and similar organizations were aligned with the interests of city officials and perhaps informed by the adjustment process of earlier waves of European immigrants, but they also helped Puerto Rican migrants enact agency in developing programs and organizations that centered their particular needs and experiences. Like Mexican Americans, Puerto Ricans found themselves working within existing frameworks to provide resources for their community, and at times, Americanization programs offered them just that.

During this time, the local media highlighted the migrants in the city as they negotiated life in Chicago. The *Chicago Daily Tribune* ran stories praising public schoolteachers for working with Puerto Rican students and providing them with "special language training" that enabled them to better adjust to life in the city.[31] Programs to help students acquire English were initiated by groups such as the Catholic Alumni Club, which offered tutoring at the De Paul Settlement House. "One feature of the program," according to an article in May 1964, "is to give culturally deprived youngsters the opportunity to talk with someone interested in them in a situation as much unlike a school room as possible."[32] A student featured in that article "has been offered a [full] scholarship to a parochial high school if his English vocabulary and reading comprehension improve." As the article implied, for students who faced multiple school transfers, these programs served as a source of stability. However, the article failed to mention or recognize the institutional problems hindering their schooling opportunities. Again, the language issue was just one of the concerns of community members, who were also contending with limited employment and housing opportunities and the prevailing racial politics that continued to obstruct their movement across the city, at times manifested as violence at the hands of police. Although Puerto Ricans were a transient community because of their limited access to housing, these limitations were not as severe or as institutionalized as those experienced by African Americans. At times, the "racially ambiguous Spanish-speaking" population served as a physical buffer between whites and the perceived threats they saw from

African Americans.[33] Further, "resigning oneself to accepting Puerto Rican neighbors meant not having to accept black ones perhaps."[34] This is not to say that Puerto Ricans (and Mexicans) escaped battles with racial discrimination across the city, as the population was racially heterogeneous. Their struggle with housing discrimination and instability continued to force them out of their initial settlement sites in the subsequent decades. Moreover, discussions about education for racially ambiguous Spanish-speaking populations sometimes excluded the communities they sought to transform and were led by individuals with their own agendas.

Organizations across the city, including the Board of Education and the Welfare Council, continued to meet to discuss the issue of educating Puerto Rican migrants. In 1955, a Chicago-based advocacy group, the Pan American Board of Education, organized a forum to discuss Latin American students. The group led a discussion about educating Puerto Rican students, titled "Puerto Rico, Our Ambassador of Good Will," with the participation of Gretta Brown and other Chicago school administrators.[35] Leading the discussion was Albert E. Goodrich, a former president of the Pan American Board of Education and a member of Willis's committee on Puerto Rican schooling concerns. Goodrich had spent two years working in schools on the island before serving as principal of McKinley High School on Chicago's Near West Side and then as principal of Wells High School, which served a growing Puerto Rican population in the West Town community. Meeting the needs of Puerto Rican students in city schools became a collaborative effort, but the community itself continued to be left out of conversations regarding their needs. City and government officials continued their quest to transform the population, but under their own terms. The Human Relations Center at the University of Chicago gathered valuable information on the local Puerto Rican population and brought together various groups to discuss issues affecting newcomers. At one gathering of school officials and city agencies, officials asked about the status of Puerto Rican students at a particular school: "20 percent of the children in our school do not speak English. [The] Puerto Rican problem is just this. We place them in a classroom situation and that is one way to get them to learn to speak and one way is to get a teacher who helps them to get their (early) help, but there is a (group) who go into a classroom where they have to fight out their own problems."[36] Without an established curriculum across the city to assist Spanish-speaking students, and with Puerto Ricans populating various communities throughout Chicago, schools and organizations questioned what strategies would be most helpful. Integrating students into monolingual classrooms seemed to be a viable option, with groups now looking to include Puerto Ricans in creating long-term plans. As participants recognized, "if you can get leadership among themselves, if they can be trained to be leaders among their own people you will help solve coming problems."[37] But in addition to encouraging leaders within the community, the group gathered by the Human Relations Center turned to the issue of schoolchildren and came up with ideas for integrating the newcomers into educational programs. With suggestions ranging from greeting new students in a friendly way and creating special orientation rooms to developing sensitivity toward the children's needs, members of the Human Relations Center expressed their desire to better understand and address the newcomers' social problems.[38]

In a 1957 report, the Welfare Council continued to praise the educational opportunities available to children and adults. Chicago, it proclaimed, had "more than 100 places in the city where one can enroll in English classes especially designed for persons who speak another language."[39] Once again, language proficiency was targeted as the only tool that could help the population. As one study suggests, "the effect of school as an agent of socialization . . . is not limited to the teaching of English, but this is its most obvious and dramatic manifestation," because the English-speaking Puerto Rican child "will be a major linking factor for his family with the institutions of the larger society."[40] Although language continued to play a role in the schooling concerns of Puerto Ricans, this report suggested that teachers' prejudices, cultural problems, and community problems (including racial conflict among Black and Puerto Rican students and gang activities at school) were also still areas of concern.[41] Schools became the spaces most seriously affected by the dominant group's misinformation and biases about Puerto Ricans, and by extension, schoolchildren faced the greatest harm, as they came to view themselves as the Puerto Rican problem.

In an article headlined "These Puerto Ricans Like It Here," the *Chicago Tribune* portrayed young Puerto Ricans as similar to any other American youth, consumers of American customs, not "square" like their island counterparts.[42] But although some Puerto Rican youth may have considered themselves similar to their "American" or white counterparts, city agencies still labeled them as "poor joiners," with a mere 4 percent participating in community or civic organizations within their new Chicago communities.[43] Creating opportunities for Puerto Ricans and others to embrace their new lives continued to be the theme across city agencies. One Americanization program initiated by the Chicago Board of Education graduated over 3,600 students in 1960.[44] At their graduation ceremony, then–Illinois governor William Stratton informed students, "Responsibility is a key element of good citizenship. History has shown that the nation most likely to endure is that nation which has citizens most fully aware of their responsibilities." For those working to transform nonwhite populations, especially (im)migrants, "the optimism lay in the expectation that education would triumph over divisions of nationality."[45] However, for Puerto Ricans and groups such as African Americans and Native Americans, "citizenship," whether legally or culturally defined, would do very little to ensure their access to a just educational experience. The Puerto Rican population was greatly invested in creating and sustaining organizations, such as Los Caballeros de San Juan, that were better positioned to respond to their everyday concerns and afforded them a connection to cultural practices and celebrations. But however well intended these groups may have been, the city continued to create its own narrative regarding Puerto Ricans' life in Chicago.

It was easy for groups to celebrate their work with and for Puerto Rican students while avoiding discussions about the structural limitations that hindered their full participation and success in city schools. In post-*Brown* Chicago, conversations about the direct connections between housing and school segregation were rare. A 1961 *New York Times* article touting the success of Puerto Ricans in Chicago made unsubstantiated claims about segregation: "Puerto Rican children generally have learned English. . . . There is no segregation of minority groups in schools here. Everyone is assigned to the nearest school. Relations of the Puerto Rican students with both native whites and Negroes have been smooth, just as have relations among adults of these groups. Nor has there been any notable Puerto Rican involvement in juvenile delinquency or crime here."[46] To the outsider, city children, in particular children of color, enjoyed an almost idyllic schooling life. Although students were allowed to enroll in local schools, as the article noted, settlement patterns in Chicago continued to fall closely along racial and class lines, with harmful effects in city classrooms. A combination of Mayor Daley's administration and Willis's school leadership in the late 1950s and early 1960s inspired the African American community to organize against the persistent and systematic marginalization of their community. African Americans in Chicago challenged school segregation by seeking transfers from overcrowded community schools to less crowded white-majority schools. In the mid-1950s, Willis moved quickly to build new schools to meet the growing demand, but by 1963, the number of students skyrocketed to over 500,000, soon outpacing the construction of new buildings.[47] Operation Transfer was launched in 1961, with over a hundred parents asking to have their children be transferred to different schools, but even though the program was backed by various civil rights organizations, their transfer requests for their children were promptly denied.[48] The ensuing suit, *Webb v. Board of Education of the*

City of Chicago (1961), "while failing to bring about school desegregation . . . did highlight the basic arguments for school desegregation in Chicago."[49] On October 22, 1963, close to 225,000 schoolchildren stayed home from school or took to the streets as part of "Freedom Day."[50] The boycott was organized by a coalition of Black religious and community groups to challenge not only the increasing school segregation but also the lack of resources available to community schools and Willis's lack of leadership in addressing their needs. As they considered placing Black children in mobile classrooms rather than allow them to attend white-majority schools, the Chicago Board of Education and Willis made their views clear regarding the needs of students of color.[51]

The concerns of the African American and Puerto Rican communities regarding school segregation (and its consequences) drew the attention of Francis Keppel, who in 1962 began a term as U.S. commissioner of education under President John F. Kennedy, followed by a position in President Lyndon B. Johnson's Department of Health, Education, and Welfare. In 1965, Keppel famously withheld $30 million in federal school funding from Chicago due to the schools' persistent segregation under Mayor Daley.[52] Daley used his political clout to "encourage" Johnson to remove Keppel from his position and allow Chicago to avoid accountability. The education of Puerto Rican residents and other communities of color was in the hands of officials such as Daley and Willis, whose visions were not always aligned with the needs of their growing school-age population. From New York to California, cities became hotspots for community challenges to local and federal policies that limited access to equitable educational opportunities for students of color. Public schools "became entangled with ethnic politics," battles headed by parents and students hoping to see both the promise of *Brown* and the Civil Rights Act come to fruition in their schooling lives.[53]

By 1966, students and community members had begun to organize. They demanded the ouster of principals and teachers who failed to meet the needs of the local communities and whose biased ideologies regarding Puerto Rican and African American students permeated students' educational experience. For instance, Principal Mildred Chuchut of Jenner School proclaimed, "You can't trust these students. . . . You can't trust the Negroes and Puerto Ricans; you have to treat them rough!"[54] Opposition to these comments led to the creation of two groups, Concerned Teachers of Jenner School and Concerned Parents of Jenner School. Parents and community members staged a three-day boycott, keeping a reported 95 percent of the student body out of school.[55] But this walkout was only the beginning of an emerging era of school-based activism by Chicago's African American and Latina/o/x communities, and it reflected a national school reform movement led by those most affected by inadequate schooling. Communities across the country had utilized the courts in the 1940s and 1950s to fight segregation and unequal schooling systems. The civil rights movement and the post-*Brown* years moved this struggle into the streets and schools themselves. In school districts in New York, Detroit, Boston, and other cities, local groups battled "the burdens of desegregation" and "unequal educational opportunity."[56] In 1963, members of Boston's African American community, with the support of the NAACP, held a "Stay Out for Freedom Day" or "Freedom Stayout" as a collective action, highlighting the Boston School Committee's failure to respond to sustained school segregation.[57] Over eight thousand students boycotted Boston schools on June 18, 1963, as parents and community groups organized events aimed at meeting the needs of their community's children.[58] For parents in New York City, organizations created through President Johnson's War on Poverty programs gave families a way to challenge the systems that blocked their children's access to a quality education. One such organization, United Bronx Parents/Padres Unidos del Bronx, worked to "challeng[e] not only inferior schools in one underserved community but also the mind-set of New York City Board of Education officials, who labeled that community's children as victims of an impoverished culture that did not value education."[59] The work of a Puerto Rican woman named Evelina López-Antonetty was instrumental in organizing community responses to the inadequate schooling opportunities for Black and Puerto Rican children.[60] Parents, community members, and most importantly students continued to see schools as central to their overall community struggles. Chicago's Puerto Ricans similarly became part of this larger nationwide move from the courthouse to the schoolhouse and the community streets.

Civil Unrest as Catalyst for School Reform

By the mid-1960s, more than eleven thousand Puerto Rican schoolchildren had been targeted by the Chicago Board of Education's "teaching English as a second language" project, created "to help newcomers adjust to city life and to an English-speaking community."[61] Migration to Chicago was entering its third decade, and for some, Chicago was their second site of migration, but these facts were overlooked by officials, who still viewed the population as monolithic. Administrators continued to focus on English language acquisition, but as the second generation of English-speaking Puerto Rican students emerged in Chicago, language limitations were increasingly irrelevant to issues of inequality. For some racialized groups, it was difficult to demonstrate the correlation between residential segregation and schooling inequality until the Illinois legislature, in 1963, began requiring Chicago to collect data on schools' racial composition.[62] But the lack of reliable demographic data prior to 1963 meant that obtaining accurate information about Puerto Rican students was a cumbersome process.[63] According to Isidro Lucas's work on Puerto Rican dropouts, even after 1963 the schools identified Puerto Rican students only by means of a visual count conducted by teachers, not by consulting the actual records.[64]

Identifying students accurately was only part of the problem. As demonstrated by Francesco Cordasco and Eugene Bucchioni in a study of Puerto Rican children in U.S. schools, teachers and school officials too often "view[ed] Puerto Ricans in terms of the prevailing prejudices, clichés and stereotypes," as "dirty, lazy, wiry, treacherous, aggressive, 'spics,' potential rapists, and knife wielders.' They are viewed as outsiders rapidly 'taking over' some cities."[65] Richard Margolis's report on Puerto Rican students in New York schools documented the concerns parents shared with researchers regarding schoolteachers who openly referred to their Puerto Rican students as "spics," mimicked their accents, or told them they should "go back to Puerto Rico."[66] It was unsurprising that feelings of discontent and frustration began to grow within Puerto Rican communities, including Chicago, as parents and community members realized that schools were ignoring the needs of their students and seemingly pushing them out through ill-treatment and the lack of resources invested in the population. As a result of this "fresh current of concern," Margolis claimed, "it is hardly a coincidence that school systems like Chicago and Philadelphia have recently included Puerto Rican children in their ethnic enrollment totals."[67] School districts' "awakened interest in Puerto Rican pupils," according to Margolis, "is a direct result of pressure from an awakening Puerto Rican community; and if counting the children remains a far cry from teaching them, it is nevertheless the first essential step on the path to reform."[68]

The subsequent community eruption in Chicago in 1966 demonstrates the need to pressure city officials to recognize their culpability in Puerto Rican students' educational shortcomings. In Margolis's words, "No school system, no matter how humane its intentions, is likely to come up with a comprehensive program aimed at saving Puerto Rican children unless the community suggests one and presses for its enactment."[69] After decades of administrative studies on helping Puerto Rican residents adjust successfully to life in Chicago, the community itself saw very few results. Puerto Rican residents still faced housing insecurity, limited labor opportunities, inadequate health resources, and schooling issues that for many were becoming more calamitous over time. It became clear to the two-decades-old community that any push for change would need to come from community action.

Chicago was confronted by an increasingly concerned population of African Americans, Mexican Americans, and Puerto Ricans who questioned the role of local institutions in perpetuating their subordinate status, which was evident in the many problems they still faced. Puerto Ricans, like African Americans, were concerned not only with housing and schooling but also with police brutality and abuse of power. The death of a Puerto Rican fourteen-year-old and the shooting of a young Puerto Rican man named Aracelis Cruz at the hands of local police prompted growing unease.[70] In one of the more serious encounters, the city of Chicago agreed to an $80,000 settlement in connection with the 1966 shooting and subsequent paralysis of seventeen-year-old Rigoberto Acosta.[71] Although schools had become sites of resistance for youth of color, "police brutality touched in a very immediate way the[ir] everyday experiences," as they "found themselves increasingly running up against antagonistic police officers."[72] Schools failed to offer much relief to young Puerto Ricans, Mexicans, and African Americans, who were increasingly dissatisfied with how they were treated by the education system, by the police, and by city agencies. These youth of color and their communities began to organize around their evolving status in an increasingly shifting city landscape, one very much embedded within Chicago's schools and at times spilling over to its community streets.

The growing Puerto Rican community had already seen their stake in their community threatened as they were pushed out of early settlement sites. In communities such as Lincoln Park, Puerto Ricans' claim to community space, and thus schools, was challenged by urban renewal projects that were welcomed and planned by the majority white residents and city officials. In early 1960, the local community was filled with apprehension at the news that nearly $300,000 had been allocated to Lincoln Park for the creation of a redevelopment plan, with millions more promised as redevelopment progressed.[73] As was the case in Nashville in the postwar years, "urban renewal funds helped remake the local landscape to suit elite hopes for growth and to deepen segregation."[74] Although Lincoln Park was "the new home of the pub and boutique, an area of coach lamps and filigree," it was "also the site of time-worn facades—and the anger of the poor."[75] This anger stemmed from the loss of homes and businesses for over two thousand individuals and was further fueled by the city's attempt to earmark prime vacant land for tennis clubs rather than public housing for local needy families—families who were primarily Puerto Rican and Black.[76] The small Puerto Rican enclave in Lincoln Park resisted leaving their community, with groups such as the Young Lords leading the struggle against community displacement and gentrification. Aligned with Black residents and church organizations, the Young Lords worked against urban renewal programs, attempting to secure affordable housing for community residents and improve the educational offerings available in Lincoln Park for Black and Puerto Rican students. The Lincoln Park redevelopment plan was financially backed by various entities, with conservation groups marking the area for urban renewal programs. In 1965, the plan was boosted by a capital grant of more than $10 million from the Federal Housing and Home Finance Agency.[77] Lincoln Park had been home to some Puerto Ricans since the late 1940s, with many others joining the neighborhood throughout the 1950s as they were displaced from other parts of the city.[78] The redevelopment project in Lincoln Park threatened yet another displacement and galvanized a one-time street gang, the Young Lords, to force officials to respond to their growing concerns. Led by José "Cha Cha" Jiménez, the Young Lords worked to confront the attempts (and ultimate success) by white residents and city officials to economically and physically remove poor, working-class residents from the community. Addressing housing evictions, police brutality, and school battles, the Young Lords' organizing work in Lincoln Park mirrored the emerging struggles faced by Puerto Ricans in other communities. It is no coincidence that the organization's membership during the late 1960s was composed of mostly second-generation Puerto Ricans, many of whom were high school dropouts, who had experienced life as second-class citizens in the metropolis.

Redevelopment in communities such as Lincoln Park, as well as the expansion of the University of Illinois Circle Campus (later known as the University of Illinois at Chicago) on the Near West Side, continued to displace Puerto Rican families in the 1960s. Their movement into neighborhoods such as Humboldt Park, Hermosa, and Logan Square led to the establishment of community organizations, centers, and schools catering to Puerto Ricans and their needs. Humboldt Park, in particular, would be regarded as the epitome of a Puerto Rican community for years to follow, but unfortunately, it also became a space where Puerto Ricans were further racialized as a criminal element, facing police brutality and schooling inequality.[79] After years of Puerto Ricans' involuntary transience, Humboldt Park quickly became the center of Puerto Rican life and cultural identity in Chicago, a space where the population was able to create a sense of community cohesiveness.

The concerns of Chicago's Puerto Ricans, who numbered thirty-two thousand by 1960, continued to grow.[80] For many, their unfamiliarity with the English language impaired their interactions with police officers, who often grew frustrated with the "foreigners." Yet the Welfare Council in 1957 conde-scendingly informed Puerto Ricans that the Chicago police were similar to the police force in Puerto Rico and were "cordial and helpful to those who comply with the law."[81] The growing population contended with police brutal-ity, exacerbated by a lack of Spanish-speaking service workers, high infant mortality rates, a high incidence of preventable disease, a lack of adequate health care, increasing unemployment, and educational inequalities.[82] On June 12, 1966, the day of the first Puerto Rican Day Parade in Chicago, com-munity frustrations inevitably erupted after a white police officer, Thomas Munyon, shot and wounded Aracelis Cruz. The incident occurred following a police call to investigate suspected gang activity near Milwaukee Avenue and Division Street, near the Wicker Park neighborhood.[83] Cruz allegedly followed Munyon and held a gun to the officer, whereupon Munyon drew his own weapon and shot Cruz in the leg. Almost immediately a crowd gath-ered, burning several police vehicles.[84] Community workers headed by Sister Janet Parmalee (later known as Janet Nolan) collected firsthand accounts of the community uprising: "Suddenly the police car was on fire. The crowd backed away and got strangely silent. There were muttered comments: 'Now they've really done it.' 'We want freedom,' a woman's voice said in English. 'No policeman will ever ride that car again.'" A young man remarked, "'No one can live in Chicago for eighteen years and not have problems with the police.'"[85]

Following the shooting, the intersection of Damen Avenue and Division Street became the initial site of a grim clash between Puerto Rican residents and police officers, leaving nineteen people hurt during the first day of the unrest, with both civilians and officers injured by bricks, bottles, and other debris.[86] The police presence in West Town and Humboldt Park intensified for two days, leading to further injuries as well as numerous arrests.[87] Puerto Rican community leaders accused Chicago police of failing to subdue the rioters. They urged the city to allow them to address the friction within the community in order to restore order, with Puerto Rican residents demanding "Police, go home."[88] Although the uprising was a direct result of the shooting of a young Puerto Rican man during the community's own ethnic celebra-tion, an act of community assertion, the community's response reflected a long history of police brutality, economic and political disenfranchisement, and frustration over educational inequities.

The Division Street uprising marked a significant shift in the history and understanding of Puerto Ricans in Chicago, especially in the local media's portrayal of the community and the community's response to the perceived threat to their stake in the city. Long gone was the language of Puerto Ricans as "fellow Americans," a "docile" people, eager to assimilate. The rhetoric now cast them as violent, drug-infested, and welfare-dependent. As now-politicized social agents, Chicago's Puerto Ricans organized through various venues to demand that the city address and reevaluate the issues afflicting their community in hopes of legitimizing their claims to space as equal stakeholders. The 1960s and beyond saw schools become contentious sites where both the city and the young Puerto Rican community could articulate concerns and aspirations, sometimes as a means of creating solutions for the social ills affecting residents. Community members deliberated ways to utilize the Division Street uprising and the attention it had drawn to mobilize and confront their positionality within the city.

On June 15, 1966, the day after the altercation ended, Mayor Daley met with city officials and community representatives to help bring calm. "All of us are concerned with the safety and well-being of our children and young people," he reiterated. "It [is] doubly important that all of us exercise the greatest diligence in keeping our children and young adults off the streets and near their homes."[89] Following the community uprising, more than two hundred Puerto Ricans, African Americans, and white allies, representing various faith-based, civic, and grassroots organizations, led a five-mile march to City Hall to present Daley with a three-page list of demands.[90] Ironically, a recent study of the Humboldt Park and West Town area conducted by the Chicago Commission on Human Relations had concluded that "conditions in the neighborhood were serene."[91] The riots had shocked the city of Chicago and its human relations experts, who had targeted other areas of the city as possible trouble spots for civil unrest in the summer of 1966. The 1966 incident erupted as "a new generation of Puerto Ricans sensed that persuasion was not going to bring an end to subordination and oppression."[92] This new generation of community leaders and activists no longer spoke of working within the city politics framework to create opportunity for the Puerto Rican population. Instead, they sought to create their own opportunities and organizations to confront what they saw as a lack of response from the city.

City officials were forced to quickly evaluate Puerto Ricans' living conditions and admit that they had ignored the group's needs and concerns for decades. Following the riots, the focus of Daley and other officials was on attempting to rectify the "youth problem," with Puerto Rican community representatives seeking recreational facilities, better Puerto Rican representation on youth commissions, and development of "a comprehensive community action program against social injustices."[93] Daley, on the other hand, continued to focus on the language barrier, as Chicago police, the Board of Education, and property owners spoke of the difficulties in communicating effectively with Puerto Ricans.[94]

Responding to the community's immediate and direct demands, the Commission on Human Relations hosted an open hearing in July 1966. "In June of 1966," it acknowledged, "Chicago experienced a civil disturbance which shocked the city, along the heavily Puerto Rican area on Division Street between Damen and California. This civil disorder, which was primarily directed against the police and government, caused great concern among all the responsible leaders of the city, including the Puerto Rican community."[95] After hearing testimony from individuals and groups with a variety of interests, the committee published a report in November 1966 outlining ways the city could work to address the needs of the community. It recommended nine areas for improvement, including the relationship between the police and the community, the courts and legislation, employment, and, of course, education. The recommendations for improving school relations and educational opportunities included the establishment of more "Americanization" classes in areas with Latin American residents, Spanish language training for teachers working in schools with large numbers of Spanish-speaking students, and various programs encouraging Spanish-speaking parents to participate in schools.[96] In collaboration with various organizations, city officials moved quickly to establish programs, especially youth-targeted programs, within the Puerto Rican community. Mayor Daley commented, "it is only with the active participation, cooperation, and help of the residents themselves that we will be able to effectively carry on worthwhile programs."[97] Also cooperating with city officials were over one hundred teachers from sixteen different public schools, who by mid-1966 had enrolled in special Spanish language courses established by the Chicago Board of Education.[98] Similarly, the Chicago Catholic Archdiocesan School System developed "curriculum units in the area of history, language study, and Latin American culture to expand their services to their Spanish-speaking students."[99] The 1966 uprising did not represent the Puerto Rican community's "awakening," as the community had been organizing since its first migrations in the 1940s. But the unrest forced the city to acknowledge that Puerto Ricans would no longer be content with mere promises; they now demanded action.

The organizational responses of Puerto Ricans and city administrators were seen as a direct consequence of the riots, even if they were not always effective in addressing the issues afflicting Puerto Ricans. "It was a response to the riots," recalls Samuel Betances, a Puerto Rican organizer and the founding editor of the Puerto Rican journal *The Rican*. "Number one, everyone was taken back because nobody really knew why the Puerto Rican community in Chicago was the first community ever to explode into a riot. . . . When we got together, we didn't know what to do. But we knew that education had to be part of the answer."[100]

As one report stated, "It was not until June 1966, when the 'civil disorder,' which was primarily directed against the police and government, shocked the city . . . that the problems of Puerto Rican residents were made visible and were publicly disputed for the first time."[101] Aside from increased English language instruction, Mayor Daley revealed plans to open Operation Head Start classes in several elementary schools, churches, and settlement houses.[102] Funding from the Federal Elementary and Secondary Education Act of 1965 enabled research specialists to institute bilingual programs in city schools.[103] In 1966, public schoolteacher (and later school administrator) Henry Romero utilized such funds to lead a summer teachers' institute. As Romero noted, "The first thing I tell them is that our role is to combine two cultures, not, as some would have us believe, to forsake one for the other. . . . Puerto Rican children, like strangers anywhere, are quick to grasp and ready to understand once initial barriers are broken down."[104] Romero further recognized "the implications of language difficulties" and other barriers that complicated the schooling of this population. But some school personnel resisted Romero's ideas. The principal of a Northwest Side school rebuked the views of those seeking services for their students: "My parents were Italian immigrants. I think they would have been surprised if I had been taught subjects in Italian. I think Puerto Rican youngsters here want to learn English."[105] Pulaski School principal Natalie Picchiotti, who attended a 1967 conference on Puerto Rican concerns organized by local and island agencies, disagreed with the notion that Puerto Rican students needed adequate bilingual education programs. Picchiotti had been instrumental in developing an earlier program to help teachers communicate better with Spanish-speaking students, but she admitted that she was apprehensive about using an interpreter to communicate with children, because "regardless of how much you try, the child feels you are condescending when you talk thru an interpreter."[106] Considering Picchiotti's commitment to aiding students' bilingualism through program development and building positive relationships between teachers and students, one is left to question her later opposition to bilingual education. The Puerto Rican community, however, began to articulate how they would position themselves to guide conversations about their future. Language would be just one of the concerns.

A Community Responds

Community members could no longer assume or take comfort in the idea that change would come at the hands of white administrators and city officials. Local community groups engaged in creating institutional change to ensure educational justice for their students, but also to gain a sense of autonomy in the decisions affecting their everyday lives. For example, in earlier years, groups such as Los Caballeros de San Juan had created programs that provided a sense of stability through economic and social outlets.[107] For many organizations, internal conflict threatened the possibility of community cohesiveness, while others became the target of organized threats from police and federal groups seeking to destabilize community organizing and its effectiveness.[108] Even the politically benign Spanish Action Committee of Chicago (SACC) became the target of such actions.

SACC was founded in June 1966, just after the Division Street uprising. It sought to "enable local residents to identify in an organized manner the physical and social problems of the community, to interpret these needs to city agencies, and work toward implementing some community-based programs."[109] Led by former Los Caballeros de San Juan member Juan Díaz, SACC engaged in local community politics, assisted local business leaders, attended school board meetings, and worked with residents on the removal of police officers accused of utilizing unfair tactics and discriminatory actions toward Puerto Ricans.[110] But with a growing population also came conflicting interests within the Puerto Rican community itself, including accusations that individuals and organizations were serving city officials at a cost to the community. Five founding members of SACC released a statement in September 1966 announcing their resignation and the creation of a new but similar organization, the American Spanish Speaking People's Association, and accused other members of subversive behavior. The press played an integral role in the planned disruption of these organizations and the lives of their members.[111] Ted Ramírez, one of the five SACC members who resigned, publicly disclosed alleged criminal activities of SACC member and director Juan Díaz. The five also accused Díaz of receiving financial and administrative assistance from reputed communists, and claimed that members of New York's Puerto Rican community had taken control of the Chicago organization.[112] In addition, Ramírez and others claimed that outsiders, not local community members, had been responsible for creating the list of demands presented to city officials following the 1966 uprising. According to Ramírez, "They knew nothing of our problems here. They just took over. . . . There has been no effort to bring to the people the realization that they must help themselves if they are to expect help from others."[113] Díaz, then president of the Latin American Boys Club, initially denied that there had been outside (and more importantly "communist") involvement in SACC, but he later recanted those statements, perhaps to avoid added pressure by Ramírez and other former SACC members, or to retain some community credibility. Janet Nolan recalled: "Juan Díaz!? He wanted no part of Communism. And he was always telling everybody not to do things to disturb the police and not to give the community a bad name. . . . Some of his own people from the Spanish Action Committee, including Ted and Mirta Ramírez and Victor, attacked him in the article, calling him a dictator. . . . After that, Juan Díaz was completely discredited in his community."[114]

The surveillance of Chicago's Puerto Rican community in the 1960s was part of a larger federal counterintelligence project targeting local and national activist groups focused on many different interests, including women's rights, antiwar efforts, and a wide range of racial and ethnic movements.[115] The "Red Squad," an arm of the Subversive Activities Unit of the Chicago Police Intelligence Unit, had been established in the early twentieth century as the city targeted suspected communist groups and labor unions.[116] In the 1960s, the Red Squad focused on the activities of groups such as the Black Panthers and various Puerto Rican community organizations in Chicago. Groups such as SACC saw their leadership dismantled by outside influences and false accusations aimed at destabilizing the community's leadership and work. Religious leaders and community activists Janet Nolan and Father Donald Headley, in the face of the impending Red Squad investigations, revealed just how complicated the situation was, not only for Díaz and Ted and Mirta Ramírez but for the larger Puerto Rican community as well. According to one account, the Ramírezes' sudden attack on Díaz and others was engineered by Red Squad instigators who manipulated the already tense relationship between these individuals, as one police officer infiltrated SACC and led attacks against Díaz.[117] Richard Gutman, an attorney for the Alliance to End Repression, contended that although the Ramírezes had actively utilized both the media and their community influence to discredit Díaz and SACC, they did so with no knowledge of the subversive actions of the Red Squad. As Díaz later testified, "I was confused, depressed and disappointed . . . and also ashamed. . . . And I was really hurt because I never expected Mirta or anybody to accuse me of communism and to resign from the organization. I'm still suffering from that. . . . Membership dispersed. Many of them left the town. And others went and made their own organizations. . . . Nobody wanted anything to do with us."[118]

The infiltration of community-based organizations like SACC during the 1960s indicates the impact that such groups had, as local and federal officials went to great lengths to limit their influence. These tactics were not limited to radical groups in Chicago, as over two thousand known COINTELPRO operations were launched across the country targeting political or politicized organizations. These operations were supported and initiated by the federal government, which sought to disrupt the work of groups such as the Black liberation movement, various Puerto Rican organizations, the American Indian movement, and Chicano/a organizations.[119] For Puerto Ricans in Chicago in the 1960s, their fragile relationships, diverging interests, and generational and class divides gave "outsiders" the opportunity to cause further friction.

Highlighting these fractures and factions among the leadership of local organizations is essential to understanding that the community was far from monolithic and homogeneous. Yet despite their inherent differences, the work of various and varying organizations allowed institutional change to occur. In fact, although the relationship between the Ramírezes and Díaz deteriorated due to outside influences, Ted and especially Mirta Ramírez in the late 1960s and early 1970s became active and vocal participants in improving the schooling lives of Puerto Rican students. Despite the work of such individuals, however, schools were now a battleground where Puerto Rican activists fought over differing visions for the community. Yet schools also become sites for collaborative relationships to develop among different activist groups, all of whom agreed that educational reform was important in reducing the victimization of Puerto Rican youth.

Organizations and groups such as Los Caballeros de San Juan, SACC, and the soon-to-be-established Aspira of Illinois drew attention to the schooling discrepancies faced by Puerto Rican children and worked alongside city officials to create better educational opportunities. Grassroots organizing work initiated by youth was also instrumental in advocating for change, as young people confronted the educational injustices they faced in their daily lives. High school and college students, community members, and groups such as the Young Lords led battles in the late 1960s and 1970s to bring attention to Puerto Rican students' standing in city schools. Through all of this, Puerto Rican women, following the trajectory of Muna Muñoz Lee and her counterparts in the preceding decades, continued to be instrumental in establishing resources and organizations to aid the community and in creating institutional change within established structures. Like the work of Mexican and Mexican American women, the work of Puerto Rican women is often absent from histories, especially community histories, and in many ways "their lives remained invisible."[120] The legacy of their community work, however, remains central to the story of Puerto Rican Chicago.

Puerto Rican Aspirations:
Schooling and Community Concerns after 1966

The Division Street uprising was only the beginning of the agitation as Chicago families and students became more vocal about their overall treatment. In the Chicago Board of Education's 1967 report on the annual pupil headcount, eight elementary schools in the city were labeled as "Puerto Rican schools" because of their large or increasing Puerto Rican student body.[121] One such school quickly realized that Puerto Ricans' schooling concerns stemmed not only from prevalent and prejudicial views regarding their linguistic and cultural identities but also from problems with the maintenance and repair of school buildings. For instance, poor lighting at Otis Elementary School forced teachers to curtail reading programs when their own eyesight became strained, an interruption that affected the school's 890 pupils and 39 teachers.[122] As one teacher put it, "Our school is beginning to look like a haunted house."[123] In 1967, the Chicago Board of Education sought to redraw school boundaries in the Humboldt Park community, forcing many children to transfer out of their local school. Officials gave little regard to the distance between children's homes and their assigned schools and appeared to discount the working relationships parents had already established with their current school principal. Puerto Rican parents argued that "the boundary change had something to do with the fact that most of the pupils affected were Puerto Rican," as it would create an almost completely Puerto Rican school.[124] A large number of parents attended a board meeting about the proposed change, demonstrating their active participation in their children's educational lives and their refusal to stand by passively as change was imposed on them. One board member noted, "Many of the parents attending our committee meeting had taken time off from their jobs to attend and lost pay for doing so."[125] For Puerto Ricans, "parenting strategies of the working-class mothers stemmed both from their cultural traditions and their neighborhood context, in which the physical safety of their children was not assured."[126] But alongside concerns about students' physical safety, parents also contended with their children's "educational" safety, as school personnel and curricula often failed to recognize children's Puerto Rican identity. This led community members to express their growing frustrations with city schools by using existing structures, such as parent-teacher associations and school board meetings, as well as by creating new organizations. The results included school boycotts, the creation of Puerto Rican–centric schools and curricula, and the radicalization of local organizations.[127]

Like Black community members, Puerto Rican parents sought greater stability for their children by resisting school redistricting, busing, overcrowding, and inadequate learning environments. They linked these concerns with what they saw as the city's overall disinvestment in Puerto Ricans. As Cha Cha Jiménez would later recall, Puerto Rican students were "not connecting" with schools.[128] The public school dropout rate among Puerto Rican students in the 1960s and 1970s was over 70 percent, which reflected their level of disengagement.[129] Just as Puerto Ricans saw themselves pushed out of neighborhoods across the city, the late 1960s saw their stake in community schools questioned and often ignored. From Lincoln Park to Humboldt Park, Puerto Rican students understood and internalized their limited status within schools and raised questions about the role of education in their community's socioeconomic plight. As one thirteen-year-old student wrote, "When I first get up in the morning I feel fresh and it seems like it would be a good day to me. But after I get in school, things change and they seem to turn into problems for me. And by the end of the day I don't even feel like I'm young. I feel tired."[130]

Puerto Ricans needed community intervention to reverse this feeling of exhaustion and defeat. The establishment of Aspira in 1968 was one of the most influential developments initiated by the community themselves to combat their current schooling battles by offering greater educational opportunities to Puerto Rican students.[131] According to one article, "Aspira's main objective is to help qualified youngsters thru educational counseling, scholarship and loan procurement, and leadership training."[132] Although credited as the brainchild of Mirta Ramírez, the birth of the organization's Illinois chapter was a community affair. "Juan Sangrudo Cruz, Julio Estacio, Samuel Betances, Marcelino Diaz, and Ted and Mirta Ramírez, we chipped in a hundred dollars each [to send Mirta to meet with Aspira leaders in New York City]. . . . We had heard there's a place called Aspira, so we said, 'Why do something in Chicago that may already exist. Maybe we can bring what exists in New York?' Because we always thought that New York was the capital of Puerto Ricans. If it was going to happen, New York [would] have had to make it happen already."[133]

Finding out about Aspira was the first step, but convincing its founder, community leader Dr. Antonia Pantoja, to bring the organization to Chicago would be the real challenge. Mirta Ramírez set up meetings with Aspira leadership in New York in order to promote Chicago as a site for a new chapter. According to Betances, "We put her on a Greyhound bus, 'cause we couldn't afford a plane ticket, and gave her those five hundred dollars, and Ted agreed, and we sent Mirta on an expedition to New York to find out what is Aspira, how does it work, and under what circumstances can we bring it to Chicago."[134] After an almost eight-hundred-mile journey, the young Puerto Rican mother succeeded in convincing the Aspira leadership in New York to visit Chicago and establish a chapter in the city. With the help of a Ford Foundation grant, the new chapter gave Chicago's Puerto Ricans a platform for addressing educational reform in classrooms rather than on the streets. As Ramírez maintained, "No one is going to help Puerto Ricans. If we want to take advantage of opportunities in this society, we'll have to help ourselves."[135]

Mirta Ramírez was well aware of the daily battles her community faced, because as a Puerto Rican migrant, she had experienced them herself, particularly regarding access to housing and education. Her father's death when she was twelve years old had prompted her mother to sell the family farm in Puerto Rico and migrate to New York in 1946. "The day we arrived in this place," she recalled, "was an overcast day in New York and I looked and say, 'My God, where the heck are we?' . . . At that time in New York it was right after the Second World War, and there were no apartments, no housing available, and we stay with a family for, thank God for three weeks, something like that, and my mother was able to buy a key to an apartment."[136] After leaving school and working in New York, Ramírez moved in 1948 to Chicago, where a brother resided, soon followed by moves to Florida and back to New York and Puerto Rico. In Puerto Rico, she met and married Ted Ramírez, who had returned there following military service. The couple briefly settled in New York while Ted completed his studies at New York University. Missing her family in Chicago, Mirta and her young family relocated to the city in the late 1950s. There she became involved in the local community while also attending college. Following the Division Street uprising in 1966, she sought to establish a community-based organization to address educational discrepancies, and in 1968 she ventured alone to New York City via Greyhound bus in the hope of convincing Aspira leaders to allow her to establish a Chicago branch of the organization.[137] As she recalled, after the 1966 unrest, a group of Puerto Rican residents in Chicago completed a survey about their community's needs, revealing that housing, unemployment, health, and education were their central concerns.[138]

Following the survey, Ramírez focused her attention on education.

I was going to college at the time. and I found the description of Aspira in a book that Father Fitzgerald had written in New York. . . . So I quit school and worked full time on the Aspira project. . . . I worked for two—well, actually eighteen months—to get the grant from the Ford Foundation, and it was for over a million dollars for three years, and that established Aspira as a national organization.[139]

In 1968, as the first director of Aspira's Illinois branch, she utilized the grant funds to begin work on the organization.

> I put the board of directors together, I bought the furniture, rented the place, set up the telephones . . . and I hired the first club organizer to go out to the high schools. The significance of that was that no outside agency had been working within schools. . . . It guides the student into whatever field they want to go to, and they develop leadership. . . . They're supposed to come back and help the others move up. . . . If I were to take the salaries of the thirty or so thousand Aspirantes that are just in Chicago, I'd be richer than, what's his name, Bill Gates![140]

Ramírez worked alongside city officials and community leaders to provide better educational opportunities for bilingual students by encouraging the Board of Education to hire teachers from Spanish-speaking countries on very limited funds. "We had $128,000 for all these children," she recalled, reminding the board of their responsibility, via the Elementary and Secondary Act, to provide support for students in Chicago.[141]

Ramírez played a crucial role in facilitating institutional reform, creating opportunities for the community through Aspira's work. Moreover, she is an important figure in a gendered history of Chicago. Ramírez and others remind us that "women were critical to forging livable settlements out of such inhospitable sites."[142] Throughout the history of Puerto Ricans in Chicago, Puerto Rican women from Elena Padilla and Muna Muñoz Lee onward have been instrumental in community development, especially in connection with educational opportunities for Puerto Ricans. As Isidro Lucas recalled, "Any movement of Latinos in Chicago, the women were leading . . . there is no question."[143]

María Cerda, who was appointed to the Chicago Board of Education in 1969, is also part of that history. Soon after the community uprising of 1966 and the subsequent mobilization among the Puerto Rican, Mexican American, and African American communities, Mayor Daley was forced to acknowledge the need for greater representation in city politics. Since the 1870s, the appointment of members to the school board had been left to the discretion of the mayor, and the appointees had reflected the city's existing power structures, lacking representation from the growing Latina/o and African American communities. It took the battle for school desegregation, initiated by the African American community, and the Puerto Rican community's mobilization in the late 1960s to pressure city officials into restructuring the board's makeup.[144] This would allow community input into decisions affecting primarily Latina/o and African American schoolchildren, such as busing, desegregation, and the hiring of a diverse teaching force. In 1969 Daley chose both Cerda, a Puerto Rican social worker, and Alvin J. Boutte, an African American businessperson and civic leader, to serve on the Board of Education, which faced long-standing yet pertinent problems.[145] Their appointment was denounced by some local groups, who labeled them as representative of "special interest groups" by virtue of their identities.[146] One such group, composed mainly of white Chicago homemakers, criticized the mayor's nominations, claiming discrimination against Chicago's working-class whites. A representative of Chicago's Southwest Associated Block Clubs, Ellen Noonan, argued that Cerda would "represent the Spanish-speaking people, and not us . . . nobody there will listen to us."[147] Another group member believed that in appointing Cerda, whose husband was the first Mexican American Illinois appellate judge and a founding member of LULAC in Chicago, Mayor Daley had "set an ethnic precedent" that would result in attempts by other groups to have their own communities represented on the board.[148] Of Boutte, Marilyn Moran, representing Bogan High School, said, "We want conservative representatives. . . . Mr. Boutte can only represent the liberal element because I have yet to meet a conservative Negro."[149] Such comments failed to mention whose interests had been served for decades by the overwhelmingly white school board.

Cerda's appointment to the Board of Education came at a critical time. The pivotal appointment of not just a Puerto Rican but a Puerto Rican woman provided a platform for Latina/o communities in Chicago to address and resolve their schooling concerns. The previous school year had been marked by dozens of walkouts and boycotts, some led by the students themselves, stemming from the growing dissatisfaction of African American, Puerto Rican, and Mexican American residents with their status in city schools. In 1969, Puerto Rican and Mexican parents attended Board of Education meetings to advocate for adequate bilingual education programs and an increase in the number of Spanish-speaking administrators to represent their interests.[150] Perhaps having learned from the successes of the African American and Mexican American communities in organizing for the educational needs of their children, Puerto Ricans utilized the language of community control and bilingual education to articulate their own schooling-related concerns. The Bilingual Education Act of 1968 centered the needs of language minorities in U.S. schools and was informed by the era's social, political, and economic struggles (the civil rights movement, the Vietnam War, etc.). To some extent it was "an effort to dissipate the growing anger in the nation about injustices and inequities" by improving educational opportunities for language minorities.[151] In giving Puerto Ricans another federal mandate (following *Brown*) to use in extending conversations about the everyday experiences of their children, this new legislation became central to Cerda's work. A native of Puerto Rico, Cerda had received her undergraduate degree in 1956 from the University of Puerto Rico, followed by a master's degree in social work from the University of Chicago in 1960, a trajectory similar to that of many other Puerto Rican women migrants to Chicago. Upon Cerda's appointment to the Board of Education, Puerto Rican residents generally saw her as Daley's response to the outcry from the community to remedy their lack of representation within city politics.[152] Her five-year tenure on the board gave her a platform for improving bilingual education and promoting curricula that valued Latina/o children's cultural backgrounds.

> It was a lot of work. At the time I had kids, and I had not worked for ten years [because] I wanted to be a mother at home. It was really an effort because there were many meetings. It was an exciting period, we were talking about—the big issue before me, before I came to the board, was busing. That was not as vital as it was when I came around, but there were many issues and I brought the issue of, not so much bilingual education, but what are we doing for this population that is growing, for many who don't speak the language? How are we doing getting resources to teach them? And then we went searching Puerto Rico and Mexico and brought teachers from Puerto Rico and Mexico. We started, with Sylvia Herrera, an Aspira program for twenty students at the University of Illinois to study for teaching. Many of them are working at the Board of Education now. And we did many things to . . . also deal with the problem and deal with solutions. And find resources to deal with the problem.[153]

During those five years, Cerda was a constant presence at local schools (unlike her board colleagues). She sought and obtained an increase in funding for Chicago's bilingual education programs and utilized the funds to recruit qualified teachers from Mexico and Puerto Rico.[154] Cerda's work on the school board had long-term effects on the lives of Puerto Ricans and other Latina/o students thanks to her promotion of Aspira's involvement in Chicago schools. When Samuel Betances, founder of *The Rican*, went to Chicago's Lane Technical High School to establish a chapter of Aspira, the principal was hesitant. As Betances recalls, Cerda "was very key because when we brought Aspira to Chicago in 1968, one of the things that Aspira used to do at that time was . . .

establish Aspira Clubs in the high school. So I went to Lane Tech to establish, to help establish an Aspira Club. To meet with the principal to let him know, and he said 'Absolutely not, we don't want that club here.' So I said okay, very good. So I called María Cerda, who spoke to the superintendent, who spoke to the principal, and we then had an Aspira Club at the high school."[155] In 1960s Chicago, a Puerto Rican woman with the ability to influence both the principal and the superintendent was worthy of note.

Cerda had previously served as an assistant to Mirta Ramírez at Aspira of Illinois, and she later worked for the Welfare Council of Metropolitan Chicago. Her time at these organizations gave her experience with two divergent approaches to addressing the "problem" of Puerto Rican migrants. Many city residents opposed Daley's appointment of Cerda and Boutte to the board, two liberal nominees who they assumed would play a lead role in the upcoming teachers' union negotiations and would block budget cuts to critical programs.[156] But other residents believed that Cerda's appointment would pave the way for institutional change in Chicago's schools and would benefit the Puerto Rican community. For Mexican and Puerto Rican parents, board meetings became a space where they could present a unified front in articulating the need for expanded bilingual instruction and their desire for a Spanish-speaking deputy school superintendent to represent their interests.[157] Through her later work with the (Chicago) Latino Institute during the 1970s, Cerda advocated for policies and legislation to improve opportunities for Latina/o communities. But just as important as her achievements in effecting institutional change was her work at the individual level. She was instrumental in creating a Parent Leadership Training Program for parents of public school students enrolled in bilingual education programs.[158] Through Cerda's appointment to the Chicago Board of Education and her work with the Latino Institute, Puerto Ricans and other Latina/o groups finally had a voice, even if her influence was at times limited and still read through the gender and racial politics of the era.

From Community Activism to Education Activism

The role of Puerto Rican women in the development of community-based work was evident to María Cerda. "If it weren't for us," she recalled, "there wouldn't be a community. In Aspira in New York, Puerto Rico, and wherever they are, the women are the leaders. If it weren't for women, we would not have the leadership that we have right now. In Puerto Rico women have always been strong leaders."[159] Although works by women such as Elena Padilla and Muna Muñoz Lee influenced the early days of the population's movement to the city, the leadership of Puerto Rican men and their organizations was central in the following decades. Cerda's appointment to the Board of Education and Ramírez's influence through Aspira were clear indicators of the ongoing labor of Puerto Rican women in improving the community's status. However, their work and influence would at times be overshadowed by continued struggles for access to educational resources and opportunities, and it often was written out of history. As we will see in chapter 5, even the Puerto Rican community's own print media often failed to center the voices of Puerto Rican women.

Organizations representing Puerto Ricans often focused on providing basic necessities to the community, allowing them to take control of their own lives while adjusting to a new environment in an urban center. Los Caballeros de San Juan, considered to be the best of the Puerto Rican community in terms of community representation and led by "civic minded, solid citizens who are anxious to help others," provided housing information, job placement, and a safe social outlet for Puerto Ricans.[160] In many ways, according to Felix Padilla, "Puerto Rican families in Chicago had achieved an enduring cohesion of community in which social organizations and agencies and cultural traditions played the largest part."[161] Although they differed in their organizing and leadership, groups such as Los Caballeros de San Juan and the Young Lords Organization paved the way for the school-based and community-led activism that came to define the community in the years following the 1966 uprising. The same issues the community had confronted since their initial migration later played out within Chicago's classrooms. When the city embraced Puerto Ricans as fellow Americans in the early years of their migration, schools sought ways to create *better* Americans, especially by targeting their language skills.[162] But as the Puerto Rican community began to question the city's role in their status as second-class citizens, schools became locations of conflict over community control and equity. The city experienced collective anxiety about its seemingly failed attempts to control or contain Puerto Ricans within the desired geographic and social boundaries. This anxiety dictated the strained relationship between the city and its Puerto Rican population, and schools became sites where battle lines were drawn. The community's eruption in 1966 and their ensuing school activism were intricately linked to the frustration on both sides. Improving educational opportunities, in both K–12 and higher education, would become a central theme for Puerto Ricans in the decade to follow, at times uniting a community that found itself divided by ideological differences. Puerto Rican youth, as well as other youth of color, mediated new means of resistance aimed at transforming and confronting the constant provocations they faced, whether on street corners or in classrooms. These transformative actions transcended the participants' own racial and ethnic identities, as these young people "contributed greatly to shaping the histories of the larger communities encompassing them."[163] For Puerto Ricans in Chicago, the opportunity to shape their community, on their own terms, became a key element in the struggle for Tuley and Clemente High Schools.

CHAPTER 3

Taking It to the Streets

The Puerto Rican Movement for Education in 1970s Chicago

IN 1971, ISIDRO LUCAS, representing the Council on Urban Education, released a comprehensive report titled *Puerto Rican Dropouts in Chicago: Numbers and Motivations*.[1] Lucas, originally a Catholic missionary from Spain, had become involved in issues pertaining to Puerto Rican and other Latina/o students at the urging of Aspira administrators.[2] Although willing to help, Lucas was adamant about who should serve in leadership positions in the community.

> I did not want nor did I take a leadership position in the movement that was trying to grow in Chicago for Latinos. It seemed to me that only Puerto Ricans or Mexicans or the like should take the positions of leadership. My situation was behind those lines as a second front to provide them with the data and the information. Before that there had been a lot of "our students are not being studied or served," but it was after I published the thing [*Puerto Rican Dropouts in Chicago*] that they could say indeed they are not being served, and we have the data to prove it.[3]

After answering an advertisement, Lucas began working with the newly formed organization, collecting valuable information on the status of Puerto Rican students. With a $10,000 grant he received in 1969 from the Office of Education, he examined the dropout problem among Puerto Ricans in Chicago's public schools. In a 1971 report he detailed the various factors that had led more than 70 percent of those students to leave school early. Instead of focusing only on how the education system had neglected Puerto Rican students, however, the report offered recommendations on how to serve them better.[4] Although Puerto Ricans faced myriad issues in Chicago schools, Lucas said that his work on language and bilingualism gave the community a concrete rallying point. Their struggle for control of their schools, in particular Tuley and Clemente High Schools, united them with a larger movement of school-based activism following 1968. All across the United States, a generation of students had witnessed both the gains and losses of the tumultuous 1960s, and they utilized the language of the era to understand their status as students. The lessons of the civil rights movement met the Black, Brown, and Red Power movements in urban classrooms. Chicana/o students in California and other southwestern states were vocal and engaged in school-centered activism within their local communities, including student-led school walkouts, and the scholarship detailing these communities' histories is growing.[5] In one such example, following the assassination of Dr. Martin Luther King Jr. in 1968, African American high school students in York, Pennsylvania, organized a Black Pride Day, which became the springboard for institutionalized changes in their school district.[6]

For Puerto Ricans, the socialization projects in schools that had begun on the island in 1898 faced the growing activism of students, teachers, and community members in Chicago more than seventy years later. But whose terms would define the debate? The answer to this question was still unclear. The struggle for Tuley and Clemente High Schools highlighted the organizing efforts of a community frustrated with their limited power in decisions regarding their own lives and demonstrated the population's heterogeneity. Whatever the course of mobilization or the rationale behind it, Puerto Ricans clearly were invested in working to remedy the ills that had led to their second-rate status in Chicago schools, as detailed in the work of Lucas and others.

Not everyone imagined that Puerto Ricans were interested in or able to organize around a common issue, despite the community's reaction to the 1966 uprising. A report titled *The Situation of the Puerto Rican Population in Chicago and Its Viewpoints about Racial Relations* portrayed them as passive actors in the movement for civil rights: "Puerto Ricans in the United States are defined as a cultural minority. In this capacity, they are subjected to exploitation and to a wide range of de facto limitations. Moreover, they are one of the least capable of all the minority groups of rapid life-style improvement. And, in spite of the occurrence of such spontaneous outbursts as the Chicago riot of 1966, they are not as active in the political and civil rights field as some other minorities."[7] However, Puerto Ricans' activism in the decade following 1966 belied the notion of their "relative passivity." Schools, especially, became sites of community engagement, although they were also a divisive space where individual politics and ideologies complicated the everyday experiences of

Puerto Rican schoolchildren. But however divisive the internal community struggles were, Puerto Ricans in Chicago continued to organize to confront the injustices their community faced in K–12 schools and, especially in the 1970s, in higher education. According to a group of Puerto Rican college students, "In our case as oppressed working-class Puerto Ricans one result of the '66 [riot] was that no longer was the school system going to avoid the needs of the Puerto Rican community. . . . We wanted education for liberation."[8] The fight for community control of Tuley and Clemente High Schools would highlight just how embedded the language of liberation and justice had become in the population's struggles.

Chicago's Puerto Rican students were not alone in seeking to remedy the schooling inequalities inherited from decades of racially motivated and politically charged policies aimed at severely limiting their overall success and opportunity. Various marginalized populations fought for economic and social stability in their communities. In March 1968, thousands of Mexican American and Chicana/o students across the United States participated in mass school walkouts to protest the "inferior quality of education" that generations of Latina/o children had endured.[9] The 1960s and 1970s ushered in an era of school activism initiated and organized by young people of color across the United States. Like the rest of the country, Chicago and its schools were caught up in civil unrest and racial conflict. The African American community's legacy of organizing through mass boycotts was very much alive in Chicago. In the early 1960s, residents confronted the de facto segregation of Black students and started conversations about the contributions and role of Black teachers. Educators sought a new reality for their students and drew attention to the unequal treatment of Black teachers in the Chicago Teachers Union.[10] Just as students experienced schooling segregation and inequality, Black teachers confronted decades-long frustrations with their status in city schools. These educators commonly held positions as "full-time basis" (FTB) substitute teachers, with very little choice regarding school assignments and without the rights and privileges of fully certified teachers.[11] FTB teachers often taught in their own classrooms yet held the lesser status for years because, despite their educational background, they had difficulty passing onerous certification exams. Many Black teachers viewed these exams as a discriminatory way to relegate them to subordinate positions.[12] This situation led Black educators to see their community schools as sites for challenging their own status within their profession's social hierarchy and as "centers of power" for improving conditions for Black students.[13]

The relationships among teachers, community members, and students were not always agreeable, and at times they fractured already contentious partnerships. New York City's Ocean Hill–Brownsville community faced numerous battles among stakeholders as teachers took to the streets in response to Black and Puerto Rican parents' intervention in administrative decisions in their quest for community control of schools.[14] In New York and other cities, even when stakeholders presented a united front regarding school integration, teachers' unions sometimes resented the growing influence of parents and community members, fearing that "teachers would be assessed by parents' political agendas rather than by their professional aptitude."[15] Likewise, the Chicago Teachers Union proclaimed its support of citywide desegregation plans, but not at the expense of teachers' rights.[16] Black teachers, in turn, sometimes opposed local teachers' organizing efforts, as they struggled with representation within those organizations. In some cases, Black teachers kept schools open in predominantly Black communities during strikes. These educators reiterated their commitment to their students, "[seeing] the school system as an impediment to their success."[17] Chicago's Black teachers reminded the larger community that they, like Black students, were contending with the effects of a segregated school system.

The era's activism prompted collaborations between Latina/o and African American students, whose demands at times mirrored one another's and whose fight for educational justice played out in Chicago during the 1960s and the 1970s. It is no coincidence that the increase in school-based organizing came during a shift in leadership. In 1966, James F. Redmond replaced Benjamin Willis as superintendent of Chicago Public Schools. Local civil rights activists initially saw Redmond's appointment as a positive move in the "handling" of city schools, at least in regard to desegregation; however, his integration strategy, known as the Redmond Plan, would prove to be controversial.[18] In his previous role as superintendent of New Orleans schools, Redmond had helped develop a desegregation plan that moved a small number of African American students into white schools, a process he attempted to repeat in Chicago.[19] In New Orleans, opposition to his plan, including a school boycott, had financially crippled the schools for a term. This experience informed Redmond's responses as he faced busing opposition and numerous teachers' strikes in Chicago schools.[20] Black and white residents in Chicago questioned the usefulness of Redmond's busing plan in dealing with overcrowded schools as a means to work toward desegregation. For some white parents, resistance to school desegregation was disguised as a call for community control of schools. For Black parents and community members, resistance to the Redmond Plan was at times a way to question the "presumed cultural deprivation of blacks or the imposition of school policies on individual liberties."[21] Chicago parents and other residents were not necessarily opposed to desegregation, but many wanted a more comprehensive and institutionalized solution than Redmond's plan, which they viewed as benefiting only a small percentage of the student population. Nevertheless, the ensuing school battles of the 1970s reminded school and city officials that African American and Puerto Rican residents had a great deal to say regarding their communities' educational future.

With the busing controversy in the background and the city still reeling from the riots that occurred during the 1968 Democratic National Convention in Chicago, high school students across the city questioned what they perceived as an inferior education. In 1968, more than two hundred students at Chicago's Fenger High School held a private meeting with school officials demanding that an African American teacher be hired to teach the African American history course.[22] Students at both Morgan Park High School and Fenger presented administrators with a Black "manifesto" detailing their push for the firing of school staff members whom students viewed as causing friction and divisiveness, and also detailed their advocacy for equal opportunities for Black students.[23] Across town, African American and "Latin American" students at Harrison High School fought for resources aimed at their particular communities, including the hiring of African American and Latin American school officials: "The black students said they were afraid they would not win their earlier demands. The Latin-American students said they sympathized with the blacks and wanted Latin-American school officials."[24] As scholars have noted, the spread of Third World Liberation consciousness helped fuel cooperation among Black and Brown students.[25] The Third World Liberation Front, founded at the University of California, Berkeley in 1969, was an alliance among organizations of Black students, Mexican American students, Native American students, and Asian American students. Its underlying philosophy was that by working together, the various groups would be more effective in their demands for institutional change. In Chicago, this understanding by one group of the needs of another clearly demonstrates that young people of color were aware of their overlapping interests and concerns. This solidarity was further articulated once these students progressed to postsecondary institutions.

Students at various Chicago high schools—including Harrison and Bowen on the South Side and Tuley, Wells, and Lake View on the North Side—organized school walkouts and boycotts to demand the incorporation of culturally relevant material into the curriculum and an increase in the hiring of faculty and administrators of color. On one day in 1968, more than twenty-eight thousand students boycotted thirty-eight Chicago schools, while several hundred teachers showed their support by refusing to teach their classes.[26] Over half of the African American students in the city's public schools were absent on October 15, 1968, as part of "Operation Breadbasket" (an arm of the Southern Christian Leadership in Chicago), joined by three hundred teachers.[27] When students demanded an English language course for Spanish-speaking students, a Spanish-speaking placement counselor, and "guest speakers who would appeal to the interests of the minority group," a 1968 *Chicago Tribune* headline declared that "Lake View High Staff Listens to Student Grievances."[28] The students' grievances were indeed heard following their brief boycott, but the school principal contended that the disturbance had been the work of outside agitators unfamiliar with the school. According to the article, prior to the boycott, a local community group (suspected by school officials of being Chicago's Puerto Rican Young Lords Organization) had distributed leaflets directed at Puerto Rican students, articulating the various community and schooling issues affecting their community. "No names were on the handouts," the principal stated, "but a telephone number was given. And students were urged to call this number and join a protest demonstration."[29] At a Board of Education meeting following these episodes, the superintendent answered some of the students' demands, promising to appoint African Americans as 34.1 percent of the teaching force and 21.9 percent of the administrative force, as long as their qualifications and abilities met state standards.[30] Over the next several years, Chicago students continued their struggle for school reform, forming coalitions across racial and ethnic groups. One central point of the school disturbances was the Latina/o community's dropout rate of more than 60 percent and the students' claim "that they are victims of a lack of concern by the Board of Education."[31] In speaking about the students' demands, Chicago Teachers Union president John Desmond stated: "These decisions should not be made by principals or district superintendents under the pressure of student disorders or community upheavals."[32] This type of rhetoric showed the failure by Desmond and other officials to acknowledge their own culpability and to recognize the students' and communities' agency in calling for changes.

The number of Puerto Rican students in Chicago Public Schools continued to increase in the late 1960s. The Board of Education began tracking their ethnic identity in 1968, with their numbers exceeding twenty-six thousand in 1970.[33] Although Puerto Rican students had been attending public (and parochial) schools since their initial migration to the city, the lack of accurate information regarding their numbers had made it difficult to track their overall status in schools. Now community members and researchers utilized this information to further question how schools and the city could better serve the population. The addition of Cerda and Boutte to the Board of Education meant parents had a more interested audience at board meetings. At one such meeting, Puerto Rican community members advocated on behalf of Spanish-speaking children and called for an end to the practice of automatically holding them back a year. As Diego Rangel argued, "[Being held back a year] is a tremendous factor in the drop-out rate which is estimated at 60 per cent for high schools alone."[34] Rangel also pushed back on the use of the term "Americanization" in language classes, as many Spanish-speaking children, including Puerto Ricans, were already Americans. According to one study of Puerto Rican students in Chicago, "Being held back one or more years is an important factor in dropping out, because of the humiliating aspects of it."[35] The "dropout problem" and dissatisfaction with students' perceived treatment called for attention from city officials and community members. Schools in the Puerto Rican community became battlegrounds for control, with debate over dissenting ideas about the best solutions for the growing community. Reports on the dropout problem informed these debates and made it difficult for school and city officials to continue ignoring the problem.

Isidro Lucas worked with a team of researchers, including Puerto Rican university students, to assess the situation of the community's youth in city schools. But some members of the Chicago Board of Education questioned the study's validity, viewing it as biased due to "the exclusive use of Puerto Rican interviewers," which they claimed "creat[ed] better rapport with the interviewee."[36] Lucas reported, "There were four professionals involved in the study, all acting as interviewers—the principal investigator who was a Spaniard, and three Puerto Rican research assistants. Anybody familiar with the sensitivity of a minority population as well as with the social stigma attached to the fact of being a dropout will understand the choice of primarily Puerto Rican interviewers to elicit true answers. The board criticisms can only be understood in a racist context, if the assumption is that only Anglo-American researchers could have been objective."[37] When administrators were asked what they perceived to be the leading cause of the Puerto Rican dropout rate, they named language as the prevailing factor.[38] However, in his 1971 report *Puerto Rican Dropouts in Chicago*, Lucas noted that "knowledge of English was greater among dropouts than among [high school] seniors."[39] Researchers generally found a correlation between the acquisition of English and schooling success, but they often overlooked the importance of students' retention of their native language. Lucas argued that students who were more confident of their Spanish were more likely to stay in school.[40] "In general," he reported, "schools were not found to be geared to Puerto Rican students," with "an acute self-identity crisis . . . prevalent among Chicago Puerto Rican youths."[41] Furthermore, "Puerto Rican youths in this study show the effects of having been exposed to discrimination on the basis of the American race concept. . . . The fact that there is awareness and knowledge of societal inferiority does not mean there is acceptance of this inferiority as a fact."[42] For Puerto Rican students, like the community at large, politics around race were embedded in their daily interactions, and Chicago schools perpetuated or even exacerbated those politics.

Compared to students of various racial groups nationally, Puerto Rican students in Chicago demonstrated greater defensiveness when the researchers asked questions regarding their success rates. Students tended to "blame teachers or 'somebody or something' for their lack of success."[43] According to Lucas, "Schools were found to have very little influence in increasing the staying-in rate: they did little to improve the student self-image or cultural identity."[44] Some of the students surveyed expressed a need and desire for the teaching of Puerto Rican culture and history in the schools, as students had demanded at Tuley and other Chicago high schools. The need for more Puerto Rican (or other Latina/o) teachers was featured prominently in the study. According to the report, students who had access to Puerto Rican or other Latina/o teachers were more likely to stay in school. "Most Puerto Ricans," however, "do not have in school any one teacher in particular they relate to. When they do, their chances to stay increase."[45] In 1971, only 75 out of the more than 25,000 teachers in the Chicago school system were Puerto Rican, with another 121 identifying as Mexican and 58 as Cuban.[46] Lucas wrote, "There was no drive at the time of the study to recruit Puerto Rican or Spanish-speaking teachers in Chicago, and those already working in the system had such little seniority that they were likely to become the first casualties in any economy move or personnel cutbacks."[47] It is interesting to note that parents' treatment in schools mirrored that of their children. "The schools placed themselves out of reach of the parents. According to the children, the parents visited school 'never or only when called' in over 85 percent of the cases. Nor was there any reason for the parents to visit the school—they were not welcome. Communications were seldom in the parents' language. Almost no administrator could address them in Spanish and children were called in as translators. Parent-teachers associations and parent advisory councils made no serious attempt to relate to the Puerto Rican parent."[48]

The call for the hiring of bilingual, bicultural teachers was echoed in the pages of the community-run newspaper *El Puertorriqueño*, which advocated for a teacher exchange program to increase the number of teachers from Puerto Rico.[49] Parents argued that "the employment of bilingual-bicultural Puerto Rican personnel represented the required approach to educating and preparing their children for a humanizing and liberating way of life."[50]

In Chicago Public Schools' 1972 annual teacher survey, only 91 teachers self-reported as Puerto Rican, a mere 0.35 percent of the total.[51] By the following year, that number had increased to 129. It is unsurprising that District 6, which housed "Puerto Rican" schools, reported the largest number of Puerto Rican teachers. It is likewise unsurprising that no Puerto Rican in the city's schools held a position higher than that of assistant principal.

In 1975, during the administration of newly appointed school superintendent Joseph P. Hannon, the federal Department of Health, Education, and Welfare (HEW) withheld over $100 million in funding from Chicago schools due to inadequacies in the district's bilingual education and faculty desegregation plans.[52] Under pressure to meet federal mandates, and perhaps also in response to community outcry among Puerto Rican and other Latina/os, the district utilized the Transitional Teacher Program to recruit and train people with degrees from Spanish-speaking countries to meet the demand for bilingual and bicultural educators, although the exact number of teachers hired under this program is unknown.[53] The employment of more Puerto Rican teachers was a step in the right direction, but the schools' relationship with parents and the larger community deteriorated quickly.

The dropout rate was reportedly over 70 percent for Chicago's Puerto Ricans, but verifying that figure proved difficult because researchers and school administrators could not always account for every student who voluntarily or involuntarily ceased to attend school.[54] It was clear, however, that the Puerto Rican students and families felt dissatisfied with their overall relationship with schools. The increase in Puerto Ricans' community and school activism reflected their estrangement from both schools and city; according to Lucas, students felt neither a sense of belonging at school nor an effective connection with teachers. In this environment, parents, students, and teachers at Tuley High School laid claim to their community's schooling needs. Enacting their agency despite their marginalized status in the city, the Tuley High School community created various organizations, including La Escuela Superior Puertorriqueña, commonly called La Escuelita, in 1972.[55] To one student, "The Puerto Rican High School means a chance for an education in a school that cares [about] its students."[56] The school, known also as Rafael Cancel Miranda High School and later Pedro Albizu Campos High School, offered students the opportunity to engage with their own history, but more importantly, it allowed the community to have a say in their children's education. Educational practices over the previous two decades, especially in schools such as Tuley, had complicated students' status in Chicago schools, and spaces like La Escuelita signaled the community's commitment to negotiating, resisting, and claiming their place in the city.

"The Tuley Thing . . ."

The largest numbers of Puerto Rican students were concentrated in District 3 (which included Lake View High School and LeMoyne Elementary School), District 6 (Tuley, Wells, and later Clemente High Schools), and District 7 (Waller High School, in the Lincoln Park neighborhood). At Tuley High School alone, Puerto Rican students made up over 50 percent of the enrollment in 1970, and they represented the majority at seven elementary schools across District 6. The increase in Puerto Rican students' enrollment at Tuley created a sense of urgency and forced city and school officials to acknowledge the community's demands for change. Since the late 1960s, Tuley High School, on Chicago's Near Northwest Side, had seen an influx of Puerto Rican students as more families relocated to the Humboldt Park community. In the late 1960s, the need to replace or expand the aging school building became a topic of both conversation and contention. Parents, students, educators, and city officials weighed in with varying agendas regarding the school's impending move.

In many ways Tuley High School was tied to Puerto Ricans' identity and claim to space in their new neighborhood, as some community members had already experienced being displaced or pushed out of previous neighborhoods across the city. Educational consultants hired to assist with the plan for the new high school argued, "Since schools are an integral part of the community, its residents must be involved in the planning of their schools."[57] Local organizations, including the Northwest Community Organization (NCO), the Wicker Park Neighborhood Council, and groups assisted by the Catholic Church, fought valiantly for the new high school. After years of empty assurances by school officials, the construction of a new school promised to alleviate Tuley's overcrowding. Unfortunately, although the city was willing to build the new school within the community, its recommended location was on California Street, between North Avenue and Division Street—in the heart of the Puerto Rican community, but regrettably in the middle of a public park: Humboldt Park.[58]

In 1969, the Building Commission sought to acquire 13 acres of the park for the school and related facilities, including a gymnasium, an indoor-outdoor swimming pool, and activity rooms. The recreational facilities would be run by the park district and open to the public except during school hours. To replace the land that would be lost, the commission proposed acquiring three scattered sites in the community totaling 8.5 acres, the amount of space the new school and facilities would require. In other words, they would take away the one bigger park and replace it with multiple smaller ones, making it difficult for the community to organize events involving large numbers of people, such as the annual Puerto Rican Day Parade and celebration. Alderman Thomas Keane, whose 31st District included Tuley, worked to delay the final decision about the new school site as representatives from both sides expressed their opinions. As Keane stated in 1970, "Opposition to this plan isn't just local. Many city-wide conservation groups are going to fight this taking of park land. They don't want to see a park cut up for any purpose."[59] Representatives of the Spanish Action Committee surveyed Puerto Rican residents, and the committee claimed that supporters of the site were ignoring Puerto Rican residents' views. "We have gone door to door," SACC's Juan Barretto reported, "and asked the people of the ward what they want. Puerto Rican residents make up more than half of the population of the ward; they are the ones who use Humboldt Park the most; and they don't want recreational space taken for a school."[60] In support of the proposed site, one NCO member said, "Either the school goes in Humboldt park or we'll have to knock down five blocks of houses to clear enough land."[61] A member of the Wicker Park Neighborhood Council stated, "The issue is people versus parks . . . save trees or educate children."[62] But Puerto Rican residents issued a demand: "Escuela Si, Pero en el Parque no!" (School, yes, but in the park, no!), saying that losing the park for the new high school would rob the community of one of its only outlets for recreation and escape from inadequate and congested housing.[63] A coalition of more than twenty community organizations, including Los Caballeros de San Juan, fought the building of the school, "y cuantos enemigo tenga la communidad" (and whatever enemies our community may have).[64]

But not every member of the Puerto Rican community opposed the location of the school within the park's boundaries. The local newspaper *El Puertorriqueno* questioned the intentions of Ted Ramírez, a community leader and the husband of Aspira founder Mirta Ramírez, as he publicly supported the school's construction despite the disruption it would cause to community life. "Costaría mucho dinero y tomaría mucho tiempo preparar un sitio en el área," he argued, "mientras que en el parque podemos comenzar a construir mañana mismo" (It would cost too much money and take too much time to prepare a site in the area, while in the park we could begin building tomorrow).[65] Ramírez's apparent lack of concern over the loss of park land was objectionable to community members, including Los Caballeros de San Juan. *El Puertorriqueño* pointed out Ramírez's outsider status, noting that his home address was well beyond the boundaries of Humboldt Park.[66] Tuley High School principal Dr. Herbert Fink maintained, "I don't care which site but by God we have to move. We need something you can get in quickly."[67]

In 1970, the work of community organizations was instrumental in securing the acquisition of land for a different site near Division Street and Western

Avenue. "La communidad nuestra ha sabido ponerse de pie," one community member declared, "y oponerse con dignidad y determinacion y el Parque se had salvado" (Our community has risen to its feet and with dignity and determination has resisted and the park has been saved).[68] In the view of *El Puertorriqueño*, the support of city planners in saving the park was indicative of a better relationship between the city and the Puerto Rican community. "La acción de la Comisión de Planes fue interpretada por los principals lideres de la communidad puertorriqueña, como una demostración de que el Boricua comienza a ser escuchado en los ciruclos del gobierno" (The action of the Planning Commission is interpreted by us, the leaders of the Puerto Rican community, as a signal that the Boricua will now be listened to in government circles).[69] According to this article, the victory in saving Humboldt Park had forced the white community to view the Puerto Rican community differently: as a vital and important part of the city rather than a population to be exploited for others' gain.

But relations between the self-proclaimed leaders of the Puerto Rican community and the local government were tested as the issues at Tuley High School persisted. The struggle over the new school's proposed location was actually minor in comparison to the growing tensions *within* Tuley. Parents were increasingly dissatisfied with the treatment of their children and the perceived lack of sensitivity toward Puerto Rican students on the part of the school's principal and administration. The Board of Education's seeming lack of concern about the increasing dropout rate and the public schools' overall condition led to many rallies calling for the ousting of Tuley's principal, with picket signs making it clear that "Puerto Ricans are tired of waiting."[70] The Coalition for Tuley, consisting of parents, teachers, students, and various community organizations, organized a school boycott in the fall of 1971, seeking to oust Principal Fink. The group led a march to the Board of Education's main offices to meet with officials over their concerns.[71] "Latin pupils," according to one report, were the majority of students in Chicago's District 6 on the Near Northwest Side, including the majority of the enrollment at forty-three elementary schools.[72] Puerto Ricans constituted over 47 percent of that total. In other districts on the city's Near Northwest Side, the proportion was even greater. Community members were unhappy with what they perceived as the school's overall negative treatment of its "Latin" students. Fink and others dismissed the group's claims as insincere.[73] In many ways, Fink came to represent the very bureaucracy encountered by Puerto Ricans throughout the city. Although Fink's power was limited to one school, his failure to recognize the community's needs or understand the era's student movement made him unable to work effectively alongside the growing Puerto

Rican presence in the school. This had unfortunate consequences both for him and for his students.

Enrollment at Tuley High School mirrored shifts in the district, with the proportion of Spanish-speaking students (most of them Puerto Rican) exceeding 64 percent by 1971, an increase of more than 10 percent over the previous school year.[74] And despite the specific charges against Principal Fink, Tuley's dropout rate was not unique; dropout numbers were high for Puerto Rican students all over the city. In 1971, the Chicago Board of Education presented a new plan for decreasing the dropout rate, with Tuley designated as one of nine program sites.[75] But one board member quickly and vehemently opposed the proposal, calling it "an insult to the students."[76] Board member María Cerda took issue with the board's definition of the dropout problem: "The problem is not that the students are apathetic, as the plan states. . . . It's that the school experience gives them no self-identity or self-pride."[77] She also noted that the board's plan failed to refer to a recent study (the one by Lucas) of the dropout problem among Puerto Rican students. "We need some program at Tuley," Cerda asserted, "but I don't believe in pouring money into one that doesn't define the problem."[78]

Tuley and the Humboldt Park community remained sites of contention throughout 1972 and 1973 as debates emerged over what to name the new school. As an expression of the community's Puerto Rican identity, residents proposed that it be named after a prominent figure in Puerto Rican history, Eugenio María de Hostos.[79] After the death of baseball legend and humanitarian Roberto Clemente in December 1972, students at Tuley led a brief sit-in in January 1973 to encourage the Board of Education to honor his life and the community by naming the school after him. Following the sit-in, the board's Committee to Study Names Submitted for New School Buildings, chaired by María Cerda, recommended that the school be named for Clemente.[80] Simultaneously, the board was exploring the creation of a bilingual/bicultural center at the new school, which would offer courses in Latin American and Puerto Rican history, Spanish literature, and Latin American dance and art. The goal was to "help students develop a positive identity with their own cultural heritage."[81] This, of course, is something students across the city had advocated for in the previous decade through their various walkouts and protests.

Despite this victory, problems persisted at Tuley in early 1973 as students, teachers, staff, and community members continued to call for Fink's ouster. A boycott led by Tuley counselor Carmen Valentín and others resulted in a three-hour battle with Chicago police, resulting in sixteen arrests and six police injuries. One protester, student Oscar Lopez, proclaimed, "no one in this city is aware of the problems in our community and no one cares. But we will go back to our community now and find a way to make them aware of what is going on."[82] The disturbance began when a group of parents and community residents attempted to "force their way" into the school in order to stage a sit-in calling for Fink's removal.[83] While board members and Tuley officials worked to find a peaceful solution to the turmoil, Fink was barred from the school (or perhaps discouraged from entering). Community representatives and a committee of Tuley teachers participated in negotiations to ensure that the school opened following the disruptions.[84] Both teachers and community leaders agreed on certain conditions to help bring order to Tuley, including encouraging positive behavior in the classroom, avoiding class discussions about the previous week's incidents, and forbidding outsiders to enter the school unless they were on official business.[85] The two groups, however, were divided on whether to retain Principal Fink, as teachers "maintain[ed] 'a neutral position' on the matter." Community members, on the other hand, "confirmed their 'overwhelming disapproval,'" believing that Fink's "presence and actions in the school are endangering lives and property in the community 'he used to serve.'"[86] On February 7, 1973, a *Chicago Defender* article asked the Board of Education not to ignore its "inescapable moral and administrative responsibility" regarding such issues, because "unchecked school eruptions are always fr[a]ught with the danger of plunging a whole community into the caldron of racial confrontations with tragic consequences."[87] The community had contended with these same consequences following their first uprising in 1966. Indeed, they were still awaiting the fulfillment of many promises made by the local government after the 1966 riots, including commitments to address Puerto Ricans' educational needs. Yet educational issues continued to be of pressing concern, pushing local youth to the verge of another uprising. The community activism many of these students had experienced since the mid-1960s in Chicago was manifested by daily (and Daley) reminders of how "Puerto Ricans are confined even physically to their own neighborhoods, which they do not control. Police, schools, business and public services are provided by non–Puerto Ricans."[88] The battle for control of their schools, especially Tuley High, was emblematic of Puerto Ricans' continued struggle to have a voice regarding their day-to-day lives. The naming of the school and the fight to remove Fink as principal were battles waged at just one school. Yet they perfectly represented both the challenges to Puerto Ricans' status and stake in their community and their ability to mobilize for successful change.

While more than two hundred supporters waited outside the closed Board of Education meeting on February 5, 1973, which lasted four hours, officials announced Fink's removal as Tuley's principal. Citing the decision as being "in 'the best interests of the school,'" the board faced representatives from a local principals' group, which threatened legal action on Fink's behalf.[89] "I felt very close to my students, my staff, and my community," Fink maintained, "but I made the agreement to leave with the board fairly and justly."[90] In a letter to the editor following the board's announcement, a Tuley student who supported Fink wrote,

> Two years ago, protesters demanded that our new school be named after a former governor of Puerto Rico. Now they want another name. Next year someone else may die, and we'll have more problems over a name. What about Murray F. Tuley? Just because he was not Puerto Rican, doesn't mean he no longer deserves to be honored. All high schools have their problems. Tuley is simply average. Dr. Fink has done as good a job as anyone could and we thank him for it. The problem could be settled if the people down at the board would get off their seats and find out what a majority of the students want.[91]

The removal of Principal Fink was met with mixed feelings. Some students and residents questioned whether his departure would eradicate long-standing social ills, and others were confused about the exact nature of the charges against him. One columnist asked, "What were the insensitive acts Mr. Fink is accused of?" Was the board "bowing to a group of rabble-rousing youngsters"?[92] As one seventeen-year-old student put it, "So, Fink's gone. We still have all our problems. He was just a little tiny one that made all the big ones seem bigger. So he's gone. I say, 'So what?'"[93] Puerto Rican students attending Northeastern Illinois University likewise expressed ambivalence about removing administrators if they would simply be replaced with similarly questionable personnel. "Schools," one student wrote, "can do without administrators as principals. What we need are educators who educate first and can administrate secondly."[94]

The removal of Fink as principal and the community uproar over the status of Puerto Rican students similarly highlighted the divisive politics within the Puerto Rican community, especially around political ideologies regarding the island itself. The continued status of Puerto Rico was on the minds of local community members, who were divided on the subject. At times, critics focused on such issues to denounce educators who espoused Puerto Rican independence, including Carmen Valentín. Support for Puerto Rico's independence and advocacy of Puerto Rican nationalist ideologies were especially prominent among local youth; as Isidro Lucas wrote in 1984, "The militancy that characterized the Young Lords has remained among Chicago Puerto

Ricans as far as the issue of the status of Puerto Rico is concerned."[95] For those who disagreed with Puerto Rican nationalist views, the issue became a wedge of contention used to discredit the work of local groups and individuals.[96]

The continued battle for control of Tuley and Clemente High Schools would have no clear winners or losers. It would pit teacher against teacher, student against student, and a community against itself. Local educator Carmen Valentín gained notoriety for encouraging students to boycott classes at Tuley in February 1973. Like many other Puerto Ricans, Valentín had arrived in Chicago in the 1950s with her family, who were seeking jobs and financial stability. "As a child," she recalled, "I always resented the move. Later, I realized that the reason for that massive migration was the necessity to improve the situation, and naturally I forgave [my parents] because I realized we were part of that."[97] Valentín completed her bachelor's degree at Northeastern Illinois University, then earned a master's degree at Roosevelt University in Chicago. She joined the staff at Tuley High School as a teacher, but subsequently became a counselor, working with the growing Puerto Rican population. Her involvement in Tuley's battles led to her brief removal from the school in 1973. She was assigned a desk job at the Chicago Board of Education, followed by a brief stint at Senn High School, before being reinstated as a counselor by the time Roberto Clemente High School opened in 1974.[98] As with María Cerda and Mirta Ramírez, Valentín's involvement in the school battles demonstrates the role of Puerto Rican women in formulating the community's future. Women continued to be active participants in challenging the status of a community, even when their own status or interests were challenged.

The opening of Clemente High School and the ousting of Principal Fink, crusades fought valiantly by students and community members, did little to squelch the school's turbulence. A 1974 student walkout, led by the Concerned Committee for a Better Education at Clemente High School, became an intense battle between protesters and police officers, resulting in twenty-eight arrests and dozens of injuries.[99] This time the protest was led by students, who resented Valentín's influence and the involvement of outsiders who were inundating students with political propaganda. In hopes of ending the school's turmoil, the board reassigned Valentín and two Clemente teachers, Joseph Figueroa and Antonio Burgos, to other schools.[100] The Concerned Committee sought the restoration of Figueroa, a strong opponent of Valentín, and advocated for a permanent principal to replace the ousted Fink. The group also sought to remove Valentín, to prohibit the teaching of politics except for the political content already included in the approved school curriculum, and to bring disciplinary action against teachers who introduced politics into extracurricular activities.[101] In response, SACC members held a community meeting to oppose a planned community-led follow-up rally at the school, fearing it was merely a diversion to allow "dissidents" to enter the school and cause further turmoil.[102] SACC members and others blamed the complicated political ideologies in the local community and in Puerto Rico for the issues affecting Puerto Rican students and the school. One newspaper article characterized Valentín as the root cause of all the disruptions at the school, accusing her of using her position as a platform to promote her views on the Puerto Rican independence movement and to recruit students to that cause.[103] But it is important to remember that students remained at the center of the controversy. They were not necessarily instigators or active participants, but they were the group most affected by the actions and decisions of others. Whether they supported Valentín or rallied for her removal, students stood to suffer the most if conflict continued at the highly troubled school. Some students who initially supported the work of Valentín and local community members, hoping it would bring positive change to their educational lives, later came to resent the influence of Valentín and others as they saw their own stake as students being ignored in the battles taking place across the community.

In speaking about Valentín's involvement in Fink's removal, police officers contended that "the anti-Fink campaign was just an excuse to enable Mrs. Valentín to 'radicalize those kids.'"[104] Tuley/Clemente student Robert Robles said, "It's enough. There is always trouble here. It is all games, all politics. What about my education? . . . She [Valentín] cares only about herself. Get her out of here and there will be peace at Clemente."[105] But it was unrealistic to assume that Valentín's removal would solve all the problems and restore immediate calm at the school, whose issues mirrored those of the local community. The disparate factions in the struggle for control of first Tuley and then Clemente remind us that the community was diverse, and community members of all ideological stances were interested in and capable of organizing to meet their needs. Valentín herself was not the cause of the community's problems, as the previous decades demonstrate. Instead, the community's responses to the 1966 uprising and the battles for Tuley and Clemente High Schools were intimately linked to the overall status of Puerto Ricans and the ambiguity of their lives in Chicago. Indeed, conversations begun by island officials in 1898 about how to "manage" the population sound much like the conversations framing students' lives in the 1970s. The connection to 1898 was not lost on this generation of Puerto Rican students as they entered higher education.

A Neglected Generation Responds

When Isidro Lucas published his report on Puerto Rican dropouts in 1971, the information he presented was not news to the community. But the report validated the experiences of a generation (or more) of students who had questioned the city's commitment to their schooling success. Lucas pointed out that "Puerto Ricans in the Continental United States have been and are one of the most neglected minorities."[106] That neglect continued to manifest itself in city schools and was reflected in the daily struggles faced by a generation of youth whose lives were marked by social turmoil created by teachers, police, and their own community. Puerto Rican students in Chicago were not alone in their outcry over their schooling situation, as their interests were aligned with a growing national movement. But there is much to be learned from the community's experience. Although linked to a larger national movement, the community's shift from the 1940s to the 1970s took place in the context of Puerto Rico's colonial relationship with the United States, which often presented barriers that prevented Puerto Ricans from enacting agency in their daily lives. The community's mobilization to remove a school administrator and name a school after a leading cultural figure might seem to an outsider like small or meaningless battles. But for Chicago's Puerto Ricans, these actions signified much more. Puerto Ricans' initial migration had been welcomed as a temporary solution to labor shortages on the mainland and a remedy for the island's perceived overpopulation. But in the uprisings of the 1970s, the community proclaimed their permanency in a city that had become less welcoming. As in other cities and among other populations, schools in Chicago offered an opportune space for Puerto Ricans to envision and assert their place in the metropolis.

For the fortunate students who moved on to postsecondary institutions, the struggle for educational equality took on new forms as they contended with many of the same issues they had faced in K–12 education. Although the high school dropout rate among Puerto Ricans and other Latina/o students remained high, their representation in higher learning increased during the 1970s in Chicago and the state of Illinois. Northeastern Illinois University on the city's North Side and the University of Illinois Circle Campus on the Near West Side were the institutions in Chicago with the highest number of Latina/o students. Puerto Rican students mobilized to improve their situation at both universities, forcing the institutions to acknowledge their needs even if they were not always willing to negotiate with students. The University of Illinois Circle Campus was located within a long-standing Latina/o community, serving as a reminder of the complicated relationship between settlement patterns and the educational opportunities of a frustrated young population.

CHAPTER 4

Learning to Resist, Resisting to Learn

Puerto Ricans and Higher Education in 1970s Chicago

During his senior year at Tuley High School, Miguel del Valle contemplated his post–high school plans, knowing he had little interest in entering military service or working at a factory. Del Valle, who later served almost twenty years as an Illinois state senator, was aware that Tuley lacked the resources and interventions needed to help Puerto Rican students further their education. "As a senior in high school," he recalled, "I had very little exposure to institutions of higher learning. I didn't see any effort being made to recruit Latino students at the time."[1] Feeling alone during his first year as a first-generation college student at Northeastern Illinois University, del Valle dealt with feelings of inadequacy as he compared his own education to that of his white suburban counterparts. At Northeastern, del Valle connected with students who shared his concerns and became involved with the Union for Puerto Rican Students. "It was at that time we saw the need for counseling geared toward us. We were standing alone with little direction. We were struggling with our own feelings of inadequacy, and at that time we needed to band together in order to deal with the monstrous institution."[2] Many Puerto Rican and other Latina/o students in Chicago had experienced and participated in educational protests and advocacy during their K–12 years, so it is unsurprising that they brought that activism with them to college. College students saw the connection between their limited educational status and the colonial relationship between the island and the United States. Writing in a Northeastern Illinois University student newspaper, *Que Ondee Sola*, a student asked, "How can Puerto Rican students accept the notion that they are being treated equally when the doors are closed to them through the most subtle manners; that is, through means that have standardized them out of the halls of higher learning?"[3] Students contended that the colonial system imposed on the island was also in effect in mainland higher education, excluding them from colleges and universities. Puerto Rican students' unique perspective affected how they internalized and responded to their status in higher education.

As at the secondary school level, the movement in Chicago's postsecondary institutions reflected contemporary struggles in other U.S. cities. The struggles of Black students in particular were framed in terms of a "widespread feeling of power and purpose . . ., combined with a sense of urgency and context of crisis."[4] This sense of urgency resulted in numerous campus-wide battles in the 1960s and 1970s, from San Francisco State College (now University) to Columbia University in New York, focusing mainly on instituting Black studies programs and increasing the hiring of Black professors across university programs.[5] Columbia University's proximity to a long-standing and often neglected Black community tied the growing student civil rights movement to the local community's needs. Students advocated not only for a larger role in Columbia's decision-making processes, especially regarding decisions about Black students' issues, but also for the construction of a gym for local community members.[6] On college campuses across the Southwest, Chicana/o students likewise created organizations and fought for the inclusion of programs and curricula representative of their experiences, and they worked closely with high school students and community members to merge their interests in challenging issues of schooling inequality.[7] Alongside faculty and community allies, Puerto Rican college students in New York City staged a multiyear struggle beginning in 1973 to save Hostos Community College in the Bronx. Their work in support of Hostos, a college heavily populated by working-class Puerto Rican students, demonstrated to the community "how very much ordinary people can achieve for themselves, their families, and communities when they find ways to unite in a struggle for the common benefit."[8] For a generation of students of color, activism for and in higher education mirrored the battles their parents had fought for their children's education in the 1960s. Like the New Yorkers resisting Hostos's closure, Puerto Rican students in Chicago could not separate their everyday neighborhood realities from their relationships with postsecondary institutions, especially when those very institutions stood in their backyards.

Although their high school dropout rate was still high, the number of Latina/o college and university students increased in Chicago and across the state of Illinois during the 1970s (see table 3).[9] Northeastern Illinois University and the University of Illinois Circle Campus were the institutions with the highest number of Latina/o students in Chicago. Puerto Rican and other

Table 3. Hispanic Enrollment at Illinois Public Universities, Fall 1973–Fall 1977

Institution	Fall 1973	Fall 1974	Fall 1975	Fall 1976	Fall 1977
Chicago State University	108	126	145	157	140
Eastern Illinois University	11	19	28	22	29
Governors State University	13	28	29	23	76
Illinois State University	55	55	56	125	109
Northeastern Illinois University	345	437	550	—	881
Northern Illinois University	164	168	202	202	203
Sangamon State University	8	19	16	11	7
Southern Illinois University–Carbondale	36	61	107	92	82
Southern Illinois University–Edwardsville	19	40	33	46	42
University of Illinois–Chicago	725	818	1,116	1,251	1,402
University of Illinois–Medical Center	31	30	43	49	81
University of Illinois–Urbana/Champaign	171	217	248	285	344
Western Illinois University	69	92	87	105	117
Public Universities Total	1,755	2,110	2,660	2,368	3,513

Source: Data from the annual *Data Book on Illinois Higher Education* (Springfield: State of Illinois, Board of Higher Education, 1974, 1975, 1976, 1977, 1978).

Latina/o students mobilized at both schools to improve their situation and to force the institutions to acknowledge their needs. Student efforts led to the creation of programs such as Northeastern's Proyecto Pa'lante and Comunidad Latino Adelantando Sus Estudios Secundarios (CLASES) and Circle Campus's Latino Cultural Center and the Latin American Recruitment and Educational Services (LARES). Through this work, they emphasized conversations about the role of higher education in their lives in the 1970s, focusing especially on how to utilize their relationship and proximity to their local community's history to challenge their institutions' slow responses to their needs.

Puerto Rican students called on both universities not to ignore their responsibility to the local community. To increase the number of Puerto Rican and other Latina/o students at the schools, organizers also worked toward institutionalized changes to bolster their success, such as the creation of support services, recruitment strategies, and financial aid. Students at Circle Campus proclaimed in March 1974, "The University, whose mission it is to serve the people of Chicago, has since its opening denied entrance to our people."[10] For a generation of students and community activists, "the university, as a repository of labor, educational, and ideological production and orientation, was increasingly seen as a site of revolutionary struggle and contestation."[11]

Northeastern Illinois University

During the time of turmoil at Tuley and Clemente High Schools, students across town at Northeastern Illinois University were facing similar struggles. In the inaugural issue of the Puerto Rican student newspaper *Que Ondee Sola* in 1972, Northeastern students expressed the need for organizations that could highlight Puerto Rican students' needs and realities and help them "overcome there [*sic*] own individualistic attitudes . . . caused by the brain-washing high school had put them through."[12] The Union for Puerto Rican Students—the Union for short—was organized in 1971 as a community-based advocacy group for not only Puerto Rican students but all oppressed groups. Approaching Northeastern Illinois administrators in 1971 with a list of demands, the Union sought to create a Puerto Rican Studies Center as well as a more effective recruitment program for Puerto Rican students. The group was well aware that Puerto Ricans' marginalized status in the city was related to the failure of the education system: "In most instances the system has been directly involved in developing a lack of self-identity in our children by alienating them from their original culture and promoting its prompt rejection in favor of the 'standard' American culture."[13] The students drew a connection between the alarming dropout rate among Puerto Rican high school students and the city schools' ineffectiveness in motivating them and supporting their needs. The community, they argued, had "reached the point of desperation. The educational system is perhaps the last hope that we have for survival in this society."[14] For some of these students, surviving both city schools and city politics had been a constant theme in their lives either as first-generation Puerto Ricans or as children of the first migrants.

Many had already witnessed conflicts between the community and the K–12 schools, and in the 1970s they relived those experiences at Northeastern and other institutions. Students hoped to leverage their new status as college students and the resources available to them within higher education to serve the communities from which they came. "Puerto Rican students were making a direct connection between their demands for educational reform and the general demands of the Puerto Rican barrio for equality."[15] Barrio youth encountered inadequately prepared schools and city agencies that did not recognize the relevance of the linguistic, racial, and cultural distinctiveness of Puerto Ricans in Chicago. Reflecting developments in the wider Puerto Rican community, Puerto Rican students at Northeastern and other institutions started forming their own organizations and producing their own print materials. The founding of the Union gave students a space in which to articulate their desires and needs. Maximino Torres, a former administrator and instructor at Northeastern, recalled that students' "familiarity with the experiences of the harsh environment they had endured in their community may have been the sustaining force that guided them to recognize, perhaps instinctively, the prevalent needs Hispanic American students face in higher education and to articulate recommendations to address such needs."[16] For these students, pursuing a sense of equity in their communities and in schooling became second nature, an element of their everyday cultural practices. The fourteen-year-old second-generation Puerto Rican youth looking down from his second-floor walkup apartment on Division Street on a summer night in 1966, witnessing the community's frustrations unravel below, had become the twenty-year-old first-generation college student struggling to find a place at Northeastern.

The Union argued for better advising and counseling aimed at Puerto Rican students specifically, and for more culturally relevant courses that would allow these students to see themselves within the university's curriculum. Said one student, "We felt we needed one person at the school who was acquainted with our community."[17] The nationwide fight for Black, Chicano, and Puerto Rican studies programs at postsecondary institutions served as the backdrop for students at Northeastern. Universities across the country had increasingly become sites for ideological and physical confrontations, especially for African Americans, and the Chicago area was no exception.[18] Black Students at Northwestern University in Evanston, about twenty miles north of Chicago, had faced a similar battle in 1968, calling for administrators to respond immediately to their demands. They argued that the university had been "ineffective in dealing with racism on campus" and demanded that at least 50 percent of the incoming Black students come from inner-city schools.[19] A few miles away, Puerto Rican students at Northeastern remained committed to their own academic success and asked administrators to share that commitment by developing programs aimed at helping them achieve that success. ¡Aquí Estoy!, which later became CLASES, was one such program.

With funding from the U.S. Office of Education under Title 1 of the Higher Education Act, Northeastern established ¡Aquí Estoy! in 1969 in the city's West Town community to connect with the growing Puerto Rican population following the 1966 riots.[20] With donated furniture and equipment, the program opened as a storefront center to help students achieve admission to Northeastern, as well as "to encourage students to return to their communities as professionals."[21] The program was founded by Northeastern student Rosa Hernandez (later Ramírez) and faculty member Rose Brandzel, who were both active in the West Town community, near the site of the 1966 uprising.[22] The two women hoped to help young people in the community both improve their oral English skills and gain access to higher education. Although the founding of ¡Aquí Estoy! seemed to fulfill some of the needs and requests of Puerto Ricans and other students by creating outreach relationships with the West Town community, the space became a site of contention for Puerto Rican students who questioned the university's commitment to their community. The Union staged a sit-in at the office of university president James Mullen to pressure administrators to hire faculty to teach courses on Puerto Rican history and Latino counselors and admissions representatives to work with Puerto Rican students.[23] In 1973, the Union "waged a struggle to revive" the ¡Aquí Estoy! program, hoping to play a prominent role in the hiring of its new director—a request that, students later claimed, was ignored.[24]

Hired as ¡Aquí Estoy! director in October 1973, Miguel Velazquez was a graduate of Wells High School, in the West Town neighborhood, and had earned a degree in the teaching of Spanish from the University of Illinois at Urbana-Champaign in 1970. He had taught at a Chicago high school and then worked at several local colleges and universities. In a memo to the president of the Union for Puerto Rican Students, Velazquez detailed his interest in working closely with the organization to implement programs and listen to the members' concerns. "Comments and criticisms are always welcome," he noted, and he aimed "to be available to any and everyone wishing to discuss any matters of concern, preferably related to the proposed program."[25] However, within a year of his hiring, students became dissatisfied with Velazquez and mobilized against his appointment. They alleged that he had failed to implement adequate programs during his tenure as director of ¡Aquí Estoy!, which he had renamed the Comunidad Latino Adelantando Sus Estudios Superiores. In a 1975 memo to President Mullen, the Union demanded Velazquez's ouster, alleging his "inability to have a viable, cohesive and structured program ready for implementation at the opening of the center."[26] Furthermore, students charged that Velazquez had changed the center's name, in which they and the community felt invested, without community input or discussion. They similarly questioned his commitment to the center and its students, claiming that he had "spread himself thin" by attending law school and seeking public office while serving as director.[27] In the students' view, Velazquez's vision for a program they had fought for was unaligned with their own.

Under mounting pressure from students and faculty, Northeastern administrators investigated the claims about Velazquez. Although students affiliated with the Union were calling for his removal, other students expressed sympathy or support for him. One student wrote, "The reason I felt it necessary to write this letter is because the [Union] has made it seem as though all Puerto Ricans and Latinos on this campus want the resignation of Mr. Velazquez. This is not so."[28] Vice President of Academic Affairs John Major responded to the charges that Velazquez had failed to implement programs at the center, "diluted the program from its purpose and constituency," and neglected to consult the Union about proposed changes to the name and logo of the program, among other concerns.[29] Upon reviewing documents and recommendations from various interest groups at Northeastern, Major concluded that many of the charges related to issues beyond Velazquez's control or actions within the scope of his job contract. Therefore, in February 1975, Major recommended to President Mullen that Velazquez be retained in his position: "His termination at this time as the center is about to open would deprive him of the opportunity to initiate the programs which he has planned and jeopardize the success of the center at the most critical time."[30] Despite Major's recommendation, Mullen relieved Velazquez of his duties a week later but proposed that he be allowed to complete his contract as a special assistant under Major in the office of Academic Affairs.[31] Velazquez's tenure as director was marked by a level of divisiveness that almost mirrored the community's conflict over Principal Fink and Tuley High School, even though Velazquez was a member of the same community that sought his removal.

Following Velazquez's removal as director of CLASES, Puerto Rican students celebrated what they saw as their victory. "Once again," they wrote in *Que Ondee Sola*, "the institute has returned to its rightful owners, the people."[32] But they also reminded readers that much work lay ahead, as the administration remained unresponsive to their needs.[33] This victory, they maintained, belonged to the students who had supported the Puerto Rican professors at Northeastern and who had pressured Mullen "to make the right decision."[34] But Union members also pointed out that "we must never interpret a student victory within our academic community as a token of friendship or respect for student rights on the administration's part," claiming that administrators and others in power would react only when their own positions and livelihoods were threatened.[35] Moreover, not all students or community members agreed with the decision to remove Velazquez as director of the center. Some saw his dismissal as a response that represented only a fraction of the Puerto Rican community, leading them to question the administration's commitment to all Latinos. High school students from the West Town community, where the center was located, sent a petition to Northeastern officials airing their discontent over Velazquez's firing and the possibility that Carmen Valentín would replace him.[36] "Are you going to sit back in your office letting the students get an unqualified person for the job? Then what kind of University are you running?" a young woman asked in a letter to Mullen.[37] (It is worth noting that the majority of the high school students responding to this issue were young women.) Just a month after Velazquez's dismissal, the Union's sense of victory had diminished: Union students had demanded that they be given significant input into all decisions regarding CLASES, but the administration had turned them down. It remained unclear who, exactly, would make decisions regarding the future of CLASES. This issue persisted as a source of antagonism among Northeastern's Puerto Rican students, staff, and faculty and the school administrators. As in previous decades, the Puerto Rican community's struggles for agency continued to play out in the classroom, with some of the same players continuing to figure prominently.

The Union and Northeastern officials attempted to work together to select a new director for CLASES, forming a steering committee to address the program's needs and future. In June 1975, the Union's executive board met with university officials to organize a Community Advisory Council to oversee the hiring of the new director. Students representing the Union met with administrators to ensure that their interests and concerns were considered and to avoid any conflict of interest, as the council was dominated by members of Aspira's leadership and not representative of the students now attending Northeastern.[38] Union students recommended that Carmen Valentín be hired as director of CLASES, because they believed she was the most qualified candidate.[39] However, in a memo to Union members, President Mullen stated adamantly that although he was willing to listen to the students' recommendations regarding the appointment of committee members and selection of the new director, he also intended to consider the interests and concerns of other constituents and community members.[40] If he was aware of Valentín's involvement in the community and Clemente High School, he might have preferred to avoid hiring such a divisive figure. Following a failed meeting in July 1975 between Union members and Mullen regarding the future of CLASES, each side accused the other of neglecting to work together to ensure a successful transition for the program. Mullen walked out of the meeting over disagreements about the composition of the Community Advisory Council and the hiring of the new director. "I was greatly disappointed by your unwillingness to enter dialogue," he wrote to Union members. "I must, therefore, move ahead with preparations for a most important and significant educational program."[41] He also shared his concerns with the Northeastern Illinois Board of Governors, referring to "Militant Marxist Socialist" students and alleging that they received financial backing from outside sources.[42] Although the Union represented a minority of the five hundred Latina/o students then attending Northeastern, Mullen saw the organization as "bent" on keeping alive the conflict over choosing a director for CLASES. The Union was focused on the needs of Puerto Rican and other marginalized students on campus but found little agreement with administrators regarding specific measures to meet these needs. Union members denounced what they saw as administrators' role in "playing Puerto Rican student against Puerto Rican student," creating an atmosphere of hostility and mistrust between the student group and the president's office.[43] It was clear to these students just how little influence they had in working alongside administrators to institute change.

In October 1975, Northeastern hired Jose Acevedo as its new director for CLASES. A West Town resident for more than twenty years, Acevedo had formerly held positions at the Latino Institute, Aspira, and various community and religious organizations. His appointment did little to silence the concerns of Puerto Rican students, many of whom denounced any decisions made by the administration without their input and advice. A group calling itself the Coalition of CLASES was soon organized to question the hiring process and the composition of the Community Advisory Council.[44] Mullen wrote that in putting the council together, he had consulted a list created by Union members and others and had chosen members reflecting a variety of interests. He also stated that he was willing to work with students to bring in new council members.[45]

Despite the conflicting views regarding Acevedo's appointment, CLASES moved forward. However, students continued to lead initiatives aimed at meeting the needs of Northeastern's growing Latina/o population. Proyecto Pa'lante, established following student-led activism, is part of that narrative. Like CLASES, Proyecto Pa'lante responded to student demands for the hiring of more Puerto Rican and other Latina/o faculty members, advisors, and administrators. The students hoped that this would boost the recruitment, admission, and retention of Puerto Rican students and increase the availability of financial aid information, among other goals.[46] Armed with a list of demands, the Union and Chicana/o student groups confronted Northeastern administrators in January 1972 and lobbied for a program to improve retention and recruitment of Latino students. These students understood that merely recruiting more of their community members was only the beginning; they also demanded programs and services focused on Latina/o students' specific needs to support retention. According to Maximino Torres's research on Proyecto Pa'lante, students wanted the university to provide culturally sensitive counseling and academic advising to Latina/o students, as well as comprehensive information on financial aid.[47] Moreover, they desired programs aimed at Latina/o students specifically, not marginalized communities more generally, because they did not want to be seen as playing into administrators' "'divide and conquer' strategy" or as "taking [out] their frustrations on other minority persons."[48] Puerto Rican students were aware of the importance of recruitment programs in boosting the enrollment of other students of color, and they did not want the administration to take resources from African American students to respond to the concerns of Latina/o students. In addition, they sought the creation of Proyecto Pa'lante to provide a space and a program that would affirm their cultural identity and recognize the importance of their cultural heritage to their academic success. In an interview with Maximino Torres, former president of the Union for Puerto Rican Students Samuel Flores pointed out that because Puerto Rican students "had been deprived of their cultural heritage," they "wanted courses in Puerto Rico history which . . . we were denied in our previous education."[49] Aware of the students' concerns even before the January 1972 meeting, administrators had begun conversations about providing services to the population.[50] They had sought physical space to be used for studying, tutoring, and recruitment and as meeting space for Latina/o student groups and office space for staff. By the fall of 1972, Proyecto Pa'lante was underway. In its first year, the program brought eighty freshman students to Northeastern, retaining all but three until at least the end of the first year.[51] But almost as soon as the program was established, its future and stability were threatened by internal struggles.

In the September 1974 issue of *Que Ondee Sola*, the Union welcomed the students recruited to Northeastern through Proyecto Pa'lante. The article spoke of the Union's work in dealing with administration and faculty, increasing Latina/o representation at all levels of the university, expanding financial aid, and pushing for the establishment of Proyecto Pa'lante. The Union "hope[d] that all incoming students [would] have an interest in participating in the creation and the struggles for fulfillment and social needs," because working toward similar goals would affect them as students as well as the larger Latina/o community.[52] In the fall of 1975, the newspaper again dedicated its first issue of the year to the newly admitted Latina/o freshman class, acknowledging "how it must feel to enter into a whole new atmosphere" and providing information about campus events and programs relevant to Latina/o students.[53] But even though the Union had been successful in convincing Northeastern to establish Proyecto Pa'lante, hire a Latino counselor (Maximino Torres), and initiate recruitment strategies at local high schools (including Tuley and Clemente), tensions developed between administrators and Puerto Rican students that would threaten the program's future.

Reflecting the short but conflict-ridden history of Puerto Ricans in Chicago, Puerto Rican students at Northeastern found that solving their immediate concerns did not prevent dissatisfaction and infighting from jeopardizing their progress. In September 1975, a new and short-lived student newspaper, *Lucha Estudiantil,* published an article titled "Proyecto Pa'lante Uses Alliance." The article alleged that Proyecto Pa'lante and Maximino Torres were providing the names and contact information of students in the program to the Puerto Rican Student Alliance "to propagandize their organization" and accused Torres of using his role and resources to advance the group's agenda.[54] The newspaper, sponsored by the Union, saw itself as the "genuine voice of the interest of the student body" and denounced what it saw as the "opportunism" of Proyecto Pa'lante, calling for an investigation of the project and its director.[55] In the October 1977 issue of *Que Ondee Sola,* student writers furthered scrutinized Torres's work, claiming that the program's students themselves had complained about his inadequacies as director, a lack of financial aid, and the colonial perspective of the courses Proyecto Pa'lante students were forced to take. One student wrote, "Proyecto Pa'lante with its present coordinator Maximino Torres is only interested in getting students in for September, and then totally forgets about them."[56] Torres, in his 1983 doctoral dissertation on the development and evolution of Proyecto Pa'lante, wrote about the strained relationship that developed in 1975 among the program, its staff, and the Union. He pointed out that this program, aimed at helping disadvantaged youth gain access to higher education, depended for its survival on student activism from those very youth, a situation that indicated "the neglect of American higher education toward underprivileged students."[57] Torres was concerned about what he perceived as an attempt by the Union to take over Proyecto Pa'lante, maintaining that the Union's ideological shift was "disruptive and detrimental to the educational process of the project students."[58] He accused the Union of pushing students to promote Puerto Rican independence as a condition for admission.[59] In response, both the Union and *Que Ondee Sola* criticized Proyecto for what they saw as a deliberate exclusion of Puerto Rican history courses from students' schedules. *Que Ondee Sola* "strongly" urged Torres to "discontinue his policy of boycotting" these classes. One student said, "I come to Northeastern University wanting to learn about my history and again I am denied my history."[60] However, despite the concerns and internal strife, Proyecto Pa'lante moved forward in its mission to recruit, retain, and graduate its students. The graduation rate for the first cohort of eighty students, recruited in 1972, was 45 percent.[61]

The case of students at Northeastern is important as it complicates the everyday experiences of Puerto Rican students in higher education in the 1970s and challenges monolithic understandings of the Puerto Rican community's educational practices. But more importantly, it articulates the powerful influence of student activism in transforming higher education, creating changes to promote students' ideas and needs while framing their continued commitment to their home communities. Indeed, at Northeastern, there was no clear distinction between Puerto Rican students' home communities and the higher education environment, as they practically shared the same space. The situation was similar at the University of Illinois Circle Campus.

The University of Illinois Circle Campus

At the University of Illinois Circle Campus (UICC), students and community members in the early 1970s found an experience similar to that of their counterparts at Northeastern: a state university system that was failing for the most part to recruit and retain Puerto Rican students. Although the number of Puerto Ricans in Chicago had increased by more than 10 percent over the previous decade, their numbers at UICC remained virtually unchanged.[62] Furthermore, many students admitted to UICC were channeled into remedial education programs, regardless of their scholastic qualifications. This required them to spend more than four years on their degree programs. In the spring semester of 1973, Puerto Rican students and other community members lodged a protest against what they saw as discriminatory practices directed at Puerto Rican students. The group claimed that the regular admissions office, contradicting university policy, did not attempt to recruit high school students at the three "main Latin ghetto schools," Tuley, Harrison, and Wells.[63] UICC's Educational Assistance Program (EAP) was responsible for the recruitment and assistance of certain populations through its "special quota" program. But the students and activists asserted that the EAP had failed to recruit at all of their community schools and accused it of focusing on middle-class Latino students who met regular admission requirements, sending a clear message to students at the Puerto Rican high schools: "Circle is simply not the place to apply: you can't get in."[64]

The push for programs to serve Puerto Ricans at UICC was an extension of the community activism that many of these students had witnessed during the preceding decade. They were familiar with the work of Puerto Ricans and Mexican Americans in mobilizing against the unfair and discriminatory practices that framed their experience in the city, especially around schooling concerns. The demonstrators were well aware that the Circle Campus was located on the site "of a flourishing Latino barrio . . . the focal point for all Latins in the city of Chicago."[65] Despite its location, however, UICC had not created opportunities for Latino students to gain admission to the school, and according to demonstrators, it based admissions on tests that had been found to be discriminatory against them. Puerto Rican student activists at UICC sought programs and spaces that recognized their distinctiveness and unique needs while pressing the institution to recognize its responsibility to the larger community. The Circle Campus, students maintained, "was built on a gravestone on the site of what had been the oldest Puerto Rican and Mexican community in Chicago until it was destroyed."[66] Students, along with teachers, faculty, parents of K–12 students, and other allies, advocated for better opportunities at UICC for Puerto Rican students and all of the city's Latina/o community.

The on-campus activism initiated by UICC's Puerto Rican students and community members in the 1970s highlighted the need to increase the population of Latina/o students at the Circle Campus, but the university's main campus at Urbana-Champaign had already engaged in similar discussions and struggles regarding student diversity. In the late 1960s, the Urbana-Champaign campus had increased the population of majority African American students, with a few slots allocated to Latina/o students, through a program called Project 500.[67] Perhaps spurred by the activism and student recruitment in Urbana-Champaign, Latina/o faculty and staff at UICC drafted similar recommendations to administrators. Paul Vega, who served as an advisor for the EAP, submitted a proposal to the university in 1971, highlighting the need for a viable program to serve the Puerto Rican community on campus. He asserted that the "admission policies of state supported institutions of higher education determine to a large extent who is to be given the opportunity to obtain an education," and although colleges and universities had been created to support *all* the people, many populations were poorly served.[68] Vega criticized UICC for its small number of Latin American students: just 1.5 percent of the nearly twenty thousand students. According to Vega's proposal, UICC did not acknowledge its responsibility to the "urban society, i.e., the people who live across the street."[69] Like Urbana-Champaign's Project 500, the UICC proposal called for recruiting and enrolling three hundred Latina/o students on a "special action" basis. Vega reminded administrators of their own support for and praise of the EAP's work, as the university had acknowledged the academic success of the program's Latina/o students. Furthermore, he pointed out that "the University [had] made many promises to the community when the school was being built, among them that the University would offer increased opportunity for the community residents to attend college."[70]

Administrators seemed willing to discuss the status of Latina/o students on campus, in accordance with Vega's proposal, but they did not respond quickly with a plan; nor did they appear to view Vega's recommendations as feasible. Vice Chancellor Leonard Goodall acknowledged the validity of the concerns raised in the proposal but claimed that the institution faced constraints that prevented it from acting on them.[71] After a very brief discussion of the matter, administrators recommended that Vega withdraw his proposal and amend it. In a letter to Vega, Goodall wrote that he believed the idea for a Latin American recruitment program was worth pursuing, but he encouraged Vega to rewrite the proposal to include a thorough depiction of what the program would look like, including a budget. Similarly, Goodall reminded Vega that the EAP was already utilizing 375 special admissions slots, and its support services were stretched thin.[72] After the proposal's withdrawal, it was two more years before university officials seriously engaged in conversations regarding the status of Latina/o students and UICC's responsibility to the larger community across the street and across the city. The "special admissions slots" mentioned by Goodall had been approved in 1970 by the University of Illinois system's Board of Trustees: "for experimental and special programs, spaces may be reserved at each campus for applicants of different qualifications."[73] The board touted the success of the EAP and Native American Programs on both the Circle Campus and the Urbana-Champaign campus. Representatives from the Circle Campus initially negotiated with students during the summer of 1973 to create a Latin American Recruitment Program (LARP) with an advisor dedicated to Latina/o students' needs. Latina/o students wanted a recruitment program separate from the EAP for two reasons. First, the EAP had already demonstrated its inability to recruit at certain high schools with high Latina/o enrollment. Second, the EAP had a low admissions quota, which meant that it could not guarantee slots for Puerto Rican and other Latina/o students.[74] The proposed LARP would be responsible for recruiting all Latina/o students, not just those who needed special admissions consideration, and students advocated that it be located organizationally within the Latin American Studies Program. Following negotiations, the student faction was victorious: LARP was made part of the Latin American Studies Program, and UICC recruited and admitted more than one hundred Latina/o students for the fall 1973 semester. But mirroring the struggles at Northeastern, LARP's implementation was soon followed by controversy as student activists accused administrators of reneging on their promises.[75]

When the academic year began in September 1973, the students and staff recruited to LARP during the summer months found the offices closed. "All their records were removed," according to a witness. "We were told that the records and the entire program would be merged with the school's Educational Assistance Program."[76] The move, which had been ordered by the chancellor's office, exacerbated the negative sentiment of those who already believed the EAP provided inadequate assistance to Puerto Rican and other Latino students. In addition, the move was criticized because it left the newly admitted students and staff unsure of their status. A spokesperson for the chancellor countered these charges, saying, "the Educational Assistance Program has an interracial staff, trying to recruit and offer educational and financial adjustments to increase minority group representation."[77] The change had come about because, after initially supporting the program, the Board of Trustees had noted a problem. The admissions provision the board had approved in 1970, reserving admissions slots for students with "different qualifications," limited such slots to 10 percent of the previous term's entering freshman class.[78] Therefore, a program specifically targeting Latina/o students would reduce the number of students admitted under already existing programs, such as the EAP. In other words, according to the Board of Trustees, LARP would negatively affect the recruitment of Native American students and other marginalized populations. "This would not be in keeping with our goals and it would be ironic indeed to meet a new need at the expense of other equally compelling needs."[79] The board voted to increase the alternate admissions cap from 10 percent to 12 percent of the previous term's freshman enrollment. Nevertheless, many students opposed LARP's move to the EAP, believing that it contradicted students' best interests.

On September 26, 1973, more than fifty Puerto Rican students and allies gathered at the UICC administrators' offices demanding that the university recruit more Latina/o students and that university officials follow through on the work they had initiated during the summer in support of LARP. One demonstrator claimed that Latina/o students were still underrepresented at the university. This charge was valid: although Latina/o residents constituted 8 percent of Chicago's population, they represented only 1.5 percent of UICC's student body.[80] A delegation of demonstrators, including students, community members, and faculty, met at University Hall with Chancellor Warren Cheston to question the administration's decision to consolidate the newly formed LARP with the EAP with no notice to the community. During this meeting, the administration offered to place LARP under the mantle of the Latin American Studies Program, while insisting that it remain housed and controlled by the EAP.[81] The delegation disagreed with these conditions and returned to the lobby to meet with the approximately two hundred other demonstrators. Administrators agreed to resume negotiations the following day, but according to students, the demonstrators were warned to exit the building immediately or face arrest at the hands of the police officers already present.

Students and allies returned to University Hall the next day. Once again, administrators refused to meet with the group in the lobby, but the demonstrators demanded that "Cheston descend from his 28th floor and negotiate in the lobby, in view of the harassment and indignity suffered the preceding day by those who [had] attempted to see him in his penthouse office."[82] When they held several elevators open, officials viewed this as a sign of aggression and called in the police, who threatened to arrest the demonstrators if they did not disperse. Although many did leave, a group of almost forty demonstrators remained behind, sitting in a circle in the lobby, "in an area causing no disruption or inconvenience to passersby," according to witnesses.[83] All were arrested and charged with criminal trespass, resisting arrest, and interfering with university operations.[84]

Community members from both the Circle Campus and the larger Latina/o/ community quickly mobilized to support those arrested as they faced their day in court. According to a flyer produced by supporters, the mass arrests "clearly illustrate the attitude of the university administration toward any student group. . . . Thus our struggle is your struggle."[85] Another leaflet admonished Cheston for what students viewed as his insensitivity toward Puerto Rican and Mexican students and called for the larger university community to support students in their efforts to negotiate with him.[86] At the Board of Trustees meeting on October 17, 1973, two representatives from the group of activists, Fred Alvarez and José López, presented a written statement requesting that the administration offer "amnesty" to those arrested and asking for the "refinement" of UICC's support programs for Puerto Rican and other Latina/o students.[87] In response, Cheston stated that UICC was developing a program to meet the needs of the Latina/o community but could not interfere in the legal case pending against those who had been arrested. After several meetings with UICC administrators, representatives from the Latina/o community were allowed to speak during the board meeting on April 17, 1974, expressing their dissatisfaction with they saw as the university's slow response to the controversy surrounding LARP and the needs of Latina/o students. On the previous day, the board had conducted a hearing to listen to the concerns and demands of community representatives and released a statement detailing what administrators saw as their progress in the recruitment of Latino students to both the Circle Campus and the Urbana-Champaign campus. The statement reiterated the board's "long standing commitment to support programs designed to recruit and admit students, regardless of ethnic background, who possess the qualifications necessary to meet the academic requirements of a university such as the University of Illinois."[88] It also informed students and community members that changes would be made according to the structures and "orderly procedures" guiding the university's decision-making, signaling to the activists that their tactics would not dictate the board's decisions.[89] The rhetoric of this statement echoed the language that K–12 educators and administrators had used to dismiss the work of high school activists in Chicago schools.

Following discussions and negotiations with community representatives, Cheston attempted to create a Latino Advisory Board to work alongside Circle Campus officials. However, not everyone at the university was in agreement regarding the creation or structure of the advisory group, and some feared it would set a harmful precedent. UICC staff member Sheila Castillo said that before her experience working with community groups in Chicago's Pilsen neighborhood, she would have agreed with the need for and effectiveness of a Latino Advisory Board for the university. However, after witnessing internal struggles over ideological differences and control, she was hesitant to support the creation of such a board. According to Castillo, "without a specific purpose, responsibility or authority, an advisory committee [would] not attract the reasonable persons that could make it useful," instead becoming "a stage for those who wish to gain attention."[90] UICC's associate vice chancellor of urban affairs, Michael Goldstein, shared similar concerns in a letter to Cheston. Goldstein articulated the difficulty of creating a Latino Advisory Board when, in his view, there was no real indication of which groups were truly representative of the community. He argued, "there is a great deal of fuzziness in terms of what does constitute a legitimate representative organization . . . the mere act of designating one organization or individual to such a committee imparts a certain degree of credibility."[91] Concerned administrators and staff also wanted to ensure that any members of the proposed advisory board would come from established groups focused on education. Similarly, uneasy about the influence such a board would have on administrative matters and on the chancellor, some suggested it should be organized as a "planning group" focused on developing curriculum, advising on the hiring of a director, and creating an advisory committee for the incoming director.[92] It was further suggested that the group report to an academic officer, not directly to the chancellor.

Administrators clearly had reservations about a program specifically targeting Latina/o students and about the proposed Latino Advisory Board, but

Latina/o students and their faculty and staff allies persisted in working for change. Unimpressed with UICC's slow pace in implementing programs for Latino students, a coalition of students wrote to Cheston and other administrators in March 1975 to remind them of their promises. "We understand that the University had previously agreed to these demands but we feel that there has been a lack of cooperation on the part of the University which has stifled this process."[93] In May 1975, representatives from the Latin American Studies Program delivered a comprehensive, more detailed proposal (perhaps an extension of Paul Vega's previous work), asking for the establishment of a Latin American Recruitment and Educational Services (LARES) program. The proposal reiterated the need for a program to "motivate, prepare, and recruit the largest possible number of Latin American students to attend UICC" and "promote the broadest possible Latin American cultural milieu within the University."[94] Supporters believed that fostering students' connection to their cultural heritage would boost their motivation in their studies. In addition to the creation of LARES, supporters requested space and resources for a Latino student center that would serve as a venue for social and cultural events and help connect the campus with the citywide Latino community.[95] Such a center would ease the adjustment of incoming high school students to life at the university and enrich their education. The proposal claimed that the center would provide research services and materials for those interested in Latino and Latin American culture but in no way would "prejudice" the interests of other ethnic groups.[96] In the months before the proposal's dissemination, the EAP's community liaison, José Ortiz, had shared his concerns regarding the lack of space for Latino students to congregate, study, or find resources. Writing to Vega, Ortiz noted that if finding space for the students was an issue, there were rooms near the EAP office that had not been used in more than four years.[97]

The continued pressure from students, staff, faculty, and community members ultimately yielded results. In the spring of 1975, UICC began making changes and implementing programs that eventually became LARES. Coordinator and recruiter-advisor positions were created under the Latin American Studies Program, whose leader served as the first LARES director. In 1975, its first year, with a budget of $22,000, LARES successfully recruited 101 students.[98] In addition to intensifying recruitment, LARES also developed tutoring and counseling services in collaboration with the EAP and worked with the English Department to create a section of Composition 102, taught by a bilingual professor, that would recognize Latina/o students' curricular needs.[99]

Attention soon turned to the creation of a Latino cultural center to support the newly admitted students. According to Otto Pikaza, a UICC faculty member, the center would serve several purposes. It would be a "bridge between the reality of the community and the sometimes alienating process and content of university education."[100] In addition, it would provide an educational space to highlight the culture of the fastest-growing ethnic group in Chicago and encourage Latino students to become more involved on campus. By the spring of 1976, students had secured space for the center, but no operating funds, although the university had allocated funding to remodel the space for a planned opening in the fall semester of 1976.[101] After receiving a detailed proposal about the establishment and support of the program, one administrator noted that the total amount requested, $65,000, exceeded what the university's reserve fund could cover. However, Associate Vice Chancellor Richard Johnson recognized that some funds were necessary for the program to be operational, even if this delayed the hiring of a director.[102] In Johnson's view, if all the available funds were spent on hiring a director, no money would remain for events and programs. Therefore, he supported an initial investment of $10,000 to keep the center open and to fund events and publicity.[103] This amount was far below the $65,000 originally requested by the students and their supporters.[104]

Even without a budget in place, students organized the opening of the cultural center in September 1976, naming it in honor of a beloved Puerto Rican professor at the Circle Campus who had recently died.[105] Students remembered Rafael Cintrón Ortiz for his teaching on Puerto Rican history and its impact; "his method of teaching motivated students to read and freely discuss in class all subject matter."[106] The center made it easier for students to create organizations that spoke to their own historical specificities and positionality within the university. One such group, the Chicano Boricua Union, soon recognized a need for coalition building among the Latino student population. The group's bylaws stated, "Learning from the lessons of the past, we have taken time to make an assessment of our present situation which we felt was necessary before proceeding in any program of action."[107] Furthermore, the students recognized that "in building a strong unity between Chicano and Boricua brothers and sisters it has become evident that a sense of direction must be established." Through the Chicano Boricua Union as well as the Confederation of Latin American Students and the Sociedad Estudiantil Latino-Americana, UICC students utilized the cultural center to promote their respective cultural and ethnic identities and ensure the permanency of the programs and centers they had fought to establish. Likewise, their counterparts on the Urbana-Champaign campus, organized by the student group La Colectiva Latina, had recently fought for the creation of their own campus cultural center.[108] At these institutions, higher education in the lives of Puerto Rican students "not only provided training and developed skills, it inculcated values, commitments, and modes of behavior . . . and [made students] more protective of civil rights."[109] Puerto Ricans earned this sense of accomplishment not only through their attainment of higher education, but also through their adeptness in resolving injustices—a skill they had inherited from their community in its short history in Chicago.

From the Schoolhouse to the Ivory Tower

Puerto Ricans' struggle for access to higher education in Chicago exemplifies the population's understanding of the structural inequalities that continued to limit their full participation as both city residents and students. They faced constant negotiation in their attempts to live out their full potential as city residents and students despite the many obstacles placed in their way. As in Puerto Ricans' fight for community control of schools, students at postsecondary institutions worked to remind the city of its responsibility to meet the population's educational needs. As students at both Northeastern Illinois University and the University of Illinois Circle Campus realized, their experiences in higher education were much like their earlier involvement in Chicago's K–12 schools, except that as university students, they were better able to challenge what they saw as the unfair practices of university administrators. They were also less willing now to accept administrators' words at face value and more confident about demanding concrete commitment to their needs. Their proximity to their home community and schools also played a valuable role in their organizing efforts, as the local community's needs continuously overlapped with their demands as students.

The practice of disseminating relevant information regarding the community played a prominent role in the organizing efforts of students and community members as they pushed for autonomy in telling the community's stories. As in the Black student movement in places such as Detroit, college and university newspapers became "an instrument for revolutionary struggle" for Puerto Rican students.[110] Centering the lives and voices of Puerto Ricans in Chicago became the mission of those working to create print materials, including publications initiated by university students. Before Puerto Rican-created print materials proliferated, the community events and the lives of Chicago's Puerto Ricans were framed by the dominant mainstream media, which rarely included accounts from community members themselves. The 1960s and 1970s offered Puerto Ricans the opportunity to express their growing discontent within the city, but also to create print media platforms to celebrate their lives and their commitment to the city, something not seen in other publications. These alternative media outlets gave Puerto Ricans a new way to share their needs, concerns, and issues with one another and to portray their own lives authentically. Such publications functioned as a form of organized response by Puerto Ricans to their conditions in the city, serving as a crucial venue through which parents, community members, and, most importantly, students communicated their troubled relationship with Chicago schools.

CHAPTER 5

Living and Writing in the Puerto Rican Diaspora

WORKING ON AN IN-DEPTH STORY about Chicago's Lincoln Park neighborhood on an August afternoon in 1969, writer Studs Terkel happened upon a group of police officers, community members, and local activists gathered on the corner of Dayton Street and Armitage Avenue on the city's North Side. The Young Lords had organized a community picnic to mark the opening of a childcare center at the church where they had their headquarters.[1] "When I arrived I found a great many policemen guarding the street, and the people who had come to participate were on the sidewalk."[2] Spotting Cha Cha Jiménez, the chairman of the Young Lords, Terkel asked him what was happening. Jiménez told Terkel that they had struggled to obtain a permit from the local community board to hold the event, although George Barr McCutcheon, the 43rd Ward alderman, had initially supported it.

> First they told us that we couldn't have the picnic at all, and I told them go to hell. Then they came back, and told one of the guys to come back and tell me: "could you tell him if he keeps the people on the sidewalk, that we can have the picnic," and I told them go to hell two times. So we're going to have the picnic on the sidewalk, on the street, wherever we want it. We're having free food, we're having entertainment that is coming pretty soon, we're having speakers, we're having poetry read, some cultural things, more or less to get more Puerto Rican people involved. And now they [the alderman and the board who denied the permit] did a nice thing because they got the Puerto Rican people really to see the truth.[3]

Event organizers accused McCutcheon of siding with a group of residents who opposed the picnic and who wished to force poor community members out of Lincoln Park. McCutcheon countered that he had denied the permit because of safety concerns, not for partisan reasons. Terkel spent the rest of the afternoon chronicling the evolution of the gathering, highlighting the story of the childcare center (the initial reason for the event) and the dispute between the Young Lords and McCutcheon, allowing people on both sides of the dispute to share their thoughts. Halfway through the celebration, with Puerto Rican music playing in the background, Terkel witnessed the growing tension between the event organizers and the Chicago police, with each side accusing the other of starting physical altercations, and police accusing the organizers of failing to follow orders. At one point, the officers readied their rifles.

As Terkel continued to record interviews, the crowd grew, with leaders of the Young Lords and the police attempting to make sense of the situation and find a peaceful solution. The police made an offer to some of the young men who had been involved in the physical confrontation with officers, proposing to transport them to the police station to file a report and then bring them back to the celebration. The police were also willing to allow witnesses concerned about the men's safety to accompany them to and from the station. However, the organizers did not necessarily trust the police to safely transport or detain members of their group. After meeting with David Rivera of the Young Lords, the deputy superintendent of police ultimately allowed the music and dancing to continue on the street, as the group had initially requested, but only if the Young Lords agreed to obey a curfew and to leave the streets clean. This allowed the celebration to continue, which, it was hoped, would end the unrest. The Reverend Bruce Johnson of the Armitage Street Methodist Church spoke with Terkel on the street about how the day had reached this climax. Johnson said, "It resulted from the police deciding to get tough to move them up to the curbing, and probably jostled a few people, and as anyone would as being shoved and pushed with a stick and everything else, I suppose they responded and reacted." Terkel asked Johnson what he thought the police had in mind during those tense moments when they were prepared to use their rifles. Johnson responded with both anger and sadness, saying that the police were preparing to protect themselves and "to get ready for snipers."[4]

This 1969 exchange between Terkel and the Puerto Rican community on a Chicago street corner, although an organic or "accidental" event, is important. Terkel's oral histories and interviews of average Americans were popular and acclaimed for giving listeners access to communities, events, and individuals they otherwise would not engage with in their daily lives. For the Young Lords and Puerto Ricans in Chicago, Terkel's account provided an unfiltered narration of their struggles to gain access to space and representation in a community interested in forcing them out, and in a city unsure about how to "deal with" them. Terkel's thorough chronicle of the day shed light on several complicated and interrelated issues: the conflicting sides within the larger issue of Lincoln Park's impending urbanization; the everyday realities of those threatened with police brutality; the city's evolving demographics; and the negotiation of space for the Puerto Rican community to articulate their concerns on their own terms. Until the late 1960s, Puerto Ricans in Chicago had had little opportunity to tell their own stories, and for far too long, the narrative about their lives had been told mainly by people outside their community, whom many Puerto Ricans viewed as the problem. But in telling the story of Puerto Rican Chicago, it is crucial to highlight the work of Puerto Rican community groups and residents in their own words. Especially for students and young people, the development of print materials produced by Puerto Ricans gave voice to the individual and collective struggles of a population experiencing the residual effects of a complicated and long-standing colonial relationship in the midst of a growing civil rights movement.

The mainstream media disseminated little information about the schooling and community organizing of Puerto Ricans in Chicago during the middle decades of the twentieth century. Yet until the mid-1960s, Puerto Ricans depended on mainstream media outlets to link them to the local community and inform them about the political, economic, and social news from Puerto Rico. For example, in response to the growing tensions at Tuley and Clemente High Schools, mainstream newspapers such as the *Chicago Tribune* described the struggle for control of the schools as a battle between school officials and outsiders intent on disrupting student learning. The community's own print outlets, on the other hand, provided space in which those most affected by the day-to-day struggles for justice could articulate their concerns, even when they did not all share the same views. Puerto Ricans seeking a compelling portrayal of their own lived realities, whether within schools, politics, or academia, developed community-based and community-run publications to express their needs as workers, activists, and scholars. More importantly, these print materials chronicled the campaign for educational equality and fostered a sense of community across ethnic and geographic locales. These publications included *The Rican: A Journal of Contemporary Puerto Rican Thought* (1971–1974), the local community newspaper *El Puertorriqueño* (1965–1986), the Northeastern Illinois University student newspaper *Que Ondee Sola*, (1972-) and the various newspapers of the Young Lords Organization. Developed during one of the community's most trying eras, these materials provided a rich and insightful narrative on Puerto Ricans' lives in

Chicago at a time when mainstream newspapers and journals failed to offer residents a legitimate option.[5] For a community embroiled in conflicts over community control of K–12 schools and postsecondary institutions, the ability to articulate their own narratives on their own terms highlighted their investment in their community's needs. Moreover, like the struggles in the schools and universities, these publications remind us of the conflicting views, experiences, and desires of a community seemingly in constant transition.

The Puerto Rican community's need to develop and maintain their own print media indicated their evolving status in Chicago and their recognition that they were there to stay. Although some Puerto Rican migrants to Chicago and other U.S. cities expected to return to the island someday, the emergence of youth activists among the second and third generations was proof of the population's permanency. In the mid-twentieth century, Chicago's Puerto Rican residents faced this rhetoric in the city's major newspapers and in scholarly journals that continued to view them as outsiders or temporary residents across the diaspora, despite their long-standing presence. The press and print culture in general allowed the population a space in which to challenge those notions, as a return to the homeland for these groups "was no longer feasible or of particular interest."[6] Puerto Ricans' inclusion and active participation in education, business, and politics indicated their enduring influence across the city. The development of Puerto Rican–run newspapers and journals solidified that permanency, as Puerto Ricans wrote themselves into the story of Chicago on their own terms.

School newspapers and other extracurricular activities, which typically were not closely monitored by principals and administrators, sometimes provided space for activist teachers and students to raise questions about marginalized communities' position amid the political and racial turmoil of the civil rights era.[7] For example, during the Freedom School movement led by Black activists in the mid-1960s, students utilized newspapers "to politicize the young people and adults, circulating their ideas about the nature of 'freedom,' articulating their disdain for the Jim Crow laws, and encouraging their readers to join the movement."[8] Similarly, across the state line in Wisconsin, newspapers such as *La Guardia* and *La Voz Chicana* aligned the young Chicana/o population with the Southwest's Chicana/o movement and gave them a platform for keeping local residents informed about their growing community's needs.[9] *La Guardia*, an underground newspaper published from the mid-1960s until 1982, was instrumental in Wisconsin's labor rights movement. The social, political, and economic milieu that contributed to the Latina/o population's increase in the Midwest during the early and mid-twentieth century was a factor in the rise of community-based ethnic newspapers. With respect to their purpose and mission, these publications were by no means homogeneous, nor were the communities they represented. Beyond merely reporting the news and offering advertisements, these newspapers in many ways became leadership institutions, "often serving as forums for intellectuals, writers and politicians, and often spearheading political and social movements."[10] For Puerto Ricans in urban spaces, their press became a mirror of their community's political, educational, and cultural realities, at times reflecting the growing conflict within their own neighborhoods.

Puerto Rican–run journals gave scholars a venue where they could not only articulate research agendas framed around their community's needs but also examine and include the voices of the growing Puerto Rican diaspora. These publications also offered them a platform for expressing concerns about their community's education and imagining alternatives, especially when school systems failed to address their challenges. While *The Rican*, *Que Ondee Sola*, the Young Lords' newspapers, and *El Puertorriqueño* may have been undervalued by the larger community, they served as an intellectual outlet in which Puerto Ricans across the diaspora could express the lived realities of their heterogeneous communities. Whether in the halls of academia or in *el barrio*, these print materials facilitated a sense of belonging and collaboration for a community who had been living on the margins in Chicago for more than three decades.

El Young Lord Latin Liberation News Service

The creation of organizations such as the Young Lords, the Brown Berets, and the Black Panthers was instrumental in mobilizing people of color to challenge the growing disparities limiting their schooling, housing, and labor opportunities. Formerly a Chicago street gang, the Young Lords Organization reorganized itself as a community-based collective in the late 1960s that challenged police brutality against Puerto Ricans and an urban renewal plan that had displaced many working-class and poor people of color. As the Young Lords Organization grew beyond Chicago, Puerto Ricans collaborated on further ways to improve their living conditions. More importantly, they created a culture of collaboration and exchange of ideas that transcended differences in class, gender, sex, race, and educational attainment. This "culture of collaboration" and recognition of the need to work across differences has played a prominent role in the history of this community. From its inception, Chicago's Young Lords utilized print media to disseminate critical information to the community and to communicate with members of other marginalized groups. In 1969, their monthly publication *YLO: Young Lords*

Organization printed an article titled "Why a Y.L.O. Newspaper?" The article claimed that a newspaper was needed because "a Latin American Movement is developing in Chicago for the purpose of putting an end to the injustices, suffering and exploitation which is forced upon our people."[11] Further, it stated, "A newspaper can be the focus of a permanent organization; it could provide a bridge between the peaks of activity."[12] The editors believed that "the tool of a newspaper can help aid the development of political consciousness in the community and in YLO, help develop revolutionary goals, people, strategy and contacts."[13] Furthermore, in highlighting news about schools and by youth, the Young Lords' newspapers demonstrated the organization's recognition of the community's schooling life as a site of liberation.

Although the newspaper itself remained consistent in its content and message, its publication locale and funding sources shifted several times as the organization changed its physical location and alliances with other community groups. Early issues were produced on North Lincoln Avenue at the offices of the Concerned Citizens of Lincoln Park, an organization aimed at challenging the gentrification and subsequent displacement of the community.[14] Cha Cha Jiménez retained directorship of the newspaper even when he lived underground in Tomah, Wisconsin, in what became known as the Young Lords Underground Training School.[15] "People would just pitch in," he said. "Donations and the sale of the newspaper on street corners would pay for the newspapers."[16] The Latin American Defense Organization of Chicago also provided financial support for an issue of the publication, in exchange for their organization's inclusion in the paper. *YLO*'s continual movement and insecure finances led to an inconsistent publication pattern and history, with issues sometimes appearing weekly and sometimes much more sporadically. However, it remained a community presence throughout the group's most active period, disseminating valuable and critical information at a tumultuous time for Chicago's Puerto Ricans and other Latina/o residents. Although Jiménez led the newspaper (and the organization), it was a collective effort involving other members. For example, Omar Lopez and Tony Baez (the Young Lords' minister of information and minister of education respectively) played crucial roles in several issues of the paper, and other members contributed by covering community events, reporting on injustices in Chicago and other cities, and conveying messages of support. The publication also utilized news agencies such as the Liberation News Service to keep readers linked to the struggles faced by other marginalized groups in the United States and abroad.[17]

Police brutality and harassment aimed at Puerto Rican residents, as well as other Latina/os and African Americans, was an ongoing reality for youth of color, and it became a recurring theme in the Young Lords' writings. Following the 1969 shooting death of Young Lords member Manuel Ramos at the hands of a plainclothes police officer, members organized the local community to confront both the offending officer and Mayor Daley. In its May 1969 issue, the newspaper's coverage of the death of Ramos, a married father of two, also served to remind the city of its failure to address the needs of Chicago's poor community.[18] Along with the Poor People's Coalition, the Young Patriots, and other activist groups, the Young Lords staged a takeover of Chicago's McCormick Theological Seminary, renaming it the "Manuel Ramos Memorial Building." They demanded the creation of a Puerto Rican cultural center, funds for a twenty-four-hour childcare center, affordable housing for poor and working-class people (in property owned by McCormick), and financial support for various welfare rights and leadership programs.

The newspaper's commitment was not limited to creating a space for members of the Young Lords Organization to document the troubled relationship between the city and the community, which had now become a constant target of Chicago police. Nor did the publication restrict its coverage to Chicago's Puerto Ricans. Since its inception, *YLO* had ventured outside its own ethnic and geographic boundaries, linking Puerto Ricans to their Chicana/o and African American allies and aligning Puerto Ricans' struggles with those of other marginalized groups. Through this movement, the Young Lords sought "a new society in which all people are treated as equal," with the newspaper providing a glimpse of a transnational political movement poised to do just that.[19] Stories on Malayan women workers' battle to gain unionizing rights were published alongside articles about the constant police surveillance of the Young Lords who were seeking to combat urban renewal plans in the Lincoln Park community. Intentionally or not, the Young Lords' newspaper placed different communities in conversation with one another, even communities that were alien to or even in conflict with each other. For example, Mexicans and Puerto Ricans have at times shared a troubled relationship, but as both groups found themselves in a contentious relationship with the city of Chicago, they forged alliances and mutual respect.[20]

Another article in *YLO*'s May 1969 issue demonstrates that after attending the Chicano Liberation Youth Conference, Young Lords members came to recognize the shared interests of Chicago's Puerto Ricans and Chicana/os.[21] In learning about the activism of Chicana/os, as well as their community's displacement and the police violence against them, Puerto Rican activists and community members gained a sense of belonging to a greater movement for equal rights and community empowerment. For instance, an April 1971 issue of the newspaper, which by then was being published under a new title,

El Young Lord, by members who had relocated to Wisconsin temporarily, focused on the current and historical struggles against local and national governments, many of which had proved brutal and fatal for Puerto Ricans and Chicana/os. One case recounted in the article involved a Texas family, including a young girl and her pregnant mother, who were brutalized in their home in the middle of the night by Texas police officers searching for two men accused of killing three police officers. According to the thirty-six-year-old mother, "After wounding us they made us kneel down on the floor, including the children, and told us not to make a move. When the oldest boy, 14 years old, moved they hit him on the side of the neck very hard."[22] By publishing such stories, the Young Lords helped solidify Puerto Ricans' communal ties with Chicana/os, fostering relationships that contributed to community and policy changes for both groups. The newspapers also placed the diaspora in conversation with the island's independence movement. One issue of *El Young Lord* featured both an educational piece on Puerto Rico's 1937 Ponce massacre and an article about a 1971 confrontation between Puerto Rican police and students at the University of Puerto Rico's Rio Piedras campus. This juxtaposition reminded Puerto Ricans of their ongoing struggle for political independence and "victory over imperialism."[23] The article about the Ponce massacre also reminded readers of the political ties between the island and the diaspora.

In addition to linking the community to a larger national and global movement, the Young Lords' newspapers (and organization) documented the status of Latina/o, Puerto Rican, and African American students in city schools. The urban renewal projects displacing poor and working-class families from communities such as Lincoln Park had consequences for students at Waller High School. According to an article in *El Young Lord*,

> Cerca de tres cuartros partes de las ventanas se encuentran sin vidrios y el edificio está por caerse. La escuela "sirve" principalmente a negros y latinos, adolecentes de la comunidad quienes sus familias están pobres para mandarlos a escuelas privadas y quienes también poco a poco son mudadas del area por Renovación Urbana (urban renewal). Algunos miembros de la facultad, en especial el principal, son verdaderos racistas que trabajan solamente por el dinero y nunca los importa si el estudiante aprende o no.[24]

> (Approximately three rooms have windows without glass, and the building is close to collapsing. The school serves primarily Blacks and Latinos, youth from the community whose parents are too poor to send them to private schools, and who have also little by little moved away from the community because of urban renewal. Some members of the faculty, including the principal, are real racists who work only for the money and do not care if the students are learning or not.)

After Waller had suspended more than 170 students during a six-month period, a group of Waller mothers attempted to meet with school administrators to seek the students' reinstatement, but the principal was uninterested in meeting with the women. In response, students and community allies (including parents) led a demonstration at the school in solidarity with the suspended students, who they believed had been punished for being Black or Latino. In 1971, the Chicago Board of Education, which was considering transforming Waller into a citywide magnet school, discussed what to do with students who had "failed to make academic advancement."[25] Superintendent James Redmond endorsed the creation of an "outpost" program for "certain socially maladjusted" students. In other words, in the midst of an urban renewal program that was displacing residents to satellite neighborhoods, the school system planned to outsource the education of Black and Puerto Rican students.

At Wells High School in early 1970, the Young Lords hosted an afterschool meeting for students who were interested in the organization. Police officers arrived at the meeting and accused the Young Lords of trespassing, leading to a confrontation in which rocks and other debris were thrown. A letter to YLO chronicled the incident: "We were in the lunchroom rapping to our brothers when the school's pig came over and started telling us that we were trespassing and that if anything happened, we were going to stay until the period was over and we told him so. He left and about twenty minutes later he came back and started telling that we had to go, so when we refused, he called to some other pigs and dragged us away so that we would not be able to relate to our brothers."[26] Although the Young Lords' presence at the school became a trespassing issue for police, it quickly became an opportunity for students to vent their frustrations with school administrators and support the Young Lords, a group that appeared to have a clear understanding of and familiarity with their needs. Mainstream newspapers, on the other hand, continued not to cover news about Wells and Waller High Schools or about Puerto Rican students' day-to-day reality in city schools.

Because many of the articles did not include bylines, it is difficult to decipher the full involvement of women in creating the Young Lords' newspapers. Furthermore, much of what has been written about Chicago's Young Lords Organization focuses on the leadership of its male members. However, women were not absent from the group's organizing work. Indeed, the scholarship on New York's Young Lords chapter includes the voices and contributions of the organization's women.[27] In Chicago's publications, a few articles were written by women members or the wives and female partners of male members. In one such piece, published in 1969, member Hilda Vasquez Ignatin provided a thorough history of the group's evolution from a street gang to an organization working to combat the urban renewal programs targeting their community.[28] In the January 1970 issue of *YLO*, a contributor to the "Letters to YLO" section explained why she supported her husband in his work as a member of the Young Lords Organization.[29] "He wants his people to be free. . . . I am married to a Young Lord. Whether he is alive or dead I will be sure that our children will be taught to prepare themselves to fight as long as rights are threatened."[30] These women and the others who published in the newspapers were vocal in sharing their own frustrations about the status of their community, whether as mothers, partners, or community organizers.

Looking beyond the Young Lords' and the newspapers' political ideologies, it is crucial to acknowledge the historical importance of these particular publications and their indispensable relationship with a community silenced or misinterpreted by the mainstream press. These writings typically were penned by young Puerto Ricans who had experienced the inadequacies of city schools in meeting their needs, and who as adults had confronted the city's disregard for their demands regarding economic and housing disparities. Newspapers such as the *Chicago Tribune* and *Chicago Sun-Times* provided limited coverage of Puerto Ricans in the city. According to Cha Cha Jiménez, "The *Chicago Tribune* had a history of fabricating racist lies against Latinos, Blacks, Native Americans and other poor of this city."[31] So a generation of Puerto Ricans— many of whom were native Chicagoans who attended Chicago schools and lived Chicago's racial politics—felt a desperate need to create spaces where they could critically examine their own subjectivities while retaining a sense of cultural and community cohesiveness. Yet the Puerto Rican community was not homogeneous. Although various organizations and their print media outlets sought to remedy long-standing injustices within the city, they did not always agree on all issues. Internal community conflict sometimes played out in the pages of both the Young Lords' newspapers and *El Puertorriqueño*.

El Puertorriqueño

If the Young Lords' news service aimed to liberate a marginalized community, *El Puertorriqueño* sought to keep the community well informed. Founded in 1965, "*El Puertorriqueño* became an established institution in the Puerto Rican community, wielding enormous influence over the thinking of barrio residents."[32] Utilizing the resources and relationships of Chicago's Puerto Rican business community and the growing political presence of Puerto Ricans, the newspaper provided more than just a space for recounting the ongoing social ills plaguing Puerto Ricans. It marked the permanency of the community in a way that no other media outlet had done. Although politically less radical than the Young Lords' newspapers, *El Puertorriqueño* was outspoken on issues affecting local residents while providing valuable information on topics ranging from voting rights and schooling issues to local Puerto Rican beauty pageants. The newspaper "would note the needs, the pains, and the aspirations of the Puerto Rican newcomer who, in America, fought an arduous struggle for existence."[33] While recognizing the community's struggles and the role of local city government in Puerto Ricans' marginalization, it also provided aspiring businesses and middle-class residents a space in which to represent their own evolving identities and lay claim to the city as rightful inhabitants rather than foreign outsiders, as they were frequently viewed. However, it would be mistaken to assume that *El Puertorriqueño* evolved into an assimilationist tool seeking to transform the Puerto Rican residents into "acceptable," privileged individuals. In fact, its publisher and cofounder, Claudio Flores, readily offered financial support for several of the Young Lords' ventures, specifically trips to Puerto Rico, perhaps as a way to support their work on the island or as educational opportunities.[34] Instead, the newspaper created a sense of community cohesiveness that transcended class, gender, and the racial specificities that came to define Puerto Rican Chicago. It did so by recognizing Puerto Ricans' cultural distinctiveness (including using Spanish in the newspaper) and by maintaining a strong connection to the island. In fact, one of the newspaper's regular staff writers covered news from Puerto Rico, ranging from sports rivalries between Puerto Rican towns to the construction of new roads on the island. The paper thus closely linked islanders' lives to those of the new migrants in Chicago. Readers' appetite for such stories shows that even in Chicago, the island was never far from their minds.

Celebrating Puerto Rican culture and community members' accomplishments was a common theme in *El Puertorriqueño*. The front-page story on March 15, 1968, highlighted Flores's reappointment to the Chicago Commission on Human Relations, an organization that was instrumental in helping migrants during their early years in the city. Flores's regular column, "Ramas y Espinas" (Branches and thorns), focused on local matters, often questioning the exclusion of the community's own voice from issues regarding their well-being. His column also reported on the growing presence of both Puerto Ricans and Mexicans in Chicago, linking these two groups in the pages of the newspaper. The column provided essential information regarding Puerto Ricans' contributions and civic involvement in Chicago, but neither Flores's writing nor the newspaper itself exemplified the radicalism and grassroots activism that characterized the Young Lords and, to some extent, the post-

1966 Puerto Rican community. However, although this seemingly moderate Spanish-language newspaper catered to a different audience than the Young Lords' newspapers and benefited greatly from the resources of the Puerto Rican business elite, *El Puertorriqueño* provided valuable insight on issues affecting Puerto Ricans in Chicago, including police harassment, urban renewal, and schooling concerns.

In the May 31, 1968, issue, a story on the living conditions of forty-two Puerto Rican families shared the front page with the crowning of that year's preteen Puerto Rican beauty queen. Unlike the newly crowned queen, the forty-two families spent Puerto Rican Day not riding atop a parade float but instead dealing with their dilapidated, roach-infested living quarters and the possibility of losing their homes to demolition.[35] Likewise, in January 1970, the newspaper published an article about the rights of tenants suffering from inadequate heating, and also announced the year's "Reina del Congreso de Organizaciones Puertorriqueñas" (queen of the 1970 Puerto Rican Day Parade).[36] The juxtaposition of these types of events in Puerto Ricans' lives not only demonstrates the dissonances within the community itself but also indicates the gender dynamics at play within the newspaper's pages. Women, for the most part, were either mothers or beauty queens—and sometimes both.

Although the newspaper's founders and publishers and most of its writers were Puerto Rican men, one woman's frequent writings were a unique and sometimes controversial contribution to the newspaper. Whether informing residents about their voting rights or encouraging (if not demanding) parental accountability for their children's education, Trina Davila was quite vocal. In March 1968, she reminded Puerto Ricans of their responsibility to both the city and themselves by urging readers to participate in local elections by voting or seeking an elected position, rather than assuming that those in power would automatically work for the community's interests.[37] Davila pleaded with Puerto Ricans "to not be mute any longer, and for us to fight for that which belongs to us; a place of honor in this city in which we live."[38] She commonly advised and even reprimanded Puerto Ricans regarding their actions and responsibilities, going so far as to challenge some residents' status as "poor people." In a 1968 column, Davila claimed that, in her experience, the community had been offered many opportunities, but they had settled for a mediocre life.[39] Her boldness in addressing contentious topics sometimes prompted community members and other newspapers to question her motivations and loyalty to the community she purported to help. In an open letter to Davila in a 1969 issue of *YLO*, Young Lords member Cha Cha Jiménez wrote, "I respect your intelligence, your age, and your expressed concern for the Puerto Rican people. However, you create doubts in me and many of my brothers and sisters by the narrow one-sidedness of your editorials. . . . They're not lazy people. You try to work where they work and see. And as far as the law goes, when the laws serve poor people, then we will follow them, not when they enslave us."[40] These divergent views demonstrate that the community was confronting not only its status in Chicago but also the social hierarchy evident within the community itself. *El Puertorriqueño* provided a different kind of service to Puerto Ricans, often seen as a bit more conservative or limited than the information and activist role provided by the Young Lords' newspapers, but it did indeed serve the community. For both newcomers and long-time Chicago residents, *El Puertorriqueño* offered a sense of belonging, or home, in the burgeoning city. The paper's classified section and business advertisements informed residents about housing and employment opportunities, which was a crucial service in light of Puerto Ricans' troubled history in both markets. *El Puertorriqueño*, which was published until the 1980s (longer than any other Puerto Rican publication in the city), provides critical documentation of an emerging Puerto Rican identity and consciousness; its reach crossed ethnic and class divides, and it is essential for understanding the development and cultivation of print culture within marginalized communities.

El Puertorriqueño was an important resource for families seeking relevant information about city schools. It notified readers about events such as PTA meetings and class reunions, and it highlighted students' achievements as well as their struggles with the school system. Unlike the prevailing coverage of Puerto Rican students in mainstream newspapers, *El Puertorriqueño* celebrated and recognized the hard work and successes of students who negotiated their way through schools despite the education system's shortcomings. When twenty-four Latina/o students graduated from San Miguel High School on Division Street in 1968, the newspaper prominently featured them, captioning the accompanying image "Spanish Power."[41] The publication periodically featured a section, "Noticias Escolares" (School news), that informed readers about the work being done by parents, teachers, and other school officials to improve students' lives. The column also provided information about resources for parents, such as English language classes. A May 1968 feature titled "Un Puertorriqueño Ciudadano del Mes" (Puerto Rican Citizen of the Month) honored the scholastic and community contributions of José López, then a student at Tuley High School.[42] The article enthusiastically recognized López as the Chicago Board of Education's "Youth Citizen of the Month" and the winner of a scholarship to attend Loyola University in Chicago.[43]

Although *El Puertorriqueño* was less radical than the Young Lords' newspapers, it would be incorrect to say that it lacked political consciousness or merely accepted the plight of Puerto Ricans. It provided valuable information to the community in Spanish, making it accessible to a wider audience. Furthermore, it reported on community activism, but in a more impartial way than the almost "Gonzo journalism" style of the Young Lords' newspapers. For example, during the controversy over the construction of a new school to replace Tuley, *El Puertorriqueño*'s reporting on the issue placed the opinion of Los Caballeros de San Juan at the center of the debate and regarded its members as spokespeople for the community's needs and desires, omitting the voices of those outside Los Caballeros' ideologies or membership. A community outsider would likely view the newspaper's 1970 article "Caballeros Se Oponen a Tuley en El Parque" (Caballeros oppose Tuley in the park) as implying that the battle to "save" the park for the community was spearheaded solely by Los Caballeros and exclusively by men.[44] By then, Puerto Rican women led several local organizations, including Aspira of Illinois, and a Puerto Rican woman was the sole Latina/o representative on Chicago's Board of Education. But the newspaper often failed to recognize their efforts as active participants and community leaders. Articles celebrating women's achievements were mostly absent from *El Puertorriqueño*, except, of course, when the community crowned a new beauty queen.

As a Spanish-language Puerto Rican–run publication, *El Puertorriqueño* legitimized the role of local residents who worked diligently to create institutional changes to improve their daily lives. For parents, the newspaper provided indispensable information in Spanish addressing their rights and responsibilities in the schools, helping ensure that schools did not leave them out of decision-making. But as informative as the newspaper might have been in disseminating news about schooling and celebrating students' achievements, it remained critical of activism that, in its view, was too radical, and it maintained a rather conservative stance on labor unions. For instance, a front-page article in 1971 not only announced the end of the Chicago public schoolteachers' strike, but also denounced teachers for failing to put their students' welfare ahead of their own self-interest and desire for higher wages. It claimed that Chicago's teachers were the best paid in the nation and had no reason to strike against Daley and the city, leaving children as the victims of citywide power struggles.[45] In an editorial, the newspaper highlighted the Board of Education's ineffectiveness in providing adequate resources to meet teachers' needs and argued that teachers were justified in demanding higher wages.[46]

Davila's columns and Flores's editorials reinforced *El Puertorriqueño*'s inconsistent stance on teachers' strikes and labor unions. In a 1971 column titled

"Termina Huelga de Maestros" (Teacher strike ends), Davila wrote, "Another strike has ended in this city of many pollutions in which the many strikes are a part of that pollution. What have the children and parents gained? Promises that many times are not filled."[47] Davila characterized unions as selfish entities that had failed to serve the individuals whose financial support sustained unions and their leaders. Likewise, Flores maintained in a 1971 editorial that teachers had organized unions as a means to ensure their own rights and demands, but he also claimed that teachers had chosen the bureaucratic process over their responsibility to children: "The teachers' strike is not something from another world, but instead just another strike; but one with devastating effects because it undoubtedly complicates the lives and development of young children and youth."[48] However, these writers seem not to have had a blanket disdain for teachers' organizing efforts. Writing in March 1971, Davila encouraged the creation of "la Asociación de Maestros Hispanos" (the Hispanic Teachers' Association) in the hope of supporting the work of "Hispanic" teachers in Chicago schools, who she claimed had sacrificed themselves and had fought for their children.[49] Chicago's Latina/o teachers indeed faced their own obstacles in the public schools and the Chicago Teachers Union (CTU). In the *Chicago Tribune*'s editorial pages in January 1973, Latina/o teachers published a letter titled "Latino Teachers Protest," accusing the CTU of failing to move forward with a union study on teaching English as a second language and bilingual education, even though the study was nonbinding and made only "nonmonetary demands." According to the letter, "The Latino community has long been skeptical of the CTU's concern for the Latino teacher and student. This current action indicates clearly to Chicago's 250,000 Latino population that the priorities of the CTU and those of our community have very little in common."[50] In this instance, Davila's priorities reflected the concerns of Latino teachers, despite the rhetoric of her previous editorials. Although her views were not always aligned with teachers' needs and concerns, her columns brought to light the issues of the city's education system. The journal *The Rican* offered an interesting response to the troubled reality of the population.

The Rican: A Journal of Contemporary Puerto Rican Thought

Established in Chicago in 1971, *The Rican*, according to its inaugural issue, set out "to establish a literary communication to exact an appreciation of isolated and forgotten values, perceptions, visions and experiences of second and third generation Puerto Ricans."[51] As cofounder Samuel Betances recalled, "We had no experience; we didn't know how to run anything. There was a bunch of us, coming together deciding that they should cost a dollar. I don't know why they should cost a dollar, but we decided that that's what we ought to charge, that we should come out quarterly and what would we call it. We said, 'Let's find out what journal exists in New York, and then we'll figure out how to bring it to Chicago, and bring it to Harvard, and make it available to other people, and promote it.'"[52] While a student at Harvard University, Betances and other Puerto Rican students (some with ties to Chicago) decided on the name *The Rican*, "because it was a way of saying our roots are in Puerto Rico but [their] identity is in the United States."[53] *The Rican*, its West Coast counterpart *Aztlán*, and similar journals were instrumental in providing spaces where Latina/o scholars' intellectual and literary works could reach a larger audience, challenge ill-rooted and biased notions about their scholarship, and build relationships beyond their own geographic and ethnic locales. *The Rican* created an alternative to the Anglo-centered, heavily monolingual journals that dominated academic settings, creating sites of cultural expression for scholars of color who until then had gained representation in scholarly journals only through what Norma Alarcón has termed the "special issue syndrome."[54] Unlike *Aztlán*, published at UCLA, and similar journals, *The Rican* was not housed at a particular institution, so it did not receive institutional resources or funding. The scholars who established the journal had no institutional clout in Chicago with any university or organization. Although there was a small presence of Puerto Rican students, faculty, and staff at Northeastern Illinois University at the time, the school was not interested in sponsoring *The Rican* for fear that it would become a platform for leftist politics and ideologies. According to Betances, "There was nothing in the community that we could tie it to. And when Aspira flirted with it, they wanted to make it an Aspira vehicle. And maybe we should have gone that way. Looking back, I could have sat down with Toni Pantoja [Aspira's founder]. But there was nothing to attach it to. . . . No, this came out of Harvard. This came out of a very hungry group of intellectual kids—that's what we were. We were young, inexperienced."[55]

The masthead of *The Rican*'s inaugural issue named its publisher as "The Rican Journal, Inc.," with some issues in 1974 later credited to the "Midwest Institute of Puerto Rican Studies and Culture." Both entities were nonprofit educational organizations. For journals such as *The Rican* and other publications centering the voices of scholars from marginalized populations, it was important to safeguard their editorial independence, and that meant avoiding "making a single unit their institutional home."[56] Editorial independence allowed journals to look beyond the halls of academia for contributors and include up-and-coming writers, artists, and scholars. This freedom enabled *The Rican* to publish the works of local youth whose literary voices expressed their constant struggles not only as Puerto Ricans, but as young people of color, in communities that criminalized them and limited their participation in society as U.S. citizens and as students. In addition, it is possible that *The Rican*'s editorial independence made it more attractive to young intellectuals familiar with the city's political and racial realities. Those who had experienced or participated in educational activism might deliberately have chosen to avoid publishing their work in venues sponsored by the educational establishment that had failed to meet their needs.

The journal's choice not to limit itself to a specific regional locale reflected the need to forge literary, academic, and activist ties with other communities. Some of the early contributors to *The Rican* had community ties to Chicago. Their goal was to highlight the plight of Chicago's growing population of second- and third-generation Puerto Ricans and provide a venue where Puerto Ricans all over the country could share and learn from each other's struggles. Early in its history, *The Rican* also included contributions by and about Chicana/os, whose similar tales of educational and social injustices aligned them with their Puerto Rican counterparts. In the inaugural issue of the journal, Thomas Pérez's "Dialogue with a Chicano Student" chronicled the experiences of a student named Guillermo as he maneuvered his way through an "Anglo"-controlled school system that relegated him to the margins. Guillermo recalled, "We were always in a little damn thing over here, man. We always had all the shit, the stupid books, the broken crayons. Everybody seemed like they got the new ones, except us."[57] For Guillermo, as for many others during the 1960s and 1970s, the mere assertion of a Chicano identity was met with suspicion or dismissed by teachers. The lack of curricular materials that spoke to the cultural distinctiveness of Chicana/o and other Latina/o people similarly impeded the schooling of this population, who were not newcomers to American schools.

In an article titled "Puerto Ricans and Mexican Americans in Higher Education," which appeared in the May 1974 issue, Betances talked about the unrest experienced by Puerto Rican and Chicano students seeking access to higher education and demanded that institutions stop ignoring their needs.[58] As a one-time high school dropout who had become a Harvard graduate, Betances understood the urgent need to address the educational discrepancies affecting Puerto Rican students. Throughout its short publication history, *The Rican* included reports on the status of Puerto Rican students in the United

States and literary pieces by the schoolchildren scholars continued to discuss. In 1971, eighteen-year-old Edwin Claudio's poem "A Boycott" helped archive the rich history of Puerto Rican student activism and the painful reality that students faced daily.

> Like it happened:
> Ricans got together to say No to
> an unjust education which says
> you learn the anglo way of life
> > Can you dig?
> > > Wife swapping in nice
> > > Decent suburban homes.[59]

This "unjust education" and the story of Chicago's school walkouts was the story of Puerto Rican Chicago. Claudio spoke to the power of youth in their demand for an end to educational instruction aimed at "selling" them the so-called American way of life as a solution to their community's problems. Although mainstream media outlets in Chicago covered the community's struggle over Tuley High School and Clemente High School, they often omitted accounts by Puerto Rican youth. Claudio's writing provides a humanistic view of the fight for educational rights from one of the people most affected.

The inclusion of Claudio's and other students' voices in *The Rican* allows us to piece together striking accounts of the trauma surrounding their schooling and everyday lives, written by those living through it. The journal offered these youth a venue where they could be heard and seen by a nationwide audience. That audience included incarcerated Puerto Rican men and women who provided "blurbs" in support of the journal, which were published on the back covers of some of the issues. In the words of one of these blurbists, the journal was "most relevant to our people's struggle. . . . We are trying to find these valuable materials that are so far from within our reach."[60] This wide reach was not the norm for other academic journals, most of which represented a particular academic discipline and voice and were neither written nor read by people outside those fields or behind prison walls. The journal's inclusion of incarcerated men and women acknowledged the existence of this population, recognizing them as actors in the community's efforts instead of consigning them to irrelevance.

Although grounded in its commitment to provide a platform for sharing the ideologically charged views and concerns of local community members, *The Rican* provided a space for those engaging in scholarship centered on the needs and stories of the communities from which they emerged. Indeed, the journal helped create the field of Puerto Rican studies, with seminal works by significant scholars such as Edna Acosta-Belen, Frank Bonilla, and Isidro Lucas.[61] *The Rican* not only created a space in which to place scholars in conversation with one another, but it also validated the lived experiences of youth and other community members who contributed written pieces about their daily realities, addressing topics such as substandard schooling, racism, identity problems, language issues, and the island's political status. During this era, university students and faculty, especially those from marginalized populations, entered into conversations about the need for academic programs devoted to the historical specificities of Black, Puerto Rican, Chicana/o, and Indigenous populations. *The Rican* provided a publishing venue for intellectual contributions by and for the community, in the hope that those contributions would find their way into classrooms at postsecondary institutions.

The Rican's educational impulse reflects Betances's experiences with Chicago's education system and his recognition of the need to address its inequalities. Betances had advocated for improved education as a response to the 1966 community uprising.[62] The journal he cofounded and edited gave young people a creative outlet for voicing their continual struggles with the schools. An untitled play published in the journal, written by seventh- and eighth-grade students at Chicago's Chopin Upper Grade Center, captures the daily interactions between teachers and students. In the first scene, the main character, Pedro, is sent to the principal's office following a dispute with his teacher.

PEDRO: I wasn't doing anything

MR. HERMAN: That's what you said the last time.

PEDRO: Mr. _____ doesn't teach anything. All he does is say shut up or keep quiet.

MR. HERMAN: But what you don't seem to understand is that a teacher cannot teach when students are running around the room or talking too much.

PEDRO: But that's what usually happens.

MR. HERMAN: I think you are blaming the problem on everyone else except yourself. You have to respect your teachers. They are here to teach you.

PEDRO: They can't teach, man.[63]

Placing blame on the student absolved educators of responsibility for Puerto Rican students' unease in urban schools. Although this account is fictional, it seems safe to assume that the students spoke from experience, an experience shared by students enrolled in higher education and writing about their postsecondary lives.

Que Ondee Sola

Established in 1972 as a student newspaper at Northeastern Illinois University, *Que Ondee Sola* was born out of "a dire need for self-expression and a lack of productive relevant communication in the society in which we live."[64] A committee of students from the Union for Puerto Rican Students founded the newspaper, seeing a need for a publication to report on current events relevant to Puerto Ricans and other minorities, share creative projects by students, and educate others about Puerto Rican history. Central to the newspaper's early mission was fostering a public space where underrepresented students could articulate their growing concerns, especially regarding their relationship with school administrators. Once again, the print media gave Puerto Ricans a forum for challenging long-standing misconceptions and assumptions about their role in the city's evolving politics, whether in schools or as community members. Although *Que Ondee Sola* was a campus newspaper, its student writers and editors took seriously their responsibility to the overall community, dedicating time and space to the relationship between schools and Puerto Ricans in Chicago, including the experiences of their younger counterparts at Tuley and Clemente High Schools.

In *Que Ondee Sola*'s inaugural issue, the editors' column declared that "a situation of the utmost concern in the Puerto Rican community today is the failure of desperately needed progress to have materialized. Most of this failure can be attributed to the educational system because . . . in most instances the system has been directly involved in developing a lack of self-identity in our children by alienating them from their original culture."[65] The student writers' awareness of the connection between schools and Puerto Rican youth identity reflected their own relationship with city schools and recalls Isidro Lucas's work on Puerto Rican students. Many Northeastern students had experienced the everyday challenges of attending schools that were ill-equipped to educate them or uninterested in doing so. The newspaper mirrored the concerns of many community members about Puerto Rican students' status, their "alarming drop-out rate," and the dearth of Puerto Rican teachers and administrators, especially in Puerto Rican–majority schools.[66] These concerns and students' frustration with what they saw as Northeastern's lack of sensitivity toward their needs fueled conversations within the pages of the newspaper. As in *The Rican*, *El Puertorriqueño*, and the Young Lords' publications, these conversations took place through editorial pieces, exposés, and personal creative pieces written by students.

Que Ondee Sola regularly chronicled the everyday contributions of Puerto Rican scholars, writers, and artists, as well as the potential benefits of Puerto

Rican studies curricula. As one writer stated, "It is insanity to the utmost degree to interpret the values and customs of one culture by the values and conceptions of another."[67] An article in the January 1972 issue reported that members of the Union for Puerto Rican Students had organized a group of delegates to visit colleges and universities on the East Coast to observe their Puerto Rican studies programs and courses.[68] The following month, the newspaper advocated for the creation of a Puerto Rican studies program: "it can become a reality with the help and cooperation of faculty members and the general student body."[69] Like *El Puertorriqueño* and the Young Lords' newspapers, *Que Ondee Sola* acknowledged and celebrated other Puerto Rican–run print materials. Student writers praised the work of Puerto Rican contributors to *The Rican*, even providing space in the newspaper to promote the sale of the journal, whose editor, Samuel Betances, had been an instructor at Northeastern. Edwin Claudio, whose poem "A Boycott" had appeared in *The Rican* in 1971 when he was in high school, had become a student at Northeastern. In *Que Ondee Sola*, he wrote about the importance of an intellectual forum to aid in dispelling the dominant biased views about Puerto Ricans.[70] The journal, Claudio wrote, gave readers a diverse set of views and experiences, "clearing the smog with a combination of writers who are on different intellectual plains [sic] from college professors to Puerto Rican high schoolers."[71]

In addition to supporting the writings of other Puerto Ricans, *Que Ondee Sola* acknowledged the works and struggles of other students of color at the university. Although it was adamant about its mission to write for and about Puerto Ricans, its student writers also engaged with relevant issues pertaining to other marginalized and oppressed populations. The newspaper regularly documented the struggles that both students and community members faced in their daily lives, from informing readers about Cesar Chavez and the growing migrant farmworker movement to reporting on racial violence aimed at Black and Puerto Rican students. It also published announcements of campus and community events organized by Black students at Northeastern, in one case congratulating them on working together to produce a dramatic performance about their African roots.[72] The Union regularly invited guests to campus to speak about the shared struggles of other groups and used the newspaper to promote the events. At one event, guest speaker Vernon Bellecourt, a Native American activist, addressed the need to "unify latino struggles with Native American struggles," since Puerto Ricans were also "of Indian origin," and thus both were Indigenous communities.[73] Similarly, student writers utilized the newspaper to confront the prevalent racism at the university: "Racial prejudice runs rampant in the halls of Northeastern. . . .

One need not to look any further to witness White Supremacy functioning perfectly."[74] Incidents of racial violence and intolerance against students at Northeastern persisted, and *Que Ondee Sola* reported on alleged attacks on Puerto Rican and Black students. Student writers documented what they saw as the mistreatment of a Black student senator by a white peer and described an incident in which white male students threw food on Puerto Rican students in the school's cafeteria.[75] "These incidents," reported Claudio, "have increased the tension of race relations."[76]

In August 1972, student writers attempted to link these tensions to the tragic shooting death of a white Northeastern instructor at the hands of an African American student, Nathaniel Allen, who then took his own life.[77] Students argued that the shooting was not merely a disagreement over a course grade but a direct consequence of "racially discriminatory actions which have been occurring at Northeastern for quite some time now."[78] Regardless of the reason, Allen's classmates wanted to remember him as they had known him and celebrate his love for his Black community. One student wrote, "Nate was about love among the human race and Black love and togetherness among his Black sisters and brothers. . . . he had accomplished his mission of spreading Black love among his people."[79] The newspaper also featured stories on local Puerto Rican men who fell victim to gun violence, including Orlando Quintana, a Northeastern graduate employed as a youth worker for a local organization serving Puerto Rican residents, who was fatally shot in July 1973 by an off-duty Chicago police officer during an alleged robbery.[80] Northeastern students and community members called that allegation false. Claiming that the Chicago Police Department was covering for a colleague who was under the influence of alcohol when he killed Quintana, *Que Ondee Sola* reprinted an excerpt from a bulletin published by the Puerto Rican Socialist Party in which the shooting was described as an "assassination" and "part of a genocidal plan to end with Puerto Ricans."[81] Student writers used the shooting death to call attention to the daily battles waged against Puerto Ricans, both in Chicago and on the island, claiming that "behind all of this is a plan to crush the growing struggle in our community and in Puerto Rico."[82] The newspaper regularly reminded readers about both historical and contemporary accounts of these struggles, accounts that it asserted were absent from the curriculum of the current education system.

The newspaper repeatedly pointed out connections between the status of Puerto Ricans in schools and communities, the history of colonialism on the island, and the exclusion of Puerto Ricans from schools' curricula. Student writers advocated for the creation of courses on Puerto Rican history and literature and the development of a Puerto Rican studies program. But instead of waiting for such courses to be developed, *Que Ondee Sola* took it upon itself to highlight Puerto Rican culture and history for its readership. A Puerto Rican studies program, according to the newspaper, would help undo the damage inflicted on Puerto Ricans via the education system; it would "create a sense of Puerto Rican self-determination and self-identity" and "teach the culture, history and social development of the Puerto Rican masses, which has been ignored by the present white educational system."[83] *Que Ondee Sola*'s pages were filled with articles detailing the history of colonialism in Puerto Rico and the struggle for Puerto Rican independence, and the newspaper advocated for dialogue regarding the status of both islanders and those residing across the diaspora. Each year on the anniversary of Grito de Lares, a Puerto Rican rebellion that took place in 1868, the newspaper educated new students about the importance of this first battle for the island's independence.[84] Similarly, it informed readers about key historical Puerto Rican figures and events, including Ramon Betances, Segundo Ruiz Belvis, Pedro Albizu Campos, and the Ponce massacre.[85] However, *Que Ondee Sola* differed from its counterparts—*El Puertorriqueño*, the Young Lords' newspapers, and *The Rican*—in its greater inclusion of writing by and about women. It would be inaccurate to say that issues pertaining to women were central to the newspaper's mission or that women and men were equally represented on the writing staff. Nevertheless, Puerto Rican women had a considerable presence in the newspaper, even if their voices sometimes served to remind their male peers of the need to support them and their causes.

An article from December 1972, "La Mujer Puertorriqueña en la Lucha" (The Puerto Rican woman in the struggle), chronicled the life works of women such as Luisa Capetillo, Julia de Burgos, Blanca Canales, and Lolita Lebrón.[86] The author wrote, "Entre aquellas mujeres que han aportado vastos meritos a la causa revolucionaria" (Among these women there are many merits contributed to the revolutionary cause), reminding readers of women's crucial role in the fight for Puerto Rican independence and the sacrifices they made for the community.[87] *Que Ondee Sola* also addressed social issues affecting Puerto Rican women and worked to educate readers about matters such as sterilization and sexual violence. In one such article, the newspaper reported on sterilization abuse among women on the island; according to some reports, by the 1970s, one-third of women in Puerto Rico had undergone sterilization.[88] Women members of the Union contributed articles reminding their male colleagues of the importance of supporting women's needs, but they also wrote to defend their own participation in the movement for women's rights. "Many of our brothers see the woman's movement as a vehicle to entrench and strengthen the majority cultures' dominance. Yet we may sometimes ask, 'Is it your *real* fear, my brother, that I be used against our movement? Or is it that I will assume a position, a stance that you are neither prepared nor willing to deal with?'"[89] As women of color, these writers recognized their difficulties in confronting both the gender politics within the Puerto Rican community and the implicit racial politics of the larger women's movement, reflected in their relationships and struggles with white women. Women members of the Union called for Third World women to become more aware of their needs and struggles and avoid emulating models of resistance created by groups of people who historically had oppressed and marginalized them as women of color. "The 3rd world woman will fight for her right to uniquiness [*sic*]—We will not be absorbed!"[90] Such writings challenged dominant gendered readings of the struggle for Puerto Rican independence and justice while making it clear to the men that *libertad* for Puerto Ricans had to include justice for Puerto Rican women as well. The informative historical articles about the significant contributions of women like Lolita Lebrón reminded men that women were part of the story.

In addition to advocating for a program devoted to Puerto Rican studies, reporting on the various struggles with school administrators, and inform-ing readers about historical figures and social movements, *Que Ondee Sola* promoted an overhaul of an education system that it saw as perpetuating "the concept that Puerto Ricans are an inferior race."[91] According to one article, the responsibility for dismantling the oppressive education system fell on Puerto Rican students and educators, whom the newspaper urged to pool their resources to achieve real institutional change. The article backed the notion that Puerto Rican teachers should teach Puerto Rican children and stated that teachers "must deal with this problem through the creation of an educational system, which is functional to the needs of the Puerto Rican community."[92] The writer argued that only Puerto Rican educators would understand the needs of Puerto Rican children and be invested in their well-being. Aida Sanchez, a former Tuley High School student writing in *Que Ondee Sola*, acknowledged the long-term effects of her educational experience. She expressed anger at the school system and administrators for allowing what she saw as incapable people to "teach" at the high school. For Tuley students, she wrote, "Any past educational experience has left vis-ible scars," painful memories, and recollections of a "bad education . . .," many times making it hard for the ex-Tuley students to survive in college."[93] Sanchez conceded that she had not personally had any battles with Herbert Fink when he was the principal, but she said she understood community members' actions in seeking his ouster and asserted that his poor leadership had allowed Puerto Rican students' situation to become so dire, citing the extraordinarily high dropout rate and low exam scores.[94] In May 1972, *Que Ondee Sola* published a letter addressed to "our high school students," written by one of their peers at Northeastern, Edwin Claudio. He called on the high school students to confront a system that ignored their needs and denied them a sense of their own history, but pointed out that "support on the picket line" was just the beginning.[95] Change, Claudio claimed, required more than boycotts; it was necessary to make the entire community aware of why change in schools and community was needed in the first place.

For students at Northeastern, *Que Ondee Sola* was a much-needed outlet. The newspaper gave them the opportunity to advocate for the needs of Puerto Ricans and other students of color at their university and to remind readers, including the larger community, of the complicated relationship between Puerto Ricans and education. In continuing to cover the growing tensions at schools like Tuley and Clemente, Northeastern students demonstrated their recognition that they could and should use their status and opportunities as university students to work toward transformative change for their community. It is important to note that some of the students involved in both the newspaper and the Union later become both community and political leaders, both locally and nationally.[96] *Que Ondee Sola* was the first platform for future leaders to envision and articulate the possibility of change for their own community.

Reading a Community

When Puerto Rican migration to Chicago began in the 1940s and 1950s, public discourse about Puerto Ricans was initially welcoming, although not necessarily accepting. Over the next few decades, however, the welcoming tone shifted, and popular rhetoric about the Puerto Rican community regarded them more as a problem to be solved than as guests to be greeted. This shift coincided with the rapid growth of the city's Puerto Rican population and the community's development of relationships with Mexican and Black residents. Puerto Ricans' relationships with other (and othered) communities were well documented within the pages of the publications discussed in this chapter. These publications not only allowed a space for the dissemination of information and valuable resources aimed at Puerto Ricans and other Latina/os but also solidified the creation, maintenance, and evolution of Puerto Rican identities. The community's sometimes conflicting agendas and ideologies played out in these publications, demonstrating the complicated particularities of the group's identity. Moreover, the texts provide insightful

Figure 2. Cover of *YLO* 1, no. 2 (May 1969). Young Lords Organization, Ministry of Information. Special Collections and Archives, DePaul University Library, Chicago IL, ylo-v1n2-p001.

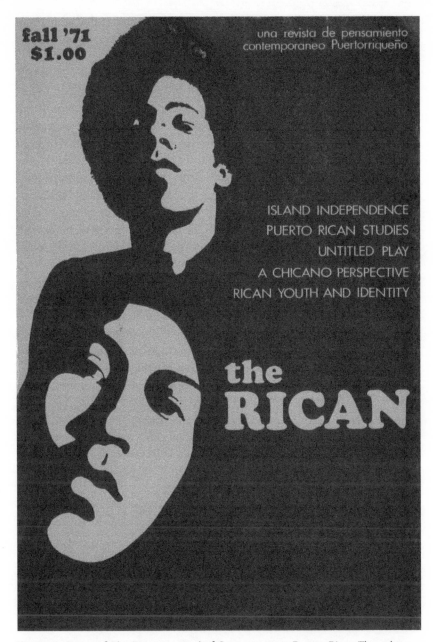

Figure 3. Cover of *The Rican: Journal of Contemporary Puerto Rican Thought,* no. 1 (Fall 1971). Chicago: Midwest Institute of Puerto Rican Studies and Culture Inc.

narratives about Puerto Ricans' lives in the city, narratives that sometimes conflict with each other and that often contradict the mainstream media's narrow and problematic depictions of Puerto Ricans.

Puerto Ricans on both the island and the U.S. mainland have historically utilized the press to critically engage within and across communities, to disseminate valuable information, and to build community. For Puerto Rican students specifically, their publications made their growing needs visible, unlike more traditional media, which often denied them a voice or even portrayed them as troubled or criminal. In the late 1960s and 1970s, the mainstream media frequently blamed students for their tumultuous relationship with Chicago's school system, failing to recognize the schools' discriminatory practices. The development of these print materials speaks to their important role in developing community for those in constant turmoil. With respect to print culture in Chicana feminist spaces, Maylei Blackwell situates "print community modes of production [as] a crucial site of historical inquiry helping us to understand the development of Chicana feminist ideology, discourse, and political praxis in a way that accounts for how ideas traveled through local formations as well as larger cross-regional circulations."[97] *El Puertorriqueño*, *The Rican*, *Que Ondee Sola*, and the Young Lords' newspapers are central to the history of Chicago's Puerto Ricans. They illustrate how Puerto Ricans viewed their own lives; whether as students, activists, workers, middle-class citizens, business owners, or political leaders, all had a valid history and a valid claim to space. These print publications marked a unique Chicago Puerto Rican identity and fueled Puerto Rican Chicagoans' quest for social justice and recognition—a quest that came to define a generation of Puerto Rican activists and students, but most importantly, a community.

Conclusion

Winning Means Hope

ON JUNE 4, 1977, Division Street looked very familiar to some members of the Humboldt Park community. On the day of the now-annual Puerto Rican Day Parade in Chicago, the community was once again set to ignite. Festival attendees enjoying the day in Humboldt Park were caught up in a violent battle, but no one could quite agree on how it had begun. Some witnesses claimed that a fight between rival gangs had been exacerbated by police officers' reaction to it. The resulting bloodshed left three men dead and dozens of people injured, in addition to causing thousands of dollars in damages across the community. Two of the deaths were the result of gunfire, with a third attributed to the riot, as the body of Domingo Torres was found among the ruins of a building that had allegedly been set on fire by rioters.[1] The June 1977 uprising followed years of economic decline and an increase in the incidence of arson across Humboldt Park. In contrast to the June 1966 uprising, according to Gina Peréz, the 1977 violence "demoralized an already weary community faced with rising unemployment, increased poverty, and sustained political marginalization."[2] Police and community members pointed fingers at each other as they grappled with the question of who, exactly, was responsible for the shooting deaths of the two young men in Humboldt Park.

Police claimed that after a gang fight broke out during the festival, they were fired upon while pursuing a suspect, Julio Osorio.[3] Officers believed that in the ensuing gunfire, Osorio fatally wounded community member Rafael Cruz before being fatally wounded himself by police. But some witnesses claimed that the police were responsible for the deaths of both men.[4] By coincidence, shortly before the disturbance at the park, a bomb exploded at the Cook County Building in downtown Chicago. Members of the local chapter of the Puerto Rican independence group Fuerzas Armadas de Liberación Nacional Puertorriqueña took credit for the blast. Although no one was injured in the bombing, it caused thousands of dollars in damages, keeping police busy that day with the investigation.[5] Community members and police were in agreement that the two events were not directly connected, although some community members believed that the bombing caused the police to react more forcefully to the festival disturbance. Lawyers for the families of two of the men who were killed alleged that the police initiated the unrest by questioning and harassing festival attendees about the bombing, "behav[ing] in an insulting, intimidating manner, causing a good deal of anger and tension among people in the park."[6] Other witnesses claimed that officers fired directly at a group of rioters who threw bottles and other debris at police.[7] The community was once again at a crossroads. According to one journalist, Humboldt Park was "a troubled 'island' without any clout," whose people continually had to remind outsiders that they were citizens and that they had experienced this turmoil once before.[8]

The 1977 uprising highlighted the Puerto Rican community's feelings of neglect at the hands of city officials, who had done little to improve their neighborhood and their lives after the 1966 Division Street uprising. In 1966, the responses had included promises of more employment, housing, and schooling opportunities, but 1977 reminded the city that most such opportunities had failed to materialize, except those for which the community itself had organized and fought. Once again, schools and education were front and center in the response to the unrest. And once again, community members and advocates told the city that its response needed to move beyond the provision of English language programs. One such advocate was Dr. Juan Cruz, the head of the Chicago Board of Education's Bilingual Education Program. He maintained that some of the fault lay with teachers who failed to help Puerto Rican students develop their full potential.[9] Another ally, who worked with youth gangs in Chicago, saw Chicago teachers as "putting in their time" and not connecting with their students' culture, with the result that "a large number of these kids aren't getting anything out of school."[10] These were the same concerns that Isidro Lucas had expressed in the early 1970s in his research on Puerto Rican dropouts and Puerto Rican students' educational disengagement.[11]

There were times when the lack of adequate schooling for Puerto Ricans in Chicago united an ideologically divided population, but at other times the schooling challenges exacerbated existing conflicts. David Tyack reminds us that when people deliberate their youths' education, they are debating the future of the nation.[12] In Chicago, the schooling of young Puerto Ricans was intertwined with the community's politically charged development. Community leaders, school administrators, and parents engaged in ongoing debates about the purposes and outcomes of students' education, as was clearly demonstrated in the struggles for Tuley and Clemente High Schools. U.S. schools have always been affected by disparities in resource allocation, resulting in educational injustices. According to educational historian James D. Anderson, the limitations experienced by generations of schoolchildren were "the main community issue around which different people could rally to promote achievement, equality, and the promise of the American dream."[13] Youth of color historically have been denied the opportunity and the right to become active participants in improving their educational lives and bringing their social realities to light, unless they engage in acts of resistance within schools. In the struggle for control of Tuley and Clemente, the actions of numerous and sometimes conflicting organizations demonstrated "the many heroic and subtle forms of resistance exercised by marginalized youth to create new possibilities."[14] But what opportunities would Chicago schools offer Puerto Rican students in the decades following the 1970s? That remained an open question.

In Chicago, the relationship between community and schools has long been inescapable, especially because of its history of ethnic enclaves and activism. A community and its schools are each systematically altered by what occurs or is denied in the other. For Puerto Ricans, schools became sites where they could challenge the racial politics that plagued their children's lives. The case of Puerto Ricans in Chicago reflects the notion that for groups of people facilitating change via their social movements, they in turn produce social structures that enable them to improve their quality of life. To understand Chicago's Puerto Ricans, it is imperative to historicize the lives of this community as they maneuvered their way within the city and its ever-changing racial landscape. But it is also crucial that we begin to examine the "historical baggage" that Chicago's Puerto Ricans have been forced to unpack for decades. We can start to understand how little space lies between the island and Chicago when we examine Puerto Ricans' transition from colonial subjects whose education was infused with ideologies of control, to community members exerting their rights and privileges as citizens. Puerto Ricans' agency in Chicago was at times limited, but their influence and mark would remain permanently.

The status and identity of Chicago's Puerto Ricans in the mid-twentieth century was influenced by their constant displacement and the myriad ways in which their own identities depended on constructs of space, place, and history. In interrogating spaces such as the city of Chicago, we must understand how they are envisioned and therefore shaped by those who live in them and those who seek to change them. If we consider schooling spaces in the same way, we are better able to recognize how issues such as redistricting and busing threatened the rootedness of Chicago's Puerto Rican students and thereby shifted the racial landscape of their spaces and identities. Puerto Ricans' claims to the city and their repeated displacement from their neighborhoods became a part of their identity that continues today. The history or story of Puerto Rican Chicago tells us how the community fought not only for a *physical community* but also for a *sense of community*, with their school activism tied to their own survival. Through their creation of and participation in print culture and media, the community similarly created a space in which they could articulate their own lives on their own terms. Their vision of who they are as a people and where they hope to be is very much part of that narrative. The Puerto Rican community's constant movement across the city complicates not only our understanding of how such spaces are produced, but also the performativity that goes along with it, as community members found alternative ways to produce space with their new occupations and their own cultural and social practices. The urgency with which the city of Chicago acted upon Puerto Ricans speaks to this power dynamic, which at times left the population no choice but to challenge dominant forces through community activism. Gaining control of their community's schooling gave them a sense of hope that benefited them for decades to come.

We learn our own value and worth through our interactions in family homes, schools, and other institutions, and these "places are centers of felt value" where our needs come to be satisfied.[15] Regardless of whether our experiences are positive, these places are where we face and contend with the limitations they may represent. For Puerto Ricans, as for other marginalized groups, their move to and growth within U.S. cities forced them to reimagine their sense of home, self, and community within new spaces and the reality they represented. Their schooling experiences within their new communities strongly influenced their initial relationship with the United States, as did their status as involuntary minorities within the U.S. social structure.[16] Puerto Ricans' relationship to U.S. schools replicates their relationship to the United States as a conquered and colonized people. To paraphrase research on voluntary and involuntary minorities by John U. Ogbu and Herbert D. Simmons, the differences between schools and their marginalized populations "may lie in the differences in their community forces."[17] Schools are places that create and strengthen community.[18] Especially for Puerto Rican women, as mothers and as community leaders, schools were a site where they became part of the story in the struggle for access to education. Education was, and continues to be, a community affair. And in the city of Chicago, the community organized to claim a fair and equal education for their children, despite the institutional and institutionalized forces that sought to limit their access, thus limiting their lives.

A Promise of Simple Justice

A 1983 report on the status of school desegregation in Chicago had an interesting title: *A Promise of Simple Justice in the Education of Chicago School Children?* According to the report, Chicagoans' quality of life should not be measured merely by economic, crime, housing, or transportation statistics; rather, "Chicago's future must also be measured by the achievement of its public school children."[19] This simple justice, sought not just by Puerto Rican students but by African American and Mexican American students as well, inspired a generation of school-centered activism in the city. Public schools in Chicago had long been characterized by their racial isolation. Because the school system was based on neighborhood schools, schools reflected the racial and ethnic segregation of the neighborhoods they served. According to one account, "official restrictive covenants, and neighborhood school policies established to be consistent with them, worked to contain blacks and other minorities in specified areas of the city," and by 1956, 91 percent of elementary schools and 71 percent of high schools were single-race schools.[20] White flight from Chicago neighborhoods and public schools led to increased school segregation, despite policies initiated by the Board of Education following the Hauser Committee Report of 1964, which further called for school desegregation.[21] The school uprisings of the late 1960s and the 1970s reflected a sense of hopelessness among Chicago's students, teachers, and community members as schooling inequities continued to affect their lives. In the late 1970s, both the Illinois Board of Education and the U.S. Department of Health, Education, and Welfare reiterated the notion that inequality was still a problem in Chicago's education system, validating the decades-long claims of Chicago's Puerto Rican, African American, and Mexican American communities. After the Illinois Board of Education in 1976 informed the Chicago Board of Education that it had failed to comply with the state's rules about desegregation, the latter adopted a plan called "Access to Excellence," which aimed to "achieve compliance through a program of voluntary desegregation."[22] But in 1979, the U.S. Department of Health, Education, and Welfare rejected the Chicago board's request for federal funding, on the grounds that it continued to practice discrimination by assigning particular children to particular schools, and placed the board under investigation for possible violations of the Civil Rights Act of 1964.[23] The threat of a lawsuit forced the Board of Education to acknowledge the existence of the racial isolation that had long been felt by Chicago's Black and Latina/o students, without necessarily taking responsibility for the segregation of students.[24] The ensuing consent decree in 1980 focused on both desegregation efforts and increasing achievement among the district's most marginalized students. Regrettably, these changes would come too late to remedy the disastrous educational lives of the students who had fought in the 1960s and 1970s for simple justice. However, perhaps those students found a sense of accomplishment in the knowledge that their work and their stories had finally made a difference to future generations of students.

Puerto Ricans across the United States have long utilized their political capital as Latina/os with voting rights and their experience with the creation and maintenance of local and national organizations promoting achievement and equality for themselves and others. Locally, groups such as Los Caballeros de San Juan, the Spanish Action Committee of Chicago, Aspira, and the many student-led organizations set the stage for a social movement to transform Puerto Ricans' educational lives and demand justice. Sonia Nieto powerfully expresses Puerto Ricans' long-standing struggles and desire for change: "Although schools can do little to remove barriers related to poverty, they can create space where students can learn at high levels and demonstrate the tremendous promise that they have. When that happens, we will all be the winners."[25] But when Puerto Ricans in Chicago began to question their living conditions in the 1940s and beyond, they realized that without a viable way to improve their circumstances, life in the city would continue to be a harsh reality. Schools soon emerged as a site where Puerto Ricans could work together to confront their marginalized status. Speaking on the Tuley High School struggles, the Reverend Joseph Fitzharris summarized it best: "This is a community of hopeless people. . . . So the Tuley thing . . . well, it gave the people a chance to win something. And winning means hope."[26]

Notes

Abbreviations

CBE	Chicago Board of Education Archives
CHM	Chicago History Museum
FLMM	Employment and Migration Bureau, Fundacion Luis Muñoz Marin
LCC	Rafael Cintrón Ortiz Latino Cultural Center Archives
NEIUSC	Northeastern Illinois University Special Collections
UICSC	University of Illinois at Chicago Special Collections
WCMC Records	Welfare Council of Metropolitan Chicago Records, 1914–1978

Introduction

1. For more, see Elena Padilla, "Puerto Rican Immigrants in New York and Chicago: A Study in Comparative Assimilation" (master's thesis, University of Chicago, 1947); and Felix M. Padilla, *Puerto Rican Chicago* (Notre Dame, IN: University of Notre Dame Press, 1987).

2. Sonia Nieto, "Fact and Fiction: Stories of Puerto Ricans in U.S. Schools," *Harvard Educational Review* 68, no. 2 (Summer 1998): 133.

3. *Coloniality* refers to the matrix of power that is the consequence or living embodiment of the legacy of colonialism that remains in contemporary society after those colonial powers are dismantled. It functions in a particular way in the Americas and across Africa, leaving the former colonial spaces to contend with different aspects of those "relationships," whether politically, economically, or socially. For more information, see Anibal Quijano, "Coloniality of Power, Eurocentrism, and Latin America," *Nepantla: Views from South* 1, no. 3 (2000): 533–80.

4. M. G. Brumbaugh, in *Report of the Commissioner of Education for Porto Rico to*

the Secretary of the Interior, U. S. A., 1901 (Washington, DC: GPO, 1901), 73. American officials used the anglicized spelling "Porto Rico" in official documents and records from 1898, when it was used in the Treaty of Paris, until 1931, when Congress passed a joint resolution to change the spelling back to the Spanish "Puerto Rico," as was commonly used by islanders. See House Committee on Insular Affairs, "Correct the Spelling of the Name of the Island of Porto Rico," February 20, 1932, H. Rep. 585, 72nd Cong., 1st sess., 2.

5. Solsiree del Moral, *Negotiating Empire: The Cultural Politics of Schools in Puerto Rico, 1898–1952* (Madison: University of Wisconsin Press, 2013), 36.

6. Ibid.

7. "Bilandic, Latinos, Meet about Riots: Bilandic Meets Humboldt Leaders," *Chicago Tribune*, June 7, 1977, 1.

8. Richard Vission, "School Community Group Takes On Bd. of Ed.," *Lincoln Park Press*, March 1969, 4.

9. Jason G. Irizarry and René Antrop-González, "RicanStructuring the Discourse and Promoting School Success: Extending a Theory of Culturally Responsive Pedagogy for DiaspoRicans," *Centro: Journal of the Center for Puerto Rican Studies* 19, no. 2 (2007): 36–60; Irizarry and Antrop-González, "RicanStruction Sites: Race, Space, and Place in the Education of DiaspoRican Youth," *Taboo: The Journal of Culture and Education* 13, no. 1 (2013): 7.

10. Guy V. Henry, "Americanizing Porto Rico," *The Independent*, June 1, 1899, 1475.

11. *Report of Brig. Gen. Geo. W. Davis, U.S.V., on Civil Affairs of Puerto Rico: 1899* (Washington, DC: GPO, 1900), 180.

12. Victor Selden Clark, *Teachers' Manual for the Public Schools of Puerto Rico* (New York: Silver, Burdett and Company, 1900), 20.

13. Ibid., 20–22.

14. Del Moral, *Negotiating Empire*, 183.

15. J. F. McGrath, "The Public Schools and the Assimilation and Americanization of the Immigrant," *Journal of Education* 72, no. 22 (1910): 600.

16. Frank Cody, "Americanization Courses in the Public Schools," *English Journal* 7, no. 10 (1918): 616.

17. Ibid.

18. Noriko Asato, "Mandating Americanization: Japanese Language Schools and the Federal Survey of Education in Hawai'i, 1916–1920," *History of Education Quarterly* 43, no. 1 (2003): 10–38.

19. Cliff Stratton, *Education for Empire* (Berkeley: University of California Press, 2016), 2.

20. Thomas C. Holt, "Marking: Race, Race-Making, and the Writing of History," *American Historical Review* 100, no. 1 (1995): 15.

21. Juan José Osuna, *A History of Education in Puerto Rico* (New York: Arno Press, 1949), 123.

22. Brumbaugh, in *Report of the Commissioner of Education for Porto Rico, 1901*, 72.

23. For more on the Americanization practices in Puerto Rican schools, see Aida

Negrón de Montilla, "Americanization in Puerto Rico and the Public School System, 1900–1930" (PhD diss., New York University, 1970). Some of the items incorporated into the curriculum were attempts to impose the celebration of American holidays not observed in Puerto Rico prior to the colonization of the island by the United States, attempts to transfer the content of American courses of study to the curricula of Puerto Rican schools, and attempts to organize patriotic exercises aimed at promoting allegiance to and emulation of the United States.

24. For more information, see Pedro A. Malavet, *America's Colony: The Political and Cultural Conflict between the United States and Puerto Rico* (New York: New York University Press, 2004); Pedro A. Cabán, *Constructing a Colonial People: Puerto Rico and the United States, 1898–1932* (Boulder, CO: Westview Press, 2018); and Arlene M. Dávila, *Sponsored Identities: Cultural Politics in Puerto Rico* (Philadelphia: Temple University Press, 1997).

25. Clark, *Teachers' Manual*, 18.

26. Vicki L. Ruiz, *From Out of the Shadows* (Oxford: Oxford University Press, 1999).

27. Carlos K. Blanton, *The Strange Career of Bilingual Education in Texas, 1836–1981* (College Station: Texas A&M University Press, 2004), 70.

28. Zaragosa Vargas, *Proletarians of the North: A History of Mexican Industrial Workers in Detroit and the Midwest, 1917–1933* (Berkeley: University of California Press, 1993), 73.

29. "Letter from the Secretary of the Interior, Transmitting a Copy of the Laws Enacted at the Last Session of the Legislative Assembly of Porto Rico," June 18, 1902, S. Doc. 417, 57th Cong., 1st sess., 55. The act declared "that in all the Departments of the Insular Government and in all the Courts of this Island, and in all public offices the English language and the Spanish language shall be used indiscriminately; and, when necessary, translations and oral interpretations shall be made from one language to the other so that all parties interested may understand any proceedings or communications made therein."

30. *Report of the Commissioner of Education for Porto Rico, 1901*, 16.

31. Ibid.

32. *Report of the Commissioner of Education for Porto Rico to the Governor of Porto Rico for the Fiscal Year Ended June 30, 1907* (Washington, DC: GPO, 1907), 382.

33. Padilla, *Puerto Rican Chicago*, 8.

34. The Jones Act established the Senate of Puerto Rico and implemented the Bill of Rights of Puerto Rico. However, it allowed the U.S. president to appoint a representative on the island until the election of the first democratically elected governor of Puerto Rico in 1948. See Ramón Grosfoguel, *Colonial Subjects: Puerto Ricans in a Global Perspective* (Berkeley: University of California Press, 2003); Frances Negrón-Muntaner, *None of the Above: Puerto Ricans in the Global Era* (New York: Springer, 2007); Cabán, *Constructing a Colonial People*; and Isar P. Godreau, *Scripts of Blackness: Race, Cultural Nationalism, and US Colonialism in Puerto Rico* (Urbana: University of Illinois Press, 2015).

35. In *From Colonia to Community: The History of Puerto Ricans in New York City* (Berkeley: University of California Press, 1994), Virginia E. Sánchez- Korrol details what she calls three important migratory patterns to U.S. cities prior to 1898. The first, influenced by commercial factors, set the stage for the following two, which were more politically and economically motivated.

36. Anthropologist Oscar Lewis shared in this view, arguing that "although economic factors, such as low income and unemployment, created an atmosphere conducive to migration, we found that non-economic factors were actually more important." Lewis, *La Vida: A Puerto Rican Family in the Culture of Poverty—San Juan and New York* (New York: Random House, 1966), xxxvii–xxxviii.

37. "A key component of the industrialization program, known as *Manos a la Obra* or Operation Bootstrap, was 'industrialization by invitation.' Tax exemptions, along with low wages, were to attract U.S. investors to Puerto Rico." Carmen Teresa Whalen, "Colonialism, Citizenship, and the Making of the Puerto Rican Diaspora: An Introduction," in *The Puerto Rican Diaspora: Historical Perspectives*, ed. Carmen Teresa Whalen and Víctor Vázquez-Hernández (Philadelphia: Temple University Press, 2005), 27. The Chardón Plan, named after island official Carlos Chardón, called for a reduction in sugar production, increased industrialization, and emigration. See Whalen, *From Puerto Rico to Philadelphia: Puerto Rican Workers and Postwar Economies* (Philadelphia: Temple University Press, 2001), 11.

38. Sánchez Korrol, *From Colonia to Community*, 18.

39. Gina M. Pérez, *The Near Northwest Side Story: Migration, Displacement, and Puerto Rican Families* (Berkeley: University of California Press, 2004), 8.

40. History Task Force, Centro de Estudios Puertorriqueños, *Labor Migration under Capitalism: The Puerto Rican Experience* (New York: Monthly Review Press, 1979), 120–21.

41. Sánchez Korrol, *From Colonia to Community*, 3.

42. History Task Force, *Labor Migration under Capitalism*, 111. Faced with increased economic displacement and disparity, many Puerto Ricans were forced to either migrate to rapidly urbanizing cities or relocate to cities in either the United States or other Caribbean countries. In large cities like Río Piedras, the population increased by 180 percent in the 1920s, while the capital city of San Juan saw a 61 percent increase during this period.

43. Whalen, *From Puerto Rico to Philadelphia*, 39.

44. Office of the Commonwealth of Puerto Rico, *Know Your Fellow American Citizen from Puerto Rico* (Washington, DC: The Office, 1956), 1.

45. "Not only did Puerto Rico have a greater degree of racial mixing than its northern colonizer but its racial classification scheme comprised fluid and diverse categories that were typical for most Latin American countries." Ruth Glasser, *My Music Is My Flag: Puerto Rican Musicians and Their New York Communities, 1917–1940* (Berkeley: University of California Press, 1997), 53. It is important to understand that islanders were not devoid of color consciousness or prejudice, as is evident in the

narrative surrounding Puerto Rican identity, but those racial categories and identities differed (if only slightly) from the policies and hierarchies in the United States.

46. *Downes v. Bidwell*, 182 U.S. 244 at 341–42 (1901).

47. Cabán, *Constructing a Colonial People*, 2.

48. For more on the Emergency Quota Act, see Ashley S. Timmer and Jeffrey G. Williamson, "Immigration Policy Prior to the 1930s: Labor Markets, Policy Interactions, and Globalization Backlash," *Population and Development Review* 24, no. 4 (December 1998): 739–71.

49. Pérez, *Near Northwest Side Story*, 7.

50. José "Cha Cha" Jiménez, interview by the author, September 20, 2008.

51. Contemporary conversations on Latina/o/x communities utilize "Latinx" to signify the need to be inclusive of identities and not impose gendered identities on individuals or groups of people. However, when speaking to particular historical moments and movements, I will use the terminology appropriate for the time period.

52. Jerry González, *In Search of the Mexican Beverly Hills: Latino Suburbanization in Postwar Los Angeles* (New Brunswick, NJ: Rutgers University Press, 2018). Moving the narrative of the population not from Mexico but from the barrios of Los Angeles to suburban San Gabriel Valley, González speaks to the motivating factors that can lead to the internal migration of communities of people (displacement due to economic renewal of their original communities being one of the main factors explored in the text).

53. Nancy Raquel Mirabal, *Suspect Freedoms: The Racial and Sexual Politics of Cubanidad in New York, 1823–1957* (New York: New York University Press, 2017).

54. Lilia Fernández, *Brown in the Windy City: Mexicans and Puerto Ricans in Postwar Chicago* (Chicago: University of Chicago Press, 2012).

55. See Vargas, *Proletarians of the North*; Eileen J. Suárez Findlay, *We Are Left without a Father Here: Masculinity, Domesticity, and Migration in Postwar Puerto Rico* (Durham, NC: Duke University Press, 2015); and John H. Flores, *The Mexican Revolution in Chicago: Immigration Politics from the Early Twentieth Century to the Cold War* (Urbana: University of Illinois Press, 2018).

56. Padilla, *Puerto Rican Chicago*; Felix M. Padilla, *Latino Ethnic Consciousness: The Case of Mexican Americans and Puerto Ricans in Chicago* (Notre Dame IN: University of Notre Dame Press, 1985).

57. Ana Y. Ramos-Zayas, *National Performances: The Politics of Class, Race, and Space in Puerto Rican Chicago* (Chicago: University of Chicago Press, 2003), 3.

58. See Maura I. Toro-Morn, "Gender, Class, Family, and Migration: Puerto Rican Women in Chicago," *Gender and Society* 9, no. 6 (1995): 712–26; Marixsa Alicea, "'A Chambered Nautilus': The Contradictory Nature of Puerto Rican Women's Role in the Social Construction of a Transnational Community," *Gender and Society* 11, no. 5 (1997): 597–626; Ramos-Zayas, *National Performances*; and Pérez, *Near Northwest Side Story*.

59. See James D. Anderson, *The Education of Blacks in the South, 1860–1935* (Chapel Hill: University of North Carolina Press, 1988).

60. For more on Mexican and Puerto Rican coalition building in Chicago, see Padilla, *Latino Ethnic Consciousness*; and Fernández, *Brown in the Windy City*.

61. "Chicago Puerto Rico Youths to Get Aid," *Chicago Tribune*, November 14, 1968, 24.

62. Puerto Rican nationalists, on and off the island, have contended with U.S. policies intended to silence their movement since 1898. In 1950, Puerto Rican nationalists staged an attack on President Harry S. Truman. Then in 1954, a group of Puerto Rican nationalists, including Lolita Lebrón, engaged in a shootout at the U.S. Capitol. See Ana Y. Ramos-Zayas, "Performing the Nation," in *National Performances*, 19–42.

63. See René Antrop-González, "This School Is My Sanctuary: The Dr. Pedro Albizu Campos Alternative High School," *Centro: Journal of the Center for Puerto Rican Studies* 15, no. 2 (2003): 232–55.

64. Isidro Lucas, "A Profile of the Puerto Rican Dropout in Chicago," in *Puerto Rican Curriculum Development Workshop: A Report*, ed. Angel P. Campos (New York: Council on Social Work Education, 1974), 20–30; Lucas, *Puerto Rican Dropouts in Chicago: Numbers and Motivations* (Chicago: Council on Urban Education, 1971).

65. Laura K. Muñoz, "*Romo v. Laird*: Mexican American Segregation and the Politics of Belonging in Arizona," *Western Legal History* 26, no. 1–2 (2013): 99.

66. Rubén Donato, *The Other Struggle for Equal Schools* (Albany: State University of New York Press, 1997), 2. See Guadalupe San Miguel Jr., "Roused from Our Slumbers," in *Latinos and Education: A Critical Reader*, ed. Antonia Darder, Rodolfo D. Torres, and Henry Gutíerrez (New York: Routledge, 1997), 135–57. *Independent School District v. Salvatierra* was a class action suit against the Del Rio, Texas, school district. San Miguel argues that this was an important case in that it marked the first time the courts were asked to "exercise their power of judicial review to determine the constitutionality of the actions of a local school district with respect to the education of Mexican Americans" (146).

67. Donato, *The Other Struggle for Equal Schools*, 2.

68. Guadalupe San Miguel Jr., "The Impact of *Brown* on Mexican American Desegregation Litigation, 1950s to 1980s," *Journal of Latinos and Education* 4, no. 4 (2005): 222. Before *Brown*, attorneys trying *Gonzales v. Sheely* in Arizona utilized *Westminster* to argue on behalf of Mexican and Mexican American schoolchildren in Arizona. The judge hearing the case invoked the Equal Protection Clause, proclaiming that the segregation of schoolchildren on the basis of their racial or national origin was indeed unconstitutional. See Laura K. Muñoz, "Ralph Estrada and the War against Racial Prejudice in Arizona," in *Leaders of the Mexican American Generation: Biographical Essays*, ed. Anthony Quiroz (Boulder: University Press of Colorado, 2015), 277–99; and Jeanne M. Powers and Lirio Patton, "Between *Méndez* and *Brown*: *Gonzales v. Sheely* (1951) and the Legal Campaign against Segregation," *Law and Social Inquiry* 33, no. 1 (Winter 2008): 127–71.

69. Felícita Méndez, interview, 1987, as quoted in Jennifer McCormick and César J.

Ayala, "Felícita 'La Prieta' Méndez (1916–1998) and the End of Latino School Segregation in California," *Centro: Journal of the Center for Puerto Rican Studies* 19, no. 2 (2007): 30.

70. Angie Morrill, Eve Tuck, and the Super Futures Haunt Qollective, "Before Dispossession, or Surviving It," *Liminalities: A Journal of Performance Studies* 12, no. 1 (2016): 2, 9.

71. Yi-Fu Tuan, *Space and Place: The Perspective of Experience* (London: Edward Arnold, 1977), 128.

72. Anderson, *Education of Blacks in the South*, 1.

73. See Guadalupe San Miguel Jr., "The Status of Historical Research on Chicano Education," *Review of Educational Research* 57, no. 4 (Winter 1987): 467–80; and Ian F. Haney López, *Racism on Trial: The Chicano Fight for Justice* (Cambridge, MA: Harvard University Press, 2003).

74. San Miguel, "Status of Historical Research," 467.

75. David G. García, *Strategies of Segregation: Race, Residence, and the Struggle for Educational Equality* (Berkeley: University of California Press, 2018).

76. Mario Rios Perez, *Subjects of Resistance: Education, Race, and Transnational Life in Mexican Chicago, 1910–1940* (New Brunswick, NJ: Rutgers University Press, forthcoming).

Chapter 1. *Al Brincar el Charco*

1. "Puerto Ricans Arrive to Take Jobs in Foundry: Flown Here from San Juan; More to Come," *Chicago Daily Tribune*, September 29, 1946, 27.

2. Ibid.

3. Ibid.

4. Arnold R. Hirsch, *Making the Second Ghetto: Race and Housing in Chicago, 1940–1960* (Cambridge: Cambridge University Press, 1983), xvi.

5. For more on the 1919 Chicago Race Riot, see Andrew J. Diamond, *Mean Streets: Chicago Youths and the Everyday Struggle for Empowerment in the Multiracial City, 1908–1969* (Berkeley: University of California Press, 2009); Robin F. Bachin, *Building the South Side: Urban Space and Civic Culture in Chicago, 1890–1919* (Chicago: University of Chicago Press, 2004); and Janet Abu-Lughod, *Race, Space, and Riots In Chicago, New York, and Los Angeles* (New York: Oxford University Press, 2007). In Diamond's *Mean Streets*, we see the relationship between race and the city, as well as the violent consequences of space and masculinity, reflected in the lives of Chicago's youth, allowing us to critically examine these issues.

6. Gabriela F. Arredondo, *Mexican Chicago: Race, Identity, and Nation, 1916–39* (Urbana: University of Illinois Press, 2008), 38. As Arredondo details, Eliseo González was killed by white rioters, and José Blanco was arrested and tried for manslaughter after defending himself against the attackers. Blanco and González were mistaken for Black residents, highlighting "how unfixed these categories of white and black really were in the lived experiences of Mexicans in Chicago in 1919."

7. Flores, *Mexican Revolution in Chicago*.

8. James R. Barrett and David Roediger, "Inbetween Peoples: Race, Nationality and the 'New Immigrant' Working Class," *Journal of American Ethnic History* 16, no. 3 (1997): 3.

9. Anne Getz, "Puerto Rican Culture Brought into Schools," *Chicago Tribune*, July 14, 1966, F2.

10. Mayor's Committee on New Residents, Chicago Commission on Human Relations, *Puerto Rican Americans in Chicago: A Study of a Representative Group of 103 Households of Puerto Rican Migrants on Chicago's Northwest Side—and Their Adjustment to Big-City Living* (Chicago: Mayor's Committee, 1960).

11. Ibid., ii.

12. Padilla, *Puerto Rican Chicago*, 53.

13. See Grosfoguel, *Colonial Subjects*. While the Chardón Plan sought to promote the industrialization of the island, in some ways mirroring New Deal programs in the United States, Operation Bootstrap had a more intense impact. Through Operation Bootstrap, we see both the economic shift on the island favoring U.S. corporate interests, under the understanding that it would provide new, much-needed job opportunities to islanders, and the simultaneous creation of outmigration as an economic possibility with low-cost transportation to U.S. cities.

14. History Task Force, *Labor Migration under Capitalism*, 120–21.

15. In the 1930s, Puerto Rican nationalist movement leader Pedro Albizu Campos claimed, "The brazenness of the Yankee invaders has reached the extreme of trying to profane Puerto Rico motherhood; of trying to invade the very insides of nationality. When our women lose the transcendental and divine concept that they are not only mothers of their children but mothers of all future generations of Puerto Rico, if they come to lose that feeling, Puerto Rico will disappear within a generation." Quoted in Laura Briggs, *Reproducing Empire: Race, Sex, Science, and U.S. Imperialism in Puerto Rico* (Berkeley: University of California Press, 2001), 76.

16. According to Briggs, the perception was that Puerto Rican women, seen as backward by the United States, were in need of reproductive intervention in order to facilitate economic and social change. It was assumed that these working-class women "required contraceptives different from those used by affluent or U.S. women." Programs initially encouraged simple contraception, but later included sterilization and experimentation with earlier versions of birth control pills, giving "physicians and population control workers increasing control over working-class women's reproduction." Ibid., 140.

17. Findlay, *We Are Left without a Father Here*, 109.

18. Sánchez Korrol, *From Colonia to Community*, 29.

19. Mervin J. Sacks, "Puerto Rican Children: Results of Group Study Here Intended to Apply Locally," letter to the editor, *New York Times*, February 19, 1936, 18; C. P. Armstrong, E. M. Achilles, and M. J. Sacks, *A Report of the Special Committee on Immigration and Naturalization of the Chamber of Commerce of the State of New*

York Submitting a Study on Reactions of Puerto Rican Children in New York City to Psychological Tests (New York: Special Committee on Immigration and Naturalization, 1935).

20. E. Padilla, "Puerto Rican Immigrants in New York and Chicago," 70.

21. Ibid., 50. Padilla later argues that because of this precise "solidarity" with Mexicans in Chicago, Puerto Ricans will "tend to be Mexicanized" (98).

22. Glasser, *My Music Is My Flag*, 72–73.

23. Glasser, ibid., discusses the racial segregation present in New York at the time, and the social stigma faced by Puerto Ricans who were assumed to be or labeled as African American. Signs posted on many buildings in New York City vehemently relayed this sentiment as they read "No dogs, No Negroes, and No Spanish." Thus the most viable options for Puerto Ricans were to either residentially align themselves with African Americans or begin to form their own enclaves.

24. Ibid., 53.

25. E. Padilla, "Puerto Rican Immigrants in New York and Chicago," 35. A nuanced discussion of race in Puerto Rico is very much needed in order to challenge at times outdated views that erase the social, economic, and political hierarchies influenced by race on the island. In *Scripts of Blackness*, Godreau offers an important discussion of how U.S. colonialism influenced the socialization of racial ideologies on the island.

26. Elena Padilla, in "Puerto Rican Immigrants in New York and Chicago," reiterates the varying racial politics on the island during the time of her work, including a thorough discussion of terminology utilized to label individuals based on where they fell on the racial/economic spectrum on the island, as well as their physical location (rural vs. urban).

27. Godreau, *Scripts of Blackness*, 25.

28. Sánchez Korrol, *From Colonia to Community*, 213.

29. Ibid., 35.

30. Welfare Council of New York City, *Puerto Ricans in New York City: The Report of the Committee on Puerto Ricans in New York City* (New York: Welfare Council, 1948), 10–11.

31. Ibid., 10.

32. Ibid., 11.

33. Patricia Cayo Sexton, "Neighbors—Puerto Rican, Negro, Italian . . .," in *Puerto Rican Children in Mainland Schools: A Source Book for Teachers*, ed. Eugene Bucchioni and Francesco Cordasco (Metuchen, NJ: Scarecrow Press, 1968), 157.

34. "2 Beaten by Strangers; Puerto Ricans, in Hospitals, Know No Reasons for Attacks," *New York Times*, December 20, 1936, 6.

35. "Puerto Ricans to Be Deported," *New York Times*, March 24, 1937, 5.

36. Zaragosa Vargas, *Crucible of Struggle: A History of Mexican Americans from Colonial Times to the Present Era* (New York: Oxford University Press, 2011), 220. For more on the history of Mexican Americans in the early twentieth century, see George J. Sánchez, *Becoming Mexican American: Ethnicity, Culture and Identity in*

Chicano Los Angeles, 1900–1945 (New York: Oxford University Press, 1993); and Dionicio Nodín Valdés, *Barrios Norteños: St. Paul and Midwestern Mexican Communities in the Twentieth Century* (Austin: University of Texas Press, 2000).

37. Sánchez Korrol, *From Colonia to Community*, 32.

38. "Puerto Rico Seeks to Curb Migration: Government Plans to Show That New York May Not Be 'Port of Opportunity,'" *New York Times*, February 23, 1947, 20.

39. Sánchez Korrol, *From Colonia to Community*, 32.

40. "Migrants Relate Tales of Hardship: 18-Year-Old Girl Is One of Witnesses at Congressional Body's Hearing Here," *New York Times*, July 30, 1940, 21.

41. Ibid.

42. E. Padilla, "Puerto Rican Immigrants in New York and Chicago," 52.

43. "Attention to women's labor migrations is pivotal in understanding the increased migration of the postwar era, migrants' destinations, their economic strategies, and their efforts to recreate their household economies." Whalen, *From Puerto Rico to Philadelphia*, 5.

44. "Puerto Rico Seeks to Curb Migration."

45. History Task Force, *Labor Migration under Capitalism*, 18.

46. Welfare Council, *Puerto Ricans in New York City*, 9.

47. "Aid Planned Here for Puerto Ricans: 1,500 a Week from Island Are Arriving in City and Social Agencies Map Action," *New York Times*, January 12, 1947, 25.

48. Welfare Council, *Puerto Ricans in New York City*, 10.

49. Mayor's Committee on New Residents, *A Six Month Report of the Migration Services Department, July–December 1957* (Chicago: Commission on Human Relations, 1958), 3.

50. Padilla, *Puerto Rican Chicago*, 56.

51. Sánchez Korrol, *From Colonia to Community*, 28.

52. E. Padilla, "Puerto Rican Immigrants in New York and Chicago," 66.

53. Ibid.

54. For more information, see Padilla, *Puerto Rican Chicago*.

55. Donald Janson, "Chicago Good City to Puerto Ricans: Many Find Work and Living Better Than in New York," *New York Times*, June 4, 1961, 80.

56. Ibid., 34.

57. Del Moral, *Negotiating Empire*, 58.

58. Ibid., 183.

59. Welfare Council, *Puerto Ricans in New York City*, 36.

60. Ibid., 41.

61. Ibid., 42.

62. Sánchez, *Becoming Mexican American*, 100.

63. Ruiz, *From Out of the Shadows*, 35.

64. Marcia Chatelain, *South Side Girls: Growing Up in the Great Migration* (Durham, NC: Duke University Press, 2015). Chatelain details the relationship between space and race in the lives of young Black girls and women in Chicago. The creation

of youth-based organizations, services, and programs that focused on Black girls greatly influenced activism in the subsequent decades.

65. "U. of. C. Hailed as Inter-American Cultural Force: Educator in Puerto Rico Tells of Goals," *Chicago Daily Tribune*, November 23, 1942, 14.

66. Merida Rúa, *A Grounded Identidad: Making New Lives in Chicago's Puerto Rican Neighborhoods* (New York: Oxford University Press, 2012).

67. For more on the initial migration of the population to Chicago and the work of the University of Chicago students, see Rúa, ibid.

68. Muna Muñoz Lee to Luis Muñoz Marín, December 9, 1946, box 9B, folder 277, Employment and Migration Bureau, Fundacion Luis Muñoz Marín, San Juan, Puerto Rico (hereafter FLMM).

69. Ibid.

70. Unless otherwise noted, all translations are my own.

71. Ibid.

72. "Plight of Hired Puerto Ricans Starts Dispute: 'Deplorable Conditions' Denied by Employers," *Chicago Daily Tribune*, December 11, 1946, 30. For more on the history of Puerto Rican women's migration to Chicago, see Rúa, *Grounded Identidad*; Ramos-Zayas, *National Performances*; and Toro-Morn, "Gender, Class, Family."

73. Mayor's Committee, *Puerto Rican Americans in Chicago*, 17.

74. Carmen Isales to Luis Muñoz Marín, Seccion IV LMM Pres. Senado, Serie 3 Individuos, box 9b, folder 275, FLMM.

75. Ibid.

76. Ibid.

77. Ibid.

78. Ibid.

79. "Agency to Stop Importing Girls for Housework," *Chicago Daily Tribune*, May 17, 1947, 12.

80. "Report on Cases of Puerto Rican Laborers Brought to Chicago to Work as Domestics and Foundry Workers under Contract with Castle, Barton, and Associates, Inc.," March 22, 1947, 7, box 9b, folder 277, FLMM.

81. Ibid.

82. Leonard C. Lewin report, December 20, 1946, box 9B, folder 277, FLMM.

83. "Maid Problem," *New Republic*, April 28, 1947, 7.

84. "Agency to Stop Importing Girls for Housework," 12.

85. The works of Maura Toro-Morn, Lilia Fernández, Merida Rúa, and others inform us not only about the implications of a deeply gendered migration to Chicago, but also about the involvement of both governments and the employment agencies who recruited the women in controlling the lives (and opportunities) of the *domesticas* now in the United States. See Maura I. Toro-Morn, "Boricuas en Chicago: Gender and Class in the Migration and Settlement of Puerto Ricans," in Whalen and Vázquez-Hernández, *The Puerto Rican Diaspora*, 128–50; Fernández, *Brown in the Windy City*; and Rúa, *Grounded Identidad*.

86. See Emma Amador, "Organizing Puerto Rican Domestics: Resistance and Household Labor Reform in the Puerto Rican Diaspora after 1930," *International Labor and Working-Class History* 88 (2015): 67–86; Fernández, *Brown in the Windy City*; and Toro-Morn, "Gender, Class, Family."

87. E. Padilla, "Puerto Rican Immigrants in New York and Chicago."

88. Hirsch, *Making the Second Ghetto*, 20. The expansion of the University of Chicago across the Hyde Park community turned into a lengthy battle for Chicago's South Side Black community. Similarly, the desire to expand the Illinois Institute of Technology in the mid-twentieth century created an unfortunate merger between private and public interests in redeveloping the Near South Side. The creation of the South Side Planning Board in 1946, along with the collaborative report *An Opportunity for Private and Public Investment in Rebuilding Chicago* (Chicago: Chicago Plan Commission, 1947), co-written by the Illinois Institute of Technology, Michael Reese Hospital, the South Side Planning Board, and others, critically affected housing opportunities and integration in the community.

89. Rashad Shabazz, *Spatializing Blackness: Architectures of Confinement and Black Masculinity in Chicago* (Urbana: University of Illinois Press, 2015), 60.

90. Fernández, *Brown in the Windy City*, 60.

91. "They found a racial hierarchy that had very clearly defined poles of black and white but that had an ambiguous and unstable middle, where they sometimes could claim an ethnic identity much like 'hyphenated' European Americans but could just as easily be perceived as racially distinct (foreign and *nonwhite*) and occupy a position closer to African Americans." Ibid., 59. Fernández offers a much more nuanced understanding of the history of communities in which both Mexicans and Puerto Ricans settled, especially regarding their relationships with white European residents.

92. Waitstill H. Sharp, Chicago Council against Racial and Religious Discrimination, to Hazel Holm, Welfare Council of Metropolitan Chicago, January 23, 1951, box 48, folder 3, Welfare Council of Metropolitan Chicago Records, 1914–1978 (hereafter WCMC Records), Chicago History Museum (hereafter CHM).

93. See Arredondo, *Mexican Chicago*, for a discussion of Mexican/Mexican American settlement in Chicago in the early twentieth century. Arredondo offers a thorough discussion of the community's complicated relationship with race and masculinity within the city, and how quickly their experiences there taught them that the currency was "whiteness." "For Mexicans in Chicago, blackness seemed to represent the oppositional other against which Mexicans strove to mark themselves. They chose to measure themselves instead in terms of whiteness and American identity" (134). They would soon find out how limited this view would be in terms of housing and labor opportunities in Chicago.

94. Ibid., 85.

95. Mayor's Committee, *Puerto Rican Americans in Chicago*, 101.

96. Mayor's Committee on New Residents, *A Summary of Work of the Migration Services Department, Mayor's Committee on New Residents, January 1957–1959* (Chicago: Chicago Commission on Human Relations, 1959), 11. In subsequent decades,

particularly in the late 1970s and early 1980s, Puerto Ricans in Chicago utilized their voting rights to challenge prevailing city politics that had come to marginalize them in the early years.

97. Mary A. Young to Robert MacRae, Welfare Council of Metropolitan Chicago, January 28, 1954, box 148, folder 3, WCMC Records, CHM.

98. Ibid.

99. Ibid.

100. Helen McLane to Robert MacRae, Community Fund of Chicago, February 15, 1965, box 148, folder 3, WCMC Records, CHM.

101. "Understanding and Working with Newcomers Workshop," box 3, folder 2, Morris L. Haimowitz Papers, ca. 1950–1970 (hereafter Haimowitz Papers), CHM.

102. "Understanding Spanish Speaking Americans in Chicago," box 4, folder 3, Haimowitz Papers, CHM.

103. "Meeting on Spanish Speaking Americans," box 4, folder 3, Haimowitz Papers, CHM.

104. "Roosevelt University Again Offers In-Service Training Program for Teachers of the Americanization Division of the Chicago Public Schools," box 3, folder 2, Haimowitz Papers, CHM.

105. Robert H. MacRae, "Welfare Council of Metropolitan Chicago," April 17, 1957, 14, box 148, folder 3, WCMC Records, CHM.

106. Ibid.

107. Mayor's Committee, *Six Month Report of the Migration Services Department*, 10.

108. Ibid., 5.

109. "Roosevelt University Again Offers In-Service Training Program," box 3, folder 2, Haimowitz Papers, CHM.

110. "Understanding and Working with Newcomers Workshop," box 3, folder 4, Haimowitz Papers, CHM.

111. Mayor's Committee, *Summary of Work of the Migration Services Department*, 2.

112. Young to MacRae, January 28, 1954.

113. Ibid.

114. Ibid. For more on the direct dealing by both governments on the migratory trajectory of Puerto Ricans to Chicago, see Fernández, *Brown in the Windy City*; Pérez, *Near Northwest Side Story*; Rúa, *Grounded Identidad*; and Toro-Morn, "Gender, Class, Family." These scholars clearly lay out the contentious relationship between Puerto Rican migrants and local social agencies, who were ill-prepared to deal with Puerto Ricans and misinformed on the population.

115. Fernández, *Brown in the Windy City*, 84. Fernández notes that the issues in the city were primarily economic, and were not tied to Puerto Ricans, "but Chicago officials singled out [Puerto Ricans] as a burden" (85).

116. Ibid., 84, 85.

117. MacRae, "Welfare Council of Metropolitan Chicago," 1.

118. Ibid., 2.

119. Mayor's Committee, *Six Month Report of the Migration Services Department*, 3.

120. See Hirsch, *Making the Second Ghetto.*

121. MacRae, "Welfare Council of Metropolitan Chicago," 6. In *Brown in the Windy City*, Fernández explores the housing opportunities and limitations experienced by Puerto Rican migrants and their families.

122. Mayor's Committee, *Six Month Report of the Migration Services Department*, 7.

123. Hull House Association, "Report on the Activities of the Hull House Branch Center," August 31, 1956, box 4, folder 4, Haimowitz Papers, CHM. According to the report, officials at the branch office of Hull House worked to "serve a group of Puerto Rican newcomers to Chicago in a development made possible by a grant from the Field Foundation."

124. Davis McEntire, *Residence and Race: Final and Comprehensive Report to the Commission on Race and Housing* (Los Angeles: University of California Press, 1960), 2.

125. Ibid.

126. "Report Shows Segregation Rises in City," *Chicago Tribune*, December 23, 1962, S2.

127. Marixsa Alicea, "'Cuando nosotros vivíamos . . .': Stories of Displacement and Settlement in Puerto Rican Chicago," *Centro: Journal of the Center for Puerto Rican Studies* 13, no. 2 (Fall 2001): 170.

128. "The Harsh New World of Our Puerto Ricans," *Chicago Tribune*, November 24, 1963, F34–41.

129. Ibid.

130. García, *Strategies of Segregation*, 13.

131. Mayor's Committee, *Puerto Rican Americans in Chicago.*

132. Ibid., 93.

133. Ibid., 98.

134. Ibid.

135. Ibid., 99.

136. Ibid.

137. Hirsch, *Making the Second Ghetto*, 4–5.

138. Aldo Beckman, "Apartment Hunt All in Day's Work for Renewal Unit," *Chicago Tribune*, August 7, 1960, N1.

Chapter 2. Community Visions of Puerto Rican Schooling, 1950–1966

1. L. J. Schloerb to John M. Gandy, September 18, 1953, box 147, folder 10, WCMC Records, CHM.

2. Mary A. Young to Robert MacRae, January 28, 1954, box 148, folder 3, WCMC Records, CHM.

3. Irizarry and Antrop-González, "RicanStructuring the Discourse," 40.

4. In *Negotiating Empire*, Solsiree del Moral offers a thorough account of cultural, political, and social negotiation surrounding schooling in Puerto Rico following the Spanish-American War. According to Del Moral, teachers played an integral role in conceptualizing ideologies surrounding nation building and national identities, while simultaneously pushing for their positions within emerging island politics.

5. For more, see Richard J. Margolis, "The Losers: A Report on Puerto Ricans and the Public Schools, New York, 1968," reprinted in *Puerto Ricans and Educational Opportunity* (New York: Arno Press, 1975); and Clarence Senior, *The Puerto Ricans: Strangers Then Neighbors* (Chicago: Quadrangle Press, 1965).

6. Donato, *The Other Struggle for Equal Schools*, 64.

7. For more on *Brown v. Board of Education* (1954), see James D. Anderson, "Crosses to Bear and Promises to Keep: The Jubilee Anniversary of *Brown v. Board of Education*," *Urban Education* 39, no. 4 (2004): 359–73.

8. From housing policies and city politics to schools and labor unions, the city has historically faced battles between local communities and the machine politics that have come to define the city. See Adam Green, *Selling the Race: Culture, Community, and Black Chicago, 1940–1955* (Chicago: University of Chicago Press, 2007); Arredondo, *Mexican Chicago*; Diamond, *Mean Streets*; and James R. Barrett, *Work and Community in the Jungle: Chicago's Packinghouse Workers, 1894–1922* (Urbana: University of Illinois Press, 1990).

9. See John L. Rury, "Race, Space, and the Politics of Chicago's Public Schools: Benjamin Willis and the Tragedy of Urban Education," *History of Education Quarterly* 39, no. 2 (1999): 117–42.

10. Benjamin C. Willis, "Using the Criticism of Public Schools for Constructive Purposes," *Elementary School Journal* 55, no. 1 (September 1954): 13.

11. Superintendent Benjamin C. Willis, "Human Relations Policy of the Chicago Public Schools," CHM.

12. Rury, "Race, Space," 131.

13. Ansley T. Erickson, *Making the Unequal Metropolis: School Desegregation and Its Limits* (Chicago: University of Chicago Press, 2018), 30.

14. For more on the history of housing and community segregation of Puerto Ricans, see Fernández, *Brown in the Windy City*.

15. "Study School Courses to Aid Puerto Ricans," *Chicago Daily Tribune*, March 11, 1954, 12.

16. "Seeks to Curb Migration of Puerto Ricans: Rose Going by Plane to San Juan Today," *Chicago Tribune*, February 4, 1954, 3. Although schools in Chicago were overseen by one superintendent, they were divided into smaller districts, with each district assigned a director/assistant superintendent. In 1965, the board argued for Chicago to be divided into forty-two districts, rather than the twenty-four that existed at the time. For more on the history of Chicago schools and their structure, see Mary J. Herrick, *The Chicago Schools: A Social and Political History* (Beverly Hills, CA: Sage, 1971).

17. Schloerb to Gandy, September 18, 1953.

18. "Seeks to Curb Migration of Puerto Ricans."

19. Ibid.

20. Ibid.

21. Ibid.

22. Schloerb to Gandy, September 18, 1953.

23. Young to MacRae, January 28, 1954.

24. Gladys Priddy, "Puerto Rican Kids Perfect Their English: City Teachers Donate Instruction," *Chicago Tribune*, June 7, 1956, N13.

25. Richard Philbrick, "Praiseworthy Church Gains Recorded Here List Accomplishments of Chicago Clergy," *Chicago Tribune*, January 27, 1957, 25.

26. Thomas G. Kelliher Jr., "Hispanic Catholics and the Archdiocese of Chicago, 1923–1970" (PhD diss., University of Notre Dame, 1996), 133–34.

27. Padilla, *Puerto Rican Chicago*, 126.

28. Dorothy Washburn, "These Puerto Ricans Like It Here: They Are Now Helping Others from Their Caribbean Isle to Adjust to a New Life in a Big Northern City," *Chicago Tribune*, August 9, 1959, F33.

29. Ibid.

30. Ibid.

31. Priddy, "Puerto Rican Kids Perfect Their English."

32. "De Paul Alumni Help Teens: Pledge 6-Week Assignments," *Chicago Tribune*, May 31, 1964, N3.

33. Fernández, *Brown in the Windy City*, 152.

34. Ibid.

35. "Pan American Board of Education Will Present Program," *Chicago Tribune*, January 15, 1955, 12.

36. Untitled document, 6, box 3, folder 1, Haimowitz Papers, CHM, parentheses in original.

37. Ibid.

38. Ibid.

39. Robert H. MacRae, "Welfare Council of Metropolitan Chicago," April 17, 1957, box 148, folder 3, WCMC Records, CHM.

40. Floreal Forni, *The Situation of the Puerto Rican Population in Chicago and Its Viewpoints about Racial Relations* (Chicago: Community and Family Study Center, University of Chicago, 1971), 19.

41. Ibid., 61.

42. Washburn, "These Puerto Ricans Like It Here," F34.

43. Mayor's Committee, *Puerto Rican Americans in Chicago*, ix.

44. "3,609 Finish Adult Citizen Instructions: Classes Had Persons from 86 Nations," *Chicago Tribune*, June 16, 1960, 2.

45. Ibid.

46. Donald Janson, "Chicago Good City to Puerto Ricans: Many Find Work and Living Better Than in New York," *New York Times*, June 4, 1961, 80.

47. James R. Ralph Jr., *Northern Protest: Martin Luther King Jr., Chicago, and the*

Civil Rights Movement (Cambridge, MA: Harvard University Press, 1993), 14. Willis created a double-shift school schedule during this period of rapid increase. Two schedules were established (early and late start times), with the students divided between them, which disproportionately affected Black students. Similarly, to ease overcrowding, Willis instituted the creation and use of mobile classrooms to house students, which would come to be known as "Willis Wagons."

48. Dionne Danns, *Desegregating Chicago's Public Schools: Policy Implementation, Politics, and Protest, 1965–1985* (New York: Palgrave Macmillan, 2014), 13.

49. Ibid. For more on the African American battles to desegregate Chicago schools, see Arvarh E. Strickland, "The Schools Controversy and the Beginning of the Civil Rights Movement in Chicago," *Historian* 58, no. 4 (1996): 717–29; Dionne Danns, "Northern Segregation: A Tale of Two Cities," *History of Education Quarterly* 51, no. 1 (2011): 77–104; and Rury, "Race, Space."

50. See Elizabeth Todd-Breland, "Barbara Sizemore and the Politics of Black Educational Achievement and Community Control, 1963–1975," *Journal of African American History* 100, no. 4 (2015): 636–62.

51. In *A Political Education: Black Politics and Education Reform in Chicago since the 1960s* (Chapel Hill: University of North Carolina Press, 2018), Elizabeth Todd-Breland offers an in-depth historical account of the Black community's organizing work around schools and schooling. Like Chicago's Puerto Rican community, Todd-Breland reminds us, the city's Black community was far from homogeneous, yet very interested in ensuring that the needs of their children in city schools were met.

52. Nancy Hoffman and Robert Schwartz, "Remembrance of Things Past: An Interview with Francis Keppel and Harold Howe II," *Change* 22, no. 2 (1990): 52–57.

53. Donato, *The Other Struggle for Equal Schools*, 59.

54. "New Race Charge against Jenner School Principal," *Chicago Daily Defender*, February 1, 1966, 1.

55. Bill Van Alstine, "Three-Day Boycott at Jenner: 'Concerned Parents' Group Maps Program to Emphasize Protest," *Chicago Defender*, January 15, 1966, 1; "Jenner Principal Asks Firing of Teachers: 15 To 20 Will Be Out If Chuchut Has Her Way," *Chicago Daily Defender*, January 25, 1966, 1.

56. Erickson, *Making the Unequal Metropolis*, 3.

57. Michael Savage, "Beyond Boundaries: Envisioning Metropolitan School Desegregation in Boston, Detroit, and Philadelphia, 1963–1974," *Journal of Urban History* 46, no. 1 (2018): 129–49. Parents initially held a sit-in at the Boston School Committee meeting on June 11, 1963, with a group of demands, which were quickly dismissed. Among other things, they called on the committee to acknowledge the long-standing segregation of its schools, initiate a review of its transfer policies, and incorporate a better multicultural curriculum. The full list can be found in the online virtual exhibition "Boston before Busing, 1964–1974," Northeastern University Libraries, https://dsgsites.neu.edu/desegregation/first-sit-in/.

58. See Jeanne Theoharis and Komozi Woodard, *Freedom North: Black Freedom Struggles outside the South, 1940–1980* (New York: Palgrave Macmillan, 2003).

59. Adina Back, "'Parent Power': Evelina López Antonetty, the United Bronx Parents, and the War on Poverty," in *The War on Poverty: A New Grassroots History, 1964–1980*, ed. Annelise Orleck and Lisa Gayle Hazirjian (Athens: University of Georgia Press, 2011), 185.

60. For more on Evelina López-Antonetty and Latina mothers' organizing work on behalf of their communities' children, see Mirelsie Velazquez, "Primero Madres: Love and Mothering in the Educational Lives of Latina/os," *Gender and Education* 29, no. 4 (2017): 508–24.

61. "Willis Tells of Schools' Spanish Unit," *Chicago Tribune*, June 24, 1966, 3.

62. "The Chicago Public Schools clung to this policy of color blindness until 1963." Rury, "Race, Space," 127.

63. Although Chicago Public Schools did not accurately document the demographics of their schools, the Chicago Diocese did track the numbers, especially for the Spanish-speaking community. "In-Migrants: Number, Location, and Selected Characteristics," November/December 1957, box 3, folder 4, Haimowitz Papers, CHM.

64. Lucas, "Profile of the Puerto Rican Drop Out."

65. Francesco Cordasco and Eugene Bucchioni, "Introduction," in *Puerto Rican Children in Mainland Schools*, 14. The edited volume also included pieces to aid teachers in understanding the cultural, fertility, dating, and spiritual habits of this population.

66. Margolis, "The Losers," 6.

67. Ibid., 14.

68. Ibid.

69. Ibid.

70. Lilia Fernández details the evolving police brutality faced by Puerto Ricans in Chicago in chapter 4 of *Brown in the Windy City*. She argues that conflicts between police and the community were an extension of racial tensions, both within the city as a whole and in the changing landscapes of neighborhoods, and with the increasingly white Chicago police force.

71. "$80,000 to Puerto Rican," *YLO* 1, no. 1 (March 19, 1969): 2. An article in the *Chicago Tribune* detailed the shooting of Acosta by Chicago police in the 2400 block of West Division Street. Police, fearful of a repeat of earlier confrontations with community members, kept a close watch on the area. "Court Delays Cases of 9 in Hindering Cops: Charge Interference during Arrest," *Chicago Tribune*, August 3, 1966, A1.

72. Diamond, *Mean Streets*, 253.

73. Suzanne Avery, "Suggest Cutback in Urban Renewal Plan," *Chicago Tribune*, February 18, 1960, NA1; "Revised Plan for Renewal Agreed Upon: Scrap Lincoln Pk. Project," *Chicago Tribune*, March 17, 1960, N1.

74. Erickson, *Making the Unequal Metropolis*, 35.

75. Robert Cross, "Big Noise from Lincoln Park," *Chicago Tribune*, November 2, 1969, I26.

76. Ibid.

77. In *Puerto Rican Chicago*, Felix Padilla thoroughly discusses urban renewal in Lincoln Park. In chapter 3, "Organizational Response to Ethnic Oppression," he examines the various economic policies initiated by the white community in Lincoln Park, which were aimed at alienating and pushing out people of color, particularly Puerto Ricans.

78. In *Brown in the Windy City*, Fernández details both the population's history in the Lincoln Park community and the evolution of the Young Lords Organization. "Puerto Rican youth were becoming educated in American meanings of race on the mainland, but they were also learning the language of class consciousness. In response . . . they began asserting a political identity that embraced their ascribed racial difference and demanded rights as economically oppressed and colonized people within a capitalist, imperialist society. This formed the basis of the Young Lords' platform" (176).

79. Gina Pérez argues that as Humboldt Park came to mean "Puerto Rican" in Chicago, Puerto Ricans' social and economic opportunities became quite limited by these racial/ethnic and spatial signifiers. See chapter 3, "Know Your Fellow Citizen from Puerto Rico," in *Near Northwest Side Story*.

80. For more detailed information on population demographics, see Evelyn M. Kitagawa and Karl E. Taeuber, eds., *Local Community Fact Book: Chicago Metropolitan Area, 1960* (Chicago: Chicago Community Inventory, 1963). Some, including William Muñiz, the director of the Migration Division of the Commonwealth of Puerto Rico, argued that the number of Puerto Ricans in Chicago should be higher. But "the census did not include tracts where there were less than 400 Puerto Ricans living," putting the figure at about 65,000 according to his estimates. See "Commonwealth Office Helps Puerto Rican New Arrivals," *Chicago Tribune*, August 27, 1964, W9.

81. MacRae, "Welfare Council of Metropolitan Chicago," 17.

82. Ramos-Zayas, *National Performances*, 52.

83. "Shooting Angers Crowd, Patrol Car Burned," *Chicago Daily Defender*, June 13, 1966. Felix Padilla's *Puerto Rican Chicago* offers one of the earliest detailed accounts of the uprising in chapter 4, "Evolution and Resolution of Conflict."

84. Detailed accounts of the Division Street riots are available in the Janet Nolan Ethnographic Research on Puerto Ricans in Chicago Collection, housed at DePaul University in Chicago. Michael Staudenmaier, "War on Poverty, War on Division Street: Puerto Rican Chicago in the 1960s through the Lens of the Janet Nolan Collection," *Centro: Journal of the Center for Puerto Rican Studies* 28, no. 2 (2016): 188.

85. Quoted in Staudenmaier, "War on Poverty," 188.

86. "Burn Cops' Cars; 35 Held," *Chicago Tribune*, June 13, 1966, 1.

87. "7 Shot in New Disorder: 37 in Defiant Crowd Seized on N. W. Side," *Chicago Tribune*, June 14, 1966, 1.

88. Donald Janson, "7 Shot in New Chicago Riot as Settlement Efforts Fail," *New York Times*, June 14, 1966, 1.

89. "Daley Urges Calm," *Chicago Tribune*, June 15, 1966, 2.

90. Thomas Power, "Puerto Ricans Give Demands to Daley Aids: More Than 200 Join Protest March," *Chicago Tribune*, June 29, 1966, A2.

91. "Controling [*sic*] Mobs," *Chicago Tribune*, June 14, 1966, 20.

92. Padilla, *Puerto Rican Chicago*, 154.

93. "Puerto Rican Grievances Heard by City," *Chicago Tribune*, July 16, 1966, 8.

94. "The language barrier and the problems involved in the transfer of rural Puerto Ricans to an urban society were the underlying factors behind Puerto Rican disturbances last June." Edward Schreiber, "Report on June Riot Tells Cause, Remedy," *Chicago Tribune*, December 16, 1966, 22.

95. Chicago Commission on Human Relations, *The Puerto Rican Residents of Chicago: A Report on An Open Hearing, July 15 and 16, 1966, Conducted by the Chicago Commission on Human Relations, and the Community Response to Date* (Chicago: Mayor's Committee on New Residents, Chicago Commission on Human Relations, 1966).

96. Ibid., 7.

97. Ibid., 14.

98. Ibid., 19.

99. Ibid.

100. Samuel Betances, interview by the author, September 25, 2009. Betances is a Harvard-educated Puerto Rican community member, who also founded *The Rican: A Journal of Puerto Rican Thought*. The journal created a space in the early 1970s for both community members and scholars to share their research and concerns regarding the Puerto Rican diaspora. For more on this, see Mirelsie Velazquez, "Solidarity and Empowerment in Chicago's Puerto Rican Print Culture," *Latino Studies* 12, no. 1 (2014): 88–110.

101. Forni, *Situation of the Puerto Rican Population*, 3.

102. "Mayor Daley Reveals Plans to Help City Puerto Ricans," *Chicago Tribune*, July 6, 1966, B6.

103. President Lyndon B. Johnson's historic passage of the Elementary and Secondary Education Act of 1965 sought to help disadvantaged schoolchildren improve academically through federal mandates such as Title 1 funding. As Erik W. Robelen writes, "Conceived as part of President Johnson's War on Poverty, the original statute was focused primarily on delivering federal aid to help level the educational playing field for poor and minority children. And Mr. Johnson—a former teacher at a predominantly Mexican-American school in Cotulla, Texas—had high hopes." Robelen, "40 Years after ESEA, Federal Role in Schools Is Broader Than Ever," *Education Week*, April 12, 2005, 1.

104. Anne Getz, "Puerto Rican Culture Brought into Schools," *Chicago Tribune*, July 14, 1966, F2.

105. Joan Pinkerton, "300 Attend Puerto Rican Conference," *Chicago Tribune*, May 28, 1967, 3.

106. "108 Teachers Taking Lessons in Spanish: Many Pupils Can Speak No English," *Chicago Tribune*, October 23, 1966, B6.

107. According to Felix Padilla, Los Caballeros served as the main outlet for social organization for the city's Puerto Ricans, first as an institution and then as a means

of cultural transmission. The organization, according to Padilla, offered a way for the population "to structure a self-conscious community for ethnic advancement." *Puerto Rican Chicago*, 126.

108. Serving as a counterintelligence program within the Federal Bureau of Investigation (FBI) between 1956 and 1971, COINTELPRO was utilized as a surveillance tool to both gain information on and infiltrate organizations deemed "subversive." African American, Puerto Rican, and American Indian groups became the targets of investigations. See Padilla, *Puerto Rican Chicago*; Ramos-Zayas, *National Performances*; and Pérez, *Near Northwest Side Story*.

109. Padilla, *Puerto Rican Chicago*, 165.

110. Ibid., 166.

111. Ibid., 178. In chapter 4, "Evolution and Resolution of Conflict," Padilla details the actions of the Chicago Police Department in deterring community activism and demonstrations and limiting free speech in order to diminish the community's political activism and cohesiveness.

112. Robert Wiedrich, "Quit Spanish Group, Say Reds Move In: Five Founders Tell of Virtual Take-over," *Chicago Tribune*, September 3, 1966, 17.

113. Robert Wiedrich, "Puerto Ricans Rip 'Take-over' by Outsiders: Demands Written by Others, They Charge," *Chicago Tribune*, September 4, 1966, 5.

114. Sister Janet Nolan, interview, in *The Price of Dissent: Testimonies to Political Repression in America*, by Bud Schultz and Ruth Schultz (Berkeley: University of California Press, 2001), 428.

115. Although the 1960s ushered in a new wave of surveillance of Chicago's Puerto Rican community under the Red Squad program, surveillance of the population dating back to the 1940s is well documented in FBI records. As early as the summer of 1949, the FBI took note of organizing in Chicago by members of the Nationalist Party of Puerto Rico, and by 1953 the bureau began recording and transmitting information to other FBI offices about the growing nationalist presence in Chicago. Federal Surveillance of the Partido Independentista Puertorriqueño, Archives Unbound (Gale database).

116. See Frank Donner, *Protectors of Privilege: Red Squads and Police Repression in Urban America* (Berkeley: University of California Press, 1990), 90–154; and Schultz and Schultz, *Price of Dissent*, 402–34.

117. Richard "Rick" Gutman, interview, in Schultz and Schultz, *Price of Dissent*, 429.

118. Ibid. Originally excerpted from a trial transcript of the direct examination of Juan Díaz in the case *Spanish Action Committee of Chicago v. City of Chicago*, No. 80 C 4714 (1984).

119. Pedro Cabán, "Cointelpro" (2005), *Latin American, Caribbean, and U.S. Latino Studies Faculty Scholarship*, 18, http://scholarsarchive.library.albany.edu/lacs_fac_scholar/1.

120. Emma Pérez, *The Decolonial Imaginary: Writing Chicanas into History* (Bloomington: Indiana University Press, 1999), 12.

121. Casey Banas, "City's Public Schools Now 52 Pct. Negro: Whites Drop to 41.5 Per Cent," *Chicago Tribune*, October 25, 1967, 1.

122. Casey Banas, "Poor Lighting Puts School in Dark Ages: Eyestrain Is Common Teaching Problem," *Chicago Tribune*, April 1, 1968, 20.

123. Ibid. For more on the struggles and history of the Chicago Teachers Union, see John F. Lyons, *Teachers and Reform: Chicago Public Education, 1929–1970* (Urbana: University of Illinois Press, 2008); and Herrick, *Chicago Schools*.

124. Joy Darrow, "Public Hearing Set on School Transfers," *Chicago Tribune*, December 21, 1967, W4.

125. Ibid.

126. Nitza M. Hidalgo, "Toward a Definition of a Latino Family Research Paradigm," in *Race Is . . . Race Isn't: Critical Race Theory and Qualitative Studies in Education*, ed. Laurence Parker, Donna Deyhle, and Sofia Villenas (Boulder, CO: Westview Press, 1999), 109–10.

127. For more on the creation of one such space, see René Antrop-González, "'This School Is My Sanctuary': The Dr. Pedro Albizu Campos Alternative High School," *Centro: Journal of the Center for Puerto Rican Studies* 15, no. 2 (2003): 232–55.

128. José "Cha Cha" Jiménez, interview by the author, September 20, 2008. Jiménez was a founder and long-time member of the Chicago Young Lords Organization (YLO). The YLO began as a local community gang, but evolved into a community-based activist organization. One of its early struggles involved the fight for community control of Lincoln Park High School in Chicago, as well as involvement in other schools. See Johanna Fernández, *The Young Lords: A Radical History* (Chapel Hill: University of North Carolina Press, 2019).

129. Lucas, *Puerto Rican Dropouts*, 6.

130. "Victor Y, Age 13," in *The Me Nobody Knows*, ed. Stephen M. Joseph (New York: Avon Books, 1969), 20.

131. Aspira was the brainchild of Puerto Rican educator and community activist Antonia Pantoja. Originally a New York organization aimed at alleviating the educational concerns of Puerto Ricans in the diaspora, Aspira spread to dozens of cities and focused on all Latino students. For more on its history, see Antonia Pantoja, "Puerto Ricans in New York: A Historical and Community Development Perspective," *Centro de Estudios Puertorriqueños Bulletin* 2, no. 5–8 (1989): 21–31.

132. "Chicago Puerto Rico Youths to Get Aid," *Chicago Tribune*, November 14, 1968, 24.

133. Betances, interview.

134. Ibid.

135. Carolyn Shojai, "Latins Form Group to Develop, Train Spanish Leaders," *Chicago Tribune*, March 16, 1969, N3.

136. Mirta Ramírez, interview, March 29, 2004, Mirta Ramírez Puerto Rican Oral History Project, DePaul University Center for Latino Research Records, Special Collections and Archives, DePaul University Library, Chicago. For more on Mirta

Ramírez, see Mirelsie Velazquez, "Looking Forward, Working for Change: Puerto Rican Women and the Quest for Educational Justice in Chicago," *Centro: Journal of the Center for Puerto Rican Studies* 28, no. 2 (2016): 126–53.

137. Betances, interview.

138. Ramírez, interview.

139. Ibid.

140. Ibid.

141. Ibid.

142. Vicki L. Ruiz and Virginia Sánchez Korrol, "Introduction," in *Latina Legacies: Identity, Biography, and Community*, ed. Ruiz and Sánchez Korrol (New York: Oxford University Press, 2005), 6.

143. Isidro Lucas, interview by the author, November 2014.

144. See Herrick, *Chicago Schools*, 378; and Danns, *Desegregating Chicago's Public Schools*.

145. "Two New Faces," *Chicago Tribune*, July 16, 1969, 24.

146. Peter Negronida, "Two Nominees OK'd for Board of Education: Full City Council Vote May Come Today," *Chicago Tribune*, July 29, 1969, 11.

147. Ibid.

148. Ibid.

149. Ibid.

150. Peter Negronida, "School Board Hears Gripes for 13 Hours: 117 Give Views on Education," *Chicago Tribune*, November 4, 1969, 2.

151. Ofelia García, "Educating New York's Bilingual Children: Constructing a Future from the Past," *International Journal of Bilingual Education and Bilingualism* 14, no. 2 (2011): 134.

152. Betances, interview; "Two New Faces."

153. María Cerda, interview by Lilia Fernández, June 2004. This interview is the property of Lilia Fernández.

154. Ibid.

155. Betances, interview.

156. Peter Negronida, "Daley's Selections Jeopardize His Influence over School Board," *Chicago Tribune*, July 20, 1969, 20.

157. Negronida, "School Board Hears Gripes."

158. María B. Cerda and Jean J. Schensul, "The Chicago Parent Leadership Training Program," in *Working with the Bilingual Community*, by the National Clearinghouse for Bilingual Education (Rosslyn, VA: InterAmerica Research Associates, 1979), 15–27.

159. Cerda, interview.

160. Washburn, "These Puerto Ricans Like It Here."

161. Padilla, *Puerto Rican Chicago*, 143.

162. Priddy, "Puerto Rican Kids Perfect Their English."

163. Diamond, *Mean Streets*, 8.

Chapter 3. Taking It to the Streets

1. For the purpose of his study, Lucas defined the Puerto Rican dropout as "a young person who having received a substantial part of his/her education in the continent has stopped attending school without obtaining a high school diploma, for any reason except death." *Puerto Rican Dropouts*, 19.

2. Isidro Lucas, interview by the author, November 2014.

3. Ibid.

4. Lucas, *Puerto Rican Dropouts*.

5. James B. Barrera, "The 1968 Edcouch-Elsa High School Walkout: Chicano Student Activism in a South Texas Community," *Aztlán: A Journal of Chicano Studies* 29, no. 2 (2004): 93–122. For more on the history of Chicana/o school activism, see Armando L. Trujillo, *Chicano Empowerment and Bilingual Education: Movimiento Politics in Crystal City, Texas* (New York: Routledge, 2014); Guadalupe San Miguel Jr. and Richard Valencia, "From the Treaty of Guadalupe Hidalgo to Hopwood: The Educational Plight and Struggle of Mexican Americans in the Southwest," *Harvard Educational Review* 68, no. 3 (1998): 353–413; Guadalupe San Miguel Jr., *Brown, Not White: School Integration and the Chicano Movement in Houston* (College Station: Texas A&M University Press, 2005); and Maylei Blackwell, "Contested Histories: *Las Hijas de Cuauhtémoc*, Chicana Feminisms, and Print Culture in the Chicano Movement, 1968–1973," in *Chicana Feminisms: A Critical Reader*, ed. Gabriela F. Arredondo, Aída Hurtado, Norma Klahn, Olga Nájera-Ramírez, and Patricia Zavella (Durham, NC: Duke University Press, 2003), 59–89.

6. Dwayne C. Wright, "Black Pride Day, 1968: High School Student Activism in York, Pennsylvania," *Journal of African American History* 88, no. 2 (2003): 151–62.

7. Forni, *Situation of the Puerto Rican Population*, 1.

8. "C.L.A.S.E.S.," Office of the President James Mullen Memos, box D 2/51, folder DD-1-1, Northeastern Illinois University Special Collections, NEIU Libraries, Chicago (hereafter NEIUSC).

9. Dolores Delgado Bernal, "Rethinking Grassroots Activism: Chicana Resistance in the 1968 East Los Angeles School Blowouts," in *The Subaltern Speak: Curriculum, Power, and Educational Struggles*, ed. Michael W. Apple and Kristen L. Buras (New York: Routledge, 2006), 141.

10. Dionne Danns, *Something Better for Our Children: Black Organization in the Chicago Public Schools, 1963–1971* (New York: Routledge, 2003).

11. Danns, *Desegregating Chicago's Public Schools*, 61.

12. Todd-Breland, *Political Education*, 123.

13. Ibid., 62.

14. See Jonna Perrillo, *Uncivil Rights: Teachers, Unions, and Race in the Battle for School Equity* (Chicago: University of Chicago Press, 2012).

15. Ibid., 118.

16. Danns, *Desegregating Chicago's Public Schools*, 57.

17. Ibid., 62.

18. Ibid., 19.

19. John P. Reilly, "James F. Redmond: An Urban Superintendent's Response to Selected Challenges (1966–1975)" (EdD diss., Loyola University of Chicago, 1991). Reilly offers a detailed account of Redmond and the Orleans Parish School Board's battle with local white families in their move to desegregate local schools. White community members boycotted integrated schools and implemented a near-embargo across the community in seeking to control Redmond and the school board.

20. Danns, *Desegregating Chicago's Public Schools*, 19–55.

21. Ibid., 20.

22. "Another Day of Disorders Hits Schools: Strikes, Protests and Vandalism," *Chicago Tribune*, October 10, 1968, 1.

23. Donald Mosby, "2 Schools Hit by Warning: Students Issue Demands," *Chicago Daily Defender*, October 12, 1968, 1. See Diamond, *Mean Streets*, for a more detailed account of Black student activism in Chicago during the late 1960s.

24. "Another Day of Disorders Hits Schools."

25. Diamond, *Mean Streets*, 294.

26. Peter Negronida, "28,000 Out in 2d Boycott of Schools," *Chicago Tribune*, October 22, 1968, 1; Herrick, *Chicago Schools*; Dionne Danns, "Black Student Empowerment and Chicago School Reform Efforts in 1968," *Urban Education* 37, no. 5 (2002): 631–55; Jaime Alanis, "The Harrison High School Walkouts of 1968: Struggle for Equal Schools and Chicanismo in Chicago" (PhD diss., University of Illinois Urbana-Champaign, 2010). Alanis challenges the labeling of Harrison's students as all Puerto Rican, given that the Spanish-speaking residents in the area in 1968 were primarily of Mexican descent.

27. Herrick, *Chicago Schools*, 364.

28. Peter Born, "Lake View High Staff Listens to Student Grievances," *Chicago Tribune*, November 7, 1968, N5.

29. Ibid.

30. Herrick, *Chicago Schools*, 364.

31. "Students Protest Latin Policies," *Chicago Tribune*, May 11, 1971, 4.

32. "Urges Action to Cope with School Furor: Union Asks Redmond to Clarify Policy," *Chicago Tribune*, October 12, 1968, 11.

33. Chicago Board of Education, *Racial Survey, Administrative and Teaching Personnel* (1968-), Chicago Board of Education Archives (hereafter CBE).

34. "School Board Hears from Spanish-Speaking," *Chicago Tribune*, November 9, 1969, 6.

35. Lucas, *Puerto Rican Dropouts*, 44.

36. Lucas, "Profile of the Puerto Rican Dropout," 23.

37. Ibid., 24.

38. Lucas, interview.

39. Lucas, *Puerto Rican Dropouts*, Author's Abstract.

40. Ibid., 62.

41. Ibid., 7, 25.

42. Ibid., 26.

43. Ibid., 28.

44. Ibid., Author's Abstract.

45. Ibid., 8.

46. Chicago Board of Education, *Racial Survey, Administrative and Teaching Personnel* (1971), CBE.

47. Lucas, "Profile of the Puerto Rican Drop Out," 28.

48. Ibid., 29.

49. Padilla, *Puerto Rican Chicago*, 251n5.

50. Ibid., 214.

51. Chicago Board of Education, *Racial Survey, Administrative and Teaching Personnel* (1972), CBE.

52. James A. Jackson, "Education Still Top Priority for Spanish-Speaking of City," *Chicago Tribune*, October 16, 1975, W1. Latino and African American community members protested the appointment of Hannon over Deputy Superintendent Manford Byrd. Jesse Jackson organized a community protest at the board's offices, without success. Danns, *Desegregating Chicago's Public Schools*, 77.

53. Padilla, *Puerto Rican Chicago*, 214. Padilla similarly documented the district's recruitment and training of bilingual and bicultural degree holders from American universities whose programs lacked teaching degrees.

54. Voluntary reasons for withdrawals, according to the Board of Education, included leaving school for such things as verifiable employment, because the student was needed at home by family or was getting married, and poor scholarship. Involuntary reasons for withdrawals included transferring to other day schools in the city, being excused from school temporarily due to physical or intellectual disability, and death. Lucas, *Puerto Rican Dropouts*, 14–15.

55. For more on the history of the school, which later became Pedro Albizu Campos High School, see René Antrop González and Anthony De Jesús, "Toward a Theory of Critical Care in Urban Small School Reform: Examining Structures and Pedagogies of Caring in Two Latino Community-Based Schools," *International Journal of Qualitative Studies in Education* 19, no. 4 (2006): 409–33.

56. James Jackson, "Puerto Ricans Here Set Up Free School to Aid Dropouts," *Chicago Tribune*, April 8, 1973, 50.

57. Joette Getse, "Educational Consultants Praise Chicago's Community Participation," *Chicago Tribune*, March 2, 1969, SCL8.

58. "Groups to Decide on New Humboldt Park High," *Chicago Tribune*, October 15, 1967, R2.

59. James Nathan, "Wrangle Clouds Future of Site for New Tuley High," *Chicago Tribune*, January 25, 1970, NW5.

60. James Nathan, "Residents Protest Tuley High School Approval Delay," *Chicago Tribune*, December 28, 1969, NW3.

61. Eugene Siskel, "N. C. O. Congress Backs High School Site," *Chicago Tribune*, March 2, 1969, NW10.

62. "City Officials Get Tour of Tuley High, Humboldt Park Site," *Chicago Tribune*, April 23, 1970, N2.

63. "Nueva Escuela Tuley Si! En el Parque Humbolt No!," *El Puertorriqueño*, January 15–21, 1970, 5.

64. Ibid.

65. "Caballeros Se Oponen a Tuley en El Parque," *El Puertorriqueno*, March 5–11, 1970, 2.

66. For more on the history of the newspaper, see Velazquez, "Solidarity and Empowerment."

67. "City Officials Get Tour."

68. "Se Salvo el Humboldt Park," *El Puertorriqueno*, April 6–30, 1970, 2.

69. Ibid., 9.

70. "Latin American Students Rally," *Chicago Tribune*, May 12, 1971, B9.

71. "Demand Principal's Ouster," *Chicago Tribune*, October 8, 1971, 3.

72. "Latin Pupils Constitute 10.4% of City Enrolment," *Chicago Tribune*, November 23, 1971, C14.

73. Robert Nolte, "Latins Plan Boycott to Oust Tuley Chief," *Chicago Tribune*, October 7, 1971, A2.

74. Ibid.

75. Jack Houston, "School Board to Open 9 Outposts for Dropouts," *Chicago Tribune*, October 21, 1971, N2.

76. "Board Dismisses Dropout Curb Plan," *Chicago Tribune*, November 18, 1971, N3.

77. Ibid.

78. Ibid.

79. Carlos Caribe Ruíz, "Acuerdan Nombrar Escuela Tuley Eugenio Maria de Hostos," *El Puertorriqueno*, December 10–16, 1970, 3. Hostos was a prominent figure on the island, known for his work in education, literature, and philosophy, and was also an advocate for Puerto Rican independence.

80. "Report of Committee to Study Names Submitted for New School Building of the City of Chicago," January 31, 1973, CBE.

81. "Preliminary Proposal Submission: A Secondary Bilingual/Bicultural Center" (1973), CBE.

82. Fredric Soll and Edith Herman, "Tuley Protesters Battle Police," *Chicago Tribune*, February 1, 1973, 3.

83. Ibid.

84. Fredric Soll and Peter Negronida, "Tuley Staff, Protesters Agree to Open School," *Chicago Tribune*, February 2, 1973, 3.

85. Ibid.

86. Ibid.

87. "Tuley High School," *Chicago Defender*, February 7, 1973, 15.

88. Lucas, *Puerto Rican Dropouts*, 26.

89. "Principal at Tuley Ousted: District Head Acts in Dispute," *Chicago Tribune*, February 6, 1973, 1.

90. Ibid.

91. Bob Buchanan, "Tuley Student Speaks," *Chicago Tribune*, February 7, 1973, 12.

92. A. Fitzgerald, "Tuley Park: What a Sin," *Chicago Defender*, February 19, 1973, 4.

93. Fredric Soll and James Jackson, "'The Tuley Thing . . . It Gave People a Chance to Win,'" *Chicago Tribune*, February 18, 1973, 43.

94. Aida Sanchez, "The Tuley Experience," *Que Ondee Sola* 1, no. 12 (March 15, 1973): 7.

95. Isidro Lucas, "Puerto Rican Politics in Chicago," in *Puerto Rican Politics in Urban America*, ed. James Jennings and Monte Rivera (Westport, CT: Greenwood Press, 1984), 107.

96. For more on the struggle over the status of Puerto Rico and the narratives about organizational responses to the political movement, see Margaret Power, "From Freedom Fighters to Patriots: The Successful Campaign to Release the FALN Political Prisoners, 1980–1999," *Centro: Journal of the Center for Puerto Rican Studies* 25, no. 1 (2013): 146–79; Ramos-Zayas, *National Performances*; Jeffrey O. G. Ogbar, "Puerto Rico en mi corazón: The Young Lords, Black Power and Puerto Rican Nationalism in the U.S., 1966–1972," *Centro: Journal of the Center for Puerto Rican Studies* 18, no. 1 (2006): 148–69; and Andrés Torres and José Emiliano Velázquez, eds., *The Puerto Rican Movement: Voices from the Diaspora* (Philadelphia: Temple University Press, 1998).

97. Vanessa Baerga, "Carmen Valentín: 'The Historical Moment I Was Living In Presented Me with This Option of Struggle, and I Accepted It,'" trans. Jan Susler, National Boricua Human Rights Network, December 22, 2009, https://boricuahumanrights.org.

98. Soll and Herman, "Tuley Protesters Battle Police."

99. Rudy Unger and Patricia Leeds, "28 in Student Protest Seized; 22 Cops Injured," *Chicago Tribune*, November 13, 1974, 3.

100. Ibid.

101. Ibid.

102. "Units Plan to Avert Trouble at Clemente," *Chicago Tribune*, November 14, 1974, 6.

103. "Who's Winning at Clemente?," *Chicago Tribune*, November 16, 1974, N16.

104. John O'Brien, "Ex-Chicago Teacher Called 'Godmother' of FALN Here," *Chicago Tribune*, April 11, 1980, A4.

105. Rick Soll, "Many Forces at Work at Clemente," *Chicago Tribune*, November 14, 1974, 6.

106. Lucas, *Puerto Rican Dropouts*, 9.

Chapter 4. Learning to Resist, Resisting to Learn

1. Miguel del Valle, interview with Maximino Torres, June 12, 1981, as quoted in Torres, "An Attempt to Provide Higher Educational Opportunity to Hispanics: The

Evolution of Proyecto Pa'lante at Northeastern Illinois University—1971–1976" (PhD diss., Loyola University Chicago, 1983), 324, 328.

2. Ibid., 331.

3. Maximino Torres, "Becoming a Counselor for Puerto Rican Students in a University in the United States," *Que Ondee Sola* 1, no. 4 (March 21, 1972): 3.

4. Martha Biondi, *The Black Revolution on Campus* (Berkeley: University of California Press, 2012), 1.

5. This is not a complete list, but for more on the Black student movement of the 1960s and 1970s, see Peniel E. Joseph, "Dashikis and Democracy: Black Studies, Student Activism, and the Black Power Movement," *Journal of African American History* 88, no. 2 (2003): 182–203; Richard D. Benson, *Fighting for Our Place in the Sun: Malcolm X and the Radicalization of the Black Student Movement, 1960–1973* (New York: Peter Lang, 2015); William C. Gibbons, Adrienne Petty, and Sydney C. Van Nort, "Revolutionary Times Revisited: Students' Interpretations of the City College of New York Student Protest and Takeover of 1969," *History Teacher* 47, no. 4 (2014): 511–28; Delores P. Aldridge and Carlene Young, eds., *Out of the Revolution: The Development of Africana Studies* (Lanham, MD: Lexington Books, 2000); Ibram H. Rogers, "The Black Campus Movement and the Institutionalization of Black Studies, 1965–1970," *Journal of African American Studies* 16, no. 1 (2012): 21–40; Rogers, "The Black Campus Movement: The Case For a New Historiography," *The Sixties* 4, no. 2 (2011): 171–86; Wayne C. Glasker, *Black Students in the Ivory Tower: African American Student Activism at the University of Pennsylvania, 1967–1990* (Amherst: University of Massachusetts Press, 2009); and Jon N. Hale, *The Freedom Schools: Student Activists in the Mississippi Civil Rights Movement* (New York: Columbia University Press, 2016).

6. Stefan M. Bradley, *Harlem vs. Columbia University: Black Student Power in the Late 1960s* (Urbana: University of Illinois Press, 2010); Bradley, "'Gym Crow Must Go!' Black Student Activism at Columbia University, 1967–1968," *Journal of African American History* 88, no. 2 (2003): 163–81.

7. See Maylei Blackwell, ¡*Chicana Power!: Contested Histories of Feminism in the Chicano Movement* (Austin: University of Texas Press, 2016); Darius V. Echeverría, *Aztlán Arizona: Mexican American Educational Empowerment, 1968–1978* (Tucson: University of Arizona Press, 2014); Roderick A. Ferguson, *We Demand: The University and Student Protests* (Berkeley: University of California Press, 2017); Carlos Muñoz, *Youth, Identity, Power: The Chicano Movement* (London: Verso, 2007); Margarita Berta-Ávila, Anita Tijerina Revilla, and Julie López Figueroa, eds., *Marching Students: Chicana and Chicano Activism in Education, 1968 to the Present* (Reno: University of Nevada Press, 2011); Guadalupe San Miguel Jr., *Chicana/o Struggles for Education: Activism in the Community* (College Station: Texas A&M University Press, 2013); and David Montejano, *Quixote's Soldiers: A Local History of the Chicano Movement, 1966–1981* (Austin: University of Texas Press, 2010).

8. Gerald Meyer, "Save Hostos: Politics and Community Mobilization to Save a College in the Bronx, 1973–1978," *Centro: Journal of the Center for Puerto Rican Studies* 15, no. 1 (2003): 97.

9. Enrollment statistics and trends can be found in the Illinois Board of Higher Education's annual *Data Book on Illinois Higher Education* (1974-).

10. "Demonstration against the University Circle Campus, Monday March 4, 1974, 12 Noon," Rafael Cintrón Ortiz Latino Cultural Center Archives, University of Illinois at Chicago (hereafter LCC).

11. Joseph, "Dashikis and Democracy," 191–92.

12. "The Union: Our History at Northeastern," *Que Ondee Sola* 1, no. 1 (January 27, 1972): 3.

13. "Mass-Media for Education," *Que Ondee Sola* 1, no. 1 (January 27, 1972): 4.

14. Ibid.

15. Padilla, *Puerto Rican Chicago*, 184.

16. Torres, "Attempt to Provide Higher Educational Opportunity," 38.

17. Ibid., 331.

18. For a discussion of Black student activism in higher education, see Eddie R. Cole, *The Campus Color Line: College Presidents and the Struggle for Black Freedom* (Princeton, NJ: Princeton University Press, 2020); Glasker, *Black Students in the Ivory Tower*; Thomas Aiello, "Violence Is a Classroom: The 1972 Grambling and Southern Riots and the Trajectory of Black Student Protest," *Louisiana History: The Journal of the Louisiana Historical Association* 53, no. 3 (2012): 261–91; Joy Ann Williamson-Lott, "The Battle over Power, Control, and Academic Freedom at Southern Institutions of Higher Education, 1955–1965," *Journal of Southern History* 79, no. 4 (2013): 879–920; Williamson-Lott, *Jim Crow Campus: Higher Education and the Struggle for a New Southern Social Order* (New York: Teachers College Press, 2018); and Williamson-Lott, "'We Hope for Nothing, We Demand Everything': Black Students at the University of Illinois at Urbana-Champaign, 1965–1975" (PhD diss., University of Illinois at Urbana-Champaign, 1998).

19. Northwestern University Black Students, "If Our Demands Are Impossible, Then Peace between Us Is Impossible Too," in *Black Nationalism in America*, ed. John H. Bracey Jr. (Indianapolis: Bobbs-Merrill, 1970), 477.

20. Alice Gaber, "¡Aquí Estoy!—Here I Am," *American Education* 7, no. 1 (January/February 1971): 18–22.

21. Ibid., 22.

22. "C.L.A.S.E.S.," 1, Office of the President James Mullen Memos, box D 2/51, folder DD-1-1, NEIUSC.

23. Ibid.

24. Ibid.

25. Miguel A. Velazquez to Jaime Delgado, November 1973, Office of the President James Mullen Memos, box D 2/51, folder DD-1-1, NEIUSC.

26. Union for Puerto Rican Students, "Demands for the Dismissal of Miguel A. Velasquez [*sic*] as Director of C.L.A.S.E.S.," memo to Dr. James H. Mullen, February 17, 1975, Office of the President James Mullen Memos, box D 2/51, folder DD-1-1, NEIUSC.

27. Ibid.

28. Aida Illeana Laboy to Vice President of Student Affairs Major, January 22, 1975, Office of the President James Mullen Memos, box D 2/51, folder DD-1-1, NEIUSC.

29. John K. Major, "Mr. Miguel Velazquez and C.L.A.S.E.S.," memo to President Mullen, February 19, 1975, Office of the President James Mullen Memos, box D 2/51, folder DD-1-1, NEIUSC.

30. Ibid.

31. President James H. Mullen to Miguel Velazquez, February 25, 1975, Office of the President James Mullen Memos, box D 2/51, folder DD-1-1, NEIUSC.

32. "Student Victory," *Que Ondee Sola*, Special Edition, February 1975, 1.

33. Ibid.

34. Ibid.

35. Ibid., 1–2.

36. Irma Acevedo to President James Mullen, March 21, 1975, Office of the President James Mullen Memos, box D 2/51, folder DD1-1, NEIUSC.

37. Ibid.

38. James Mullen to Luis Gutierrez, June 25, 1975, Office of the President James Mullen Memos, box D 2/51, folder dated July 23, 1975: "Memo to Luis Gutierrez, Pres. Union for Puerto Rican Students, Dispute re: C.L.A.S.E.S.," NEIUSC.

39. Union for Puerto Rican Students, memo to President Mullen, June 23, 1975, Office of the President James Mullen Memos, box D 2/51, folder DD-1-1, NEIUSC.

40. Mullen to Gutierrez, June 25, 1975.

41. Ibid.

42. Mullen to Don Walters, July 18, 1975, Office of the President James Mullen Memos, box D 2/51, folder dated July 18, 1975: "Memo to B.O.G. re: Social Movement in Union for Puerto Rican Students," NEIUSC.

43. Union for Puerto Rican Students to President Mullen, July 23, 1975, Office of the President James Mullen Memos, box D 2/51, folder dated July 23, 1975: "Memo to Luis Gutierrez, Pres. Union for Puerto Rican Students, Dispute re: C.L.A.S.E.S.," NEIUSC.

44. Coalition of C.L.A.S.E.S. to NEIU Board of Governors, Office of the President James Mullen Memos, box D 2/51, folder DD-1-1, NEIUSC.

45. James Mullen to Don Walters, December 22, 1975, Office of the President James Mullen Memos, box D 2/51, folder DD-1-1, NEIUSC.

46. Padilla, *Puerto Rican Chicago*, 187.

47. Torres, "Attempt to Provide Higher Educational Opportunity."

48. Ibid., 114.

49. Ibid., 116.

50. Ibid., 164–67.

51. Ibid., 176.

52. "¡Envolvimiento Estudiantil!," *Que Ondee Sola* 4, no. 1 (September 1974): 6.

53. "Welcome Latino Freshman!," *Que Ondee Sola* 5, no. 1 (September 1975): 1.

54. "Proyecto Pa'lante Uses Alliance," *Lucha Estudiantil*, September 1975, 1. *Lucha Estudiantil* was a short-run newspaper created by members of the Union for Puerto

Rican Students. According to the inaugural issue, its mission was "to defend the genuine interests of the student body; to confront and unmask the administration; as we put the student body on alert before the 'liberalism' of the other newspapers."

55. Ibid.

56. "Maximo Torres Does It Again!!," *Que Ondee Sola*, October 21, 1977, 3.

57. Torres, "Attempt to Provide Higher Educational Opportunity," 198.

58. Ibid., 200.

59. Ibid., 202.

60. "Editorial," *Que Ondee Sola*, October 1976, 11.

61. Torres, "Attempt to Provide Higher Educational Opportunity," 207.

62. Untitled fact sheet, 1973, binder A-1, LCC. The fact sheet was compiled by student activists during the 1973 protests. Other items related to the history of student activism at UIC can be found in the Rafael Cintrón Ortiz Latino Cultural Center Records, box 19, folder 489, Special Collections and University Archives, University of Illinois at Chicago (hereafter UICSC).

63. Ibid.

64. Ibid.

65. Ibid.

66. Puerto Rican Advisory Board, "Discrimination against Puerto Ricans at Circle Campus," August 1973, binder A, folder "Student Protest Flyers, 1973–1976," LCC.

67. For more on the student struggles at the University of Illinois at Urbana-Champaign, see Joy Ann Williamson, *Black Power on Campus: The University of Illinois, 1965–75* (Urbana: University of Illinois Press, 2003).

68. Paul Vega, "Admission of Additional Latin American Students to the University of Illinois at Chicago Circle Campus through Special Action" [1971], 1, Office of the Chancellor Records, Chancellor's Central Files, Series 2, Subseries 3, box 159, folder 1508, UICSC.

69. Ibid., 3.

70. Ibid., 4.

71. Vice Chancellor Leonard E. Goodall to Paul Vega, March 19, 1971, Office of the Chancellor Records, Chancellor's Central Files, Series 2, Subseries 3, box 159, folder 1508, UICSC.

72. Ibid.

73. University of Illinois Board of Trustees Meeting, July 18, 1973, 337. Meeting minutes for the University of Illinois Board of Trustees can be found at https://www .bot.uillinois.edu/meetings/minutes.

74. Untitled fact sheet, 2.

75. Binder A, folder titled "UHS Sit-In Documents, 1973," LCC.

76. "Latins Charge Racism: Circle Recruiting Hit," *Chicago Today*, September 27, 1973, 10.

77. Ibid.

78. University of Illinois Board of Trustees meeting minutes, July 18, 1973, 337.

79. Ibid.

80. "Demand More Latins at Circle," *Chicago Tribune*, September 27, 1973, B9.

81. "Circle Campus vs. the Latin Community of Chicago" (1973), 2, binder A, folder "Student Protest Flyers, 1973–1976," LCC.

82. Ibid.

83. Ibid.

84. "38 Seized in Latin Protest at U. I . Circle," *Chicago Tribune*, September 28, 1973, 3.

85. Flyer, "Court Day For the 39 People Arrested at U of I (Circle), Thursday October 4, 9AM," binder A, folder "Student Protest Flyers, 1973–1976," LCC.

86. "Cheston Discriminates" (1973), binder A, folder "Student Protest Flyers, 1973–1976," LCC.

87. University of Illinois Board of Trustees meeting minutes, October 17, 1973, 378.

88. University of Illinois Board of Trustees meeting minutes, April 17, 1974, 548.

89. Ibid.

90. Sheila Castillo to Michael B. Goldstein, August 2, 1974, Office of the Chancellor Records, Chancellor's Central Files, Series 2, Subseries 3, box 159, folder 1508, UICSC.

91. Ibid.

92. Patricia McFate to Dr. Warren B. Cheston, August 12, 1974, Office of the Chancellor Records, Chancellor's Central Files, Series 2, Subseries 3, box 159, folder 1508, UICSC.

93. Latin American Students' Coalition to Chancellor Warren E. Cheston and Others, March 31, 1975, Office of the Chancellor Records, Chancellor's Central Files, Series 1, Subseries 1, box 60, folder 807, UICSC.

94. "Proposal for the Establishment of the Latin American Recruitment and Educational Services (LARES) as Presented by Latin American Studies," May 9, 1975, Office of the Chancellor Records, Chancellor's Central Files, Series 1, Subseries 1, box 60, folder 807, UICSC.

95. Otto Pikaza, "Addendum Concerning the Creation of a Latin American Cultural Center," May 28, 1975, Office of the Chancellor Records, Chancellor's Central Files, Series 1, Subseries 1, box 60, folder 807, UICSC.

96. Ibid., 3.

97. Jose Ortiz, Community Liaison to EAP, memorandum to Paul Vega, September 30, 1974, Committee—Latin American Cultural Center, Office of the Chancellor Records, Chancellor's Central Files, Series 1, Subseries 1, box 60, folder 807, UICSC.

98. Ira W. Langston and E. E. Oliver, *A Study of Special Support Programs at the Chicago Circle Campus of the University of Illinois: A Summary Report of Research Memorandum No. 77-8* (Urbana: University of Illinois, University Office of School and College Relations, 1977).

99. Ibid., 27.

100. Ibid.

101. Vice Chancellor Eugene Wagner to the Latin American Cultural Center Committee, June 1, 1976, Office of the Chancellor Records, Chancellor's Central Files, Series 1, Subseries 1, box 84, folder 1010, UICSC.

102. Associate Vice Chancellor Richard Johnson to Chancellor Donald H. Riddle, October 5, 1976, Office of the Chancellor Records, Chancellor's Central Files, Series 1, Subseries 1, box 84, folder 1010, UICSC.

103. Ibid.

104. "Centro Cultural Rafael Cintrón Ortiz/Rafael Cintrón Ortiz Center for Latin American Culture," Office of the Chancellor Records, Chancellor's Central Files, Series 1, Subseries 1, box 84, folder 1010, UICSC.

105. "Latin American Cultural Center Committee to All Faculty, Students, and Concerned Community," September 27, 1976, Office of the Chancellor Records, Chancellor's Central Files, Series 1, Subseries 1, box 84, folder 1010, UICSC. Born in Arroyo, Puerto Rico, in 1946, Rafael Cintrón Ortiz became a beloved figure on campus as a professor in the Latin American Studies Program. He died in February 1976. His personal papers are archived at the LCC. For biographical information, see "Rafael Cintrón Ortiz," Rafael Cintrón Ortiz Latino Cultural Center, http://latinocultural .uic.edu/about/rafael-cintron-ortiz/.

106. *El Grito Estudiantil* (Union Pro-Estudiantes Puertorriqueños), Special Issue, February 1976, binder A, LCC.

107. Papers of the Chicano Boricua Union, 1974–1975, binder E, LCC.

108. Arisve Esquivel, "On Whose Terms? The (In)visibility of the Latina/o Community at the University of Illinois at Urbana-Champaign," *Counterpoints* 195 (2003): 123–43. Unbeknownst to students, administrators at the Circle Campus warned their colleagues in Urbana-Champaign to avoid the turmoil they had faced in Chicago dealing with their Latina/o students.

109. Padilla, *Puerto Rican Chicago*, 189.

110. Joseph, "Dashikis and Democracy," 191.

Chapter 5. Living and Writing in the Puerto Rican Diaspora

1. The church taken over by the Young Lords, known then as the Armitage Street Methodist Church, was rebranded as the People's Church.

2. Studs Terkel, *Fiesta: A Chicago Happening*, pt. 2, August 23, 1969, Studs Terkel Radio Archive, https://studsterkel.digitalrelab.com/?s=file=9062.

3. Ibid.

4. Ibid.

5. See Velazquez, "Solidarity and Empowerment."

6. Nicolás Kanellos, "A Brief History of Hispanic Periodicals in the United States," in *Hispanic Periodicals in the United States, Origins to 1960: A Brief History and Comprehensive Bibliography*, by Nicolás Kanellos and Helvetia Martell (Houston: Arte Público Press, 2000), 6.

7. Scott Baker, "Pedagogies of Protest: African American Teachers and the History of the Civil Rights Movement, 1940–1963," *Teachers College Record* 113, no. 12 (2011): 2777–803.

8. Jon Hale, "'The Student as a Force for Social Change': The Mississippi Freedom Schools and Student Engagement," *Journal of African American History* 96, no. 3 (2011): 336.

9. Marc Simon Rodriguez, "A Movement Made of 'Young Mexican Americans Seeking Change': Critical Citizenship, Migration, and the Chicano Movement in Texas and Wisconsin, 1960–1975," *Western Historical Quarterly* 34, no. 3 (2003): 274–99; Jesús Salas and David Giffey, *Struggle for Justice: The Migrant Farm Worker Labor Movement in Wisconsin* (Milwaukee: Wisconsin Labor History Society, 1998).

10. Kanellos, "Brief History of Hispanic Periodicals," 7.

11. "Why a YLO Newspaper?," *YLO* 1, no. 1 (March 19, 1969): 1. Unless stated otherwise, all of the Young Lords Organization publications discussed here can be accessed via DePaul University's online digital Young Lords Newspaper Collection at https://digicol.lib.depaul.edu/digital/collection/younglords.

12. Ibid., 9.

13. Hilda Vasquez Ignatin, "Young Lords Serve and Protect," *YLO* 1, no. 2 (May 1969): 7.

14. José "Cha Cha" Jiménez, personal communication, June 26, 2012.

15. Ibid.

16. Ibid.

17. The Liberation News Service, or LNS, served as an alternative to mainstream news agencies such as the Associated Press, providing news of the counterculture of the 1960s–early 1980s. For more on the LNS and other underground press services, see James Lewes, "The Underground Press in America (1964–1968): Outlining an Alternative, the Envisioning of an Underground," *Journal of Communication Inquiry* 24, no. 4 (2000): 379–400.

18. Untitled article, *YLO* 1, no. 2 (May 1969): 3, 8.

19. "Why a YLO Newspaper?," 1.

20. Padilla, *Latino Ethnic Consciousness*; Fernández, *Brown in the Windy City*.

21. "Chicano Youth Conference," *YLO* 1, no. 2 (May 1969): 20.

22. "Texas Pigs Attack Chicano Family: Critically Wound Father, Mother and Daughter," *El Young Lord Latin Liberation News Service* 1, no. 1 (April 1, 1971): 3. The police officers entered the house of the Rodriguez family in Dallas, Texas, wounding the three family members. The two offenders whom the police had intended to arrest lived more than fifty feet away in a neighboring unit.

23. "March 21, 1937: The Ponce Massacre," *El Young Lord Latin Liberation News Service* 1, no. 1 (April 1, 1971): 13; "U.P.R. Repression," *El Young Lord Latin Liberation News Service* 1, no. 1 (April 1, 1971): 15. In the 1937 incident, a group of Puerto Rican nationalist leaders held a peaceful demonstration in the town of Ponce, where they were met by more than two hundred armed police officers, leaving over a dozen civilians dead and many more wounded. In 1971, a clash between pro-independence students and ROTC cadets on the campus of the University of Puerto Rico ended two lives.

24. "Waller High School," *El Young Lord Latin Liberation News Service* 1, no. 2 (April 15, 1971): 6.

25. "Establish an outpost for socially maladjusted dropouts under the Waller High School Satellite Program," April 14, 1971, recommendation submitted by Superintendent of Chicago Schools James F. Redmond, Waller High School Papers, CBE.

26. "Speak Out: Straight from Mousee," *YLO* 2, no. 6 (February–March 1970): 2.

27. See Darrel Enck-Wanzer, ed., *The Young Lords: A Reader* (New York: New York University Press, 2010); Jennifer Nelson, "'Abortions under Community Control': Feminism, Nationalism, and the Politics of Reproduction among New York City's Young Lords," *Journal of Women's History* 13, no. 1 (2001): 157–80; and Darrel Wanzer-Serrano, *The New York Young Lords and the Struggle for Liberation* (Philadelphia: Temple University Press, 2015).

28. Vasquez Ignatin, "Young Lords Serve and Protect," 6.

29. Isabel, "To My Sisters," *YLO* 1, no. 5 (January 1970): 2.

30. Ibid.

31. José Jiménez, General Secretary of Chicago's Young Lords Organization, to "All Press Contacts," April 1, 1974, box 1, folder 3, Collection on the Young Lords, Special Collections and Archives, DePaul University Library, Chicago.

32. Padilla, *Puerto Rican Chicago*, 142.

33. Ibid., 140–41.

34. José "Cha Cha" Jiménez, personal communication.

35. "En Peligro de Perder Hogares," *El Puertorriqueño*, May 31, 1968, 1.

36. The article on tenants' rights reminded residents of the resources available to them: "Let me remind you again that the personnel of the Center of Urban Progress is here with only the purpose of helping the community." "Falta Calor en Muchos Hogares de Chicago," *El Puertorriqueño*, January 8, 1970, 1.

37. Trina Davila, "Llegó la Hora Nuestra, Todos Para Inscribirse Para Votar," *El Puertorriqueño*, March 15–21, 1968, 4.

38. Ibid.

39. Ibid.

40. "Dear Dona Trina Davila, My Puerto Rican Sister," *YLO* 1, no. 4 (Fall 1969): 2, 13.

41. "Se Graduan de Escuela Superior 24 Hispanos en Escuela San Miguel," *El Puertorriqueño*, May 31–June 6, 1968, 11.

42. "Un Puertorriqueño Ciudadano del Mes," *El Puertorriqueño*, May 10–16, 1968, 12.

43. José E. López went on to attend both Loyola University and the University of Chicago. He became a prominent leader in the Puerto Rican community in Chicago, both as the executive director of the Puerto Rican Cultural Center of Chicago and as a frequent lecturer on Puerto Rican history at local institutions of higher education. In the 1970s, he became involved in educational activism on the University of Illinois Circle Campus, as discussed in chapter 4.

44. "Caballeros Se Oponen a Tuley en El Parque," *El Puertorriqueno*, March 5–11, 1970, 1.

45. "Termina Huelga de Maestros de las Escuelas Públicas," *El Puertorriqueño*, January 14–20, 1971, 1.

46. "Huelga de Maestros el Derecho a Unificarse," editorial, *El Puertorriqueño*, January 14–20, 1971, 3.

47. Trina Davila, "Impressiones: Termina Huelga de Maestros," *El Puertorriqueno*, January 28–February 3, 1971, 6.

48. "Huelga de Maestros el Derecho a Unificarse," 3.

49. Trina Davila, "Impressiones: La Asociación de Maestros Hispanos," *El Puertorriqueno*, March 18–24, 1971, 5.

50. Elias Argott, Juan Walker, and Patricio Perez, "Latino Teachers Protest," *Chicago Tribune*, January 18, 1973, 16.

51. "Editorial," *The Rican*, no. 1 (Fall 1971): 1.

52. Samuel Betances, interview by the author, September 25, 2009.

53. Ibid.

54. Norman Alarcón, "Hay Que Inventarnos/We Must Invent Ourselves," *Third Woman* 1, no. 1 (1981): 5.

55. Betances, interview.

56. Catherine S. Ramírez, "Alternative Cartographies: *Third Woman* and the Respatialization of the Borderlands," *Midwest Miscellany* 30 (Fall 2002): 47–62.

57. Thomas Pérez, "Dialogue with a Chicano Student," *The Rican*, no. 1 (Fall 1971): 32.

58. Samuel Betances, "Puerto Ricans and Mexican Americans in Higher Education," *The Rican* 1, no. 4 (May 1974): 27.

59. Edwin Claudio, "A Boycott," *The Rican*, no. 1 (Fall 1971): 29.

60. Blurb on the back cover of the May 1974 issue of *The Rican*, attributed to "Brother Pablo #30818, Pontiac, Illinois."

61. Edna Acosta-Belen and Frank Bonilla went on to become distinguished scholars in the field of Puerto Rican studies, with Bonilla serving as the longtime director of the Center for Puerto Rican Studies at City University of New York. Isidro Lucas became a leading researcher and advocate on issues of higher education for Puerto Ricans and other Latinos.

62. Betances, interview.

63. "Untitled Play," scene 1, *The Rican*, no. 1 (Fall 1971): 24.

64. "About the Newspaper," *Que Ondee Sola* 1, no. 1 (January 27, 1972): 1.

65. "Mass-Media for Education," *Que Ondee Sola* 1, no. 1 (January 27, 1972): 4.

66. Ibid.

67. Chuck Torre, "Descarga," *Que Ondee Sola* 1, no. 2 (February 15, 1972): 4.

68. "U.P.R.S. Delegates Return from New York," *Que Ondee Sola* 1, no. 1 (January 27, 1972): 1.

69. Hector Luis Rosario, "Sound Off," *Que Ondee Sola* 1, no. 2 (February 15, 1972): 7.

70. Edwin Claudio, "The Rican," *Que Ondee Sola* 1, no. 3 (February 29, 1972): 3.

71. Ibid.

72. "Black Exito," *Que Ondee Sola* 1, no. 4 (March 21, 1972): 2.

73. "Vernon Bellecourt Visits Uni," *Que Ondee Sola*, December 12, 1977, 2.

74. Brian Wasserman, "Racism at Northeastern," *Que Ondee Sola* 1, no. 6 (May 30, 1972): 3.

75. Edwin Claudio, "A Progress Report on the Progression of Racism in Your School," *Que Ondee Sola* 1, no. 5 (April 7, 1972): 2.

76. Ibid.

77. "Teacher Student Shot Dies," *Chicago Tribune*, July 9, 1972, D22; statement on the shooting by "We, the concerned Black and Puerto Rican students of Northeastern Illinois University," *Que Ondee Sola* 1, no. 8 (August 5, 1972): 1.

78. "We, the concerned Black and Puerto Rican students."

79. Debbie Washington, "A Black's View of the News," *Que Ondee Sola* 1, no. 8 (August 5, 1972): 5.

80. "Special Jury for Latin Death Denied," *Chicago Tribune*, August 30, 1973, A6.

81. "The Case of July 29th," *Que Ondee Sola* 3, no. 1 (August 30, 1973): 1, reprinting an excerpt from *El Matemano*, bulletin of the Puerto Rican Socialist Party—Chicago Committee, July 1973.

82. Ibid., 2.

83. Luis Gutierrez, "Puerto Rican Studies and Education," *Que Ondee Sola* 4, no. 5 (January 1975): 2.

84. "Todos a El Grito de Lares y El Grito de Dolores," *Que Ondee Sola*, September 1976, 1; "El Grito de Lares," *Que Ondee Sola*, September 1976, 7; "The Birth [of] Puerto Rican Nationalism," *Que Ondee Sola*, September 6, 1977, 1; "El Grito de Lares," *Que Ondee Sola* 4, no. 1 (September 1974): 2–5, 8.

85. "Historical Notes," *Que Ondee Sola* 5, no. 1 (September 1975): 2; "La Masacre de Ponce," *Que Ondee Sola* 1, no. 4 (March 21, 1972): 6.

86. Gini Sorrentini Blaut, "La Mujer Puertorriqueña en la Lucha," *Que Ondee Sola* 1, no. 11 (December 1, 1972): 2–4, 9. These four women are important figures in Puerto Rican history as writers, political leaders, and labor activists. For more on their lives and work, see Luisa Capetillo, *A Nation of Women: An Early Feminist Speaks Out* (Houston: Arte Público Press, 2004); Ruiz and Sánchez Korrol, *Latina Legacies*; and Julia de Burgos, *Song of the Simple Truth: The Complete Poems of Julia de Burgos* (Evanston, IL: Northwestern University Press, 1995).

87. Blaut, "La Mujer Puertorriqueña en la Lucha."

88. "Esterilizacion," *Que Ondee Sola*, September 6, 1977, 3. For more, see Iris López, *Matters of Choice: Puerto Rican Women's Struggle for Reproductive Freedom* (New Brunswick, NJ: Rutgers University Press, 2008).

89. "Perspective," *Que Ondee Sola* 4, no. 7 (March 1975): 3.

90. Ibid.

91. Gutierrez, "Puerto Rican Studies and Education," 1.

92. Ibid.

93. Sanchez, "The Tuley Experience."

94. Ibid.

95. Edwin Claudio, "Our High School Students," *Que Ondee Sola* 1, no. 6 (May 30, 1972): 5.

96. Luis V. Gutierrez would go on to have a long political career in Chicago, serving as a member of the Chicago City Council representing the 26th Ward, and later serving over two decades as the U.S. Representative for Illinois's 4th Congressional District.

97. Blackwell, "Contested Histories," 60–61.

Conclusion

1. Frederick Lowe and Derrick Blakley, "Humboldt Park Riot: 2 Die, 15 Cops Hurt; 3,000 on Rampage," *Chicago Tribune*, June 5, 1977, 1. For more on Torres's death, see David Axelford, "He Feared Rioters More Than Flames," *Chicago Tribune*, June 10, 1977, B1.

2. Peréz, *Near Northwest Side Story*, 88.

3. Paul Delaney, "Looting, Vandalism Follow Chicago Riot: Police Strength Stepped Up in Park Where Two Hispanic Men Died," *New York Times*, June 6, 1977, 1.

4. "Slain Puerto Ricans' Kin Sue for $48 Million," *Chicago Tribune*, June 17, 1977, B1.

5. Frederick Lowe and Monroe Anderson, "Blast Damages County Building," *Chicago Tribune*, June 5, 1977, 3; Delaney, "Looting, Vandalism."

6. "Slain Puerto Ricans' Kin Sue."

7. Lowe and Blakley, "Humboldt Park Riot."

8. "Humboldt Park: A Troubled 'Island' without Any Clout," *Chicago Tribune*, June 12, 1977, 1.

9. Ibid., 26.

10. Ibid.

11. Lucas, *Puerto Rican Dropouts*; Lucas, "Profile of the Puerto Rican Drop Out."

12. David B. Tyack, *The One Best System: A History of American Urban Education* (Cambridge, MA: Harvard University Press, 1974), 2.

13. James D. Anderson, introduction to pt. 3, "1950–1980: Separate and Unequal," in *School: The Story of American Public Education*, ed. Sarah Mondale and Sarah B. Patton (Boston: Beacon Press, 2001), 123–24.

14. Enora R. Brown, "Freedom for Some, Discipline for 'Others': The Structure of Inequity in Education," in *Education as Enforcement: The Militarization and Corporatization of Schools*, ed. Kenneth J. Saltman and David A. Gabbard (New York: Routledge, 2003), 136.

15. Tuan, *Space and Place*, 4.

16. John U. Ogbu and Herbert D. Simmons, "Voluntary and Involuntary Minorities: A Cultural-Ecological Theory of School Performance with Some Implications for Education," *Anthropology and Education Quarterly* 29, no. 2 (1998): 155–88.

17. Ibid., 161.

18. "Any community can be described as a collection of primary networks in which individuals are linked through the relationships of kinship or friendship or by virtue of being neighbors." Richard D. Alba, "Social Assimilation among American Catholic National-Origin Groups," *American Sociological Review* 41, no. 6 (December 1976): 1033.

19. Mary Davidson, *Interim Report: A Promise of Simple Justice in the Education of Chicago School Children?* (Chicago: Chicago Public Schools, Monitoring Commission for Desegregation Implementation, February 1983), vi, https://files.eric.ed.gov/fulltext/ED342852.pdf.

20. Chicago Board of Education, "Executive Summary, Report by the Board of Education of Student Desegregation Plan" (April 1981), 2, CHM.

21. Ibid., 3.

22. Ibid.

23. The Department of Health, Education, and Welfare rejected the board's revisions to its Access to Excellence report as inadequate and imprecise, although the Illinois Board of Education gave the report its qualified approval. According to the report, "In April of 1980, the Department of Justice indicated its conclusion that a sufficient case existed to warrant filing suit against the school district, but invited the district to negotiate." Ibid., 3–4.

24. Ibid., 3.

25. Sonia Nieto, "Puerto Rican Students in U.S. Schools: A Brief History," in *Puerto Rican Students in U.S. Schools*, ed. Sonia Nieto (Mahwah, NJ: Lawrence Erlbaum Associates, 2000), 32.

26. Soll and Jackson, "The Tuley Thing."

Index

MIRELSIE VELÁZQUEZ is an associate professor of education at the University of Oklahoma.

Latinos in Chicago and the Midwest

The University of Illinois Press
is a founding member of the
Association of University Presses.

———————————————

University of Illinois Press
1325 South Oak Street
Champaign, IL 61820-6903
www.press.uillinois.edu